ISLANDS

OF THE
NORTHEASTERN UNITED STATES
AND
EASTERN CANADA

Also by Sarah Bird Wright

FERRIES OF AMERICA
A Guide to Adventurous Travel

ISLANDS
Of the South and
Southeastern United States

ISLANDS

OF THE
NORTHEASTERN UNITED STATES
AND
EASTERN CANADA

Sarah Bird Wright

Peachtree Publishers, Ltd.
Atlanta

Published by
PEACHTREE PUBLISHERS, LTD.
494 Armour Circle, NE
Atlanta, Georgia 30324

Cover design and illustration for the ISLANDS series by Lisa Lytton-Smith
Maps by Tom Roberts

Manufactured in the United States of America

10 9 8 7 6 5 4 3 2 1

Library of Congress Cataloging in Publication Data

Wright, Sarah Bird.
    Islands of the northeastern United States and eastern Canada / Sarah Bird Wright.
      p. cm.
    Includes bibliographical references.
    ISBN 0-934601-99-2
    1. Northeastern States — Description and travel — Guide-books.
    2. Canada, Eastern — Description and travel — Guide-books.
    3. Islands — Northeastern States — Guide-books.
    4. Islands — Canada, Eastern — Guide-books. I. Title.
  F2.3.W76 1990   89-28645
  917.95 — dc20   CIP

CONTENTS

*For my husband, Lewis, with whom I
first came to know the delights
and diversions of New England, and
for our son, Alex, who is reveling in
them now.*

PRICE CATEGORIES

(Prices in Canada are approximately 15% less)

RESTAURANTS:

Average cost of a meal for one (excluding beverages, tips, and taxes)

$ Under $12 $$ $12-$20 $$$ Over $20

LODGING:

Price for a standard double, high season, exclusive of taxes:

$ Under $60 $$ $60-$100 $$$ Over $100

Note that many establishments have a wide range of prices, according to location and season.

While every care has been taken to assure the accuracy of the information in this guide, the passage of time will always bring change, and consequently the publisher cannot accept responsibility for errors that may occur. All information is based on that available at press time; the prudent traveler will avoid inconvenience by calling ahead.

INTRODUCTION

*An island always pleases my imagination, even the smallest,
as a small continent and integral part of the globe.*
— Henry David Thoreau,
**A Week on the Concord
and Merrimack Rivers**

The islands of New England and maritime Canada do not have the soft, bright, and even languid character of many southern ones, but they have a special charisma: rock-hard, sturdy, and individualistic. William Stoughton, an early governor of Massachusetts, declared that "God hath sifted a whole nation, that he might send choice grain into this wilderness." There is a stronger sense of community on a small island than in many mainland towns, and less privacy. There are few secrets: tax delinquents are known, and if the ambulance comes over on the ferry, people know who is sick. A ferry arrival at an isolated island, with mail, groceries, mattresses, champagne and flowers for weddings, is an all-purpose and sociable event, superseding most everyday concerns. New-comers learn to restrain themselves at island town meetings — and town meet-ings are one of the most ancient of New England heritages.

The present inhabitants of dozens of islands bear names of great antiquity, going back to the earliest records, belying the obsession with mobility which afflicts much of the mainland. Those which come to mind are Frenchboro in Maine, Grand Manan in New Brunswick, Canada, and the Magdalens in Quebec, Canada. A good many islanders contribute to the community in several capacities: the clerk of the summer church may run the tourist bureau, the local teacher represent the island on the county planning board, and a resort owner serve as president of the local historical society. At the same time, islanders are far from provincial. Matinicus residents, in winter, visit such far-flung places as Arizona, the Bahamas, and Vienna, and a good many eastern Canadians are more familiar with Florida than most Americans. Young people in Canada's Magdalen Islands attend universities and take jobs in Montreal.

Each of these islands is, in its way, a "splendid domain," as Oliver Wendell Holmes said of Naushon, owned by the Forbes family, near Martha's Vineyard. The topography and ambiance he describes evoke many northeastern islands: "Blue sea around it. . . . Rocks scattered about, Stone-henge-like monoliths. . . . There is nothing in the shape of kindness and courtesy that can make life beautiful, which has not found its home in that ocean-principality. It has welcomed all who were worthy of welcome, from the pale clergyman who came to breathe the sea-air with its medicinal salt and iodine, to the great statesman who turned his back on the affairs of empire, and smoothed his Olympian forehead, and flashed hs white teeth in merriment over the long table, where his wit was the keenest and his story the best." Today the "long table" may be a family-style inn on Monhegan, a sunny antique-filled breakfast room on Cape Breton, a rocky ledge with a clambake on Thacher Island, a "back-door dinner" from a restaurant on Martha's Vineyard, spread out on the sand dunes, or a luncheon in the servants' hall after a church service in Jorstadt Castle in the Thousand Islands of New York. They all, however, manage to evoke in visitors the island genie of conviviality and wit which so struck Holmes and which obtains on public as well as private islands. Those who have attained an island, especially by ferry, have a sense of discernment, of pilgrimage realized, and of worthy exploration. New England and Canadian intellectuals have had a special affinity for islands — Harry Emerson Fosdick for Mouse Island in Maine, Celia Thaxter for Appledore and Star in New Hampshire, Henry David Thoreau for Plum in Massachusetts, Willa Cather for Grand Manan in New Brunswick, and Hugh MacLennan for Cape Breton, among many others, have cherished the solitude and absence of pressure. Fosdick stated, when he and G. Ellsworth Huggins bought Mouse Island: "It is far enough from the mainland so that we can live an entirely unsophisticated life; that is to say, a man can put on a flannel shirt in the morning and go to bed in it at night if he feels like it." Informality and individuality are still hallmarks of life on most New England and Canadian islands, even in the short tourist season.

Some islands, such as Long Island and Staten Island, have been omitted because they were too large and too populated. Others could not be included because they were not accessible to the public. I have had to leave out still others because space did not permit this volume in the Islands series to be comprehensive; each is intended as an anthology of special islands and not an encyclopedia of those within a given region. For each entry, the book contains information about access, the island's general history, points of interest, sight-seeing tours and cruises, parks, beaches, camping, marinas, lodging, restaurants, rental housing, and the appropriate contact. The book is meant as a practical guide for advance planning as well as for use on the trip itself. I would hope it will also provide insights into the experience of island inhabitants and their varying perspectives — stores close on some of the Maine islands before Labor Day and not afterwards, to give the owners a holiday, and in the Thousand Islands people dread getting too old to drive a boat, not a car. Each of the islands represented has a special flavor and is accessible to the public, within certain limits. Some of those included, such as Jorstadt in the Thousand Islands and Star and Appledore in New Hampshire's Isles of Shoals, may be visited only under special circumstances. The islands in Lake Winnipesaukee and the Thimbles may only be seen from cruise ships. For the most part, however, visitors are welcome on this portfolio of islands in the Northeastern United States and Eastern Canada.

CONNECTICUT

In *Inside U.S.A.*, John Gunther described Connecticut as a "worthy little state"; it also has a long tradition of being the "land of steady habits." Both epithets are apt; the state is emblematic of New England itself, with small villages centered on green commons, accented by church steeples and farms with stone walls and barns, providing a picturesque backdrop to the forested areas. Much of the state lacks the frenetic pace of neighboring New York, and it is battling hard to retain its rural charm against encroachments from New York and Massachusetts. There are still areas with small roads winding for miles along the quiet shores of rivers. There is a sophisticated ambiance underlying the pastoral scene: tiny towns have well-stocked bookshops and yogurt and muffin shops; harbors are crowded with handsome yachts. There is great diversity, with an urban belt running from Hartford through New Haven and on to Bridgeport.

Adriaen Block sailed into the Connecticut River in 1614. During the 1630s the state was the scene of the earliest westward migration in the United States, when John Haynes, the Reverend Thomas Hooker, and the Reverend Samuel Stone moved from Cambridge, where they felt crowded, to settle Hartford, Windsor, and Wethersfield, on the Connecticut River. The Connecticut River has the two oldest ferry crossings in the country, between Chester and Hadlyme and between Rocky Hill and Glastonbury.

The state has always been boat and river-oriented. Schooners such as the *Argia*, the *Mystic Clipper*, the *Mystic Whaler*, and the *Voyager*, all leaving from Mystic, and cruise ships such as the *Sabino* from Mystic, the *Camelot Star* from Haddam, and the *Liberty Belle* from New Haven offer trips on the state's rivers, harbors, and coast. The name "Connecticut" derives from the Indian word "quinatucquet," meaning "upon the long tidal river" (i.e., the Connecticut River).

Alexis de Tocqueville summarized the state: "Connecticut . . . the little spot . . . that makes the clock peddler, the schoolmaster, and the senator. The first, gives you time; the second, tells you what to do with it; the third makes your law and your civilization." His metaphor enlarges the state from a simple to a complex one, and, in history and influence, Connecticut is immensely complex. Her islands, however, offer a means of returning to the simplicity of colonial and seafaring days; there is the primitive landscape of Selden Island, Sheffield with its lighthouse, and the Thimbles, purposely kept undeveloped. All are worth visiting.

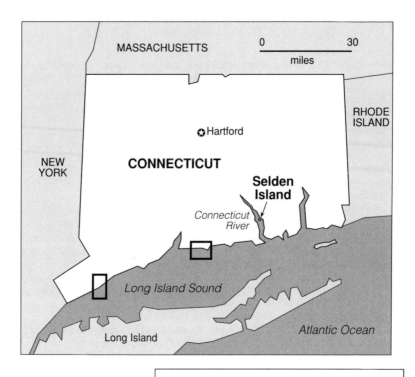

MASSACHUSETTS

0   30
miles

RHODE
ISLAND

⊕Hartford

NEW
YORK

CONNECTICUT

**Selden
Island**

*Connecticut
River*

Long Island Sound

Long Island

Atlantic Ocean

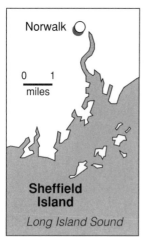

Norwalk ◖

0   1
miles

**Sheffield
Island**

Long Island Sound

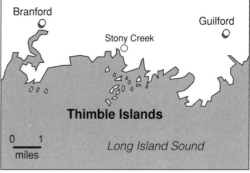

Branford ◖

Guilford ◖

Stony Creek ○

Thimble Islands

0   1
miles

Long Island Sound

CONNECTICUT

SELDEN ISLAND

Area Code 203
LOCATION Connecticut River, near Lyme.

SIZE 528 acres.

ACCESS The island is accessible by water only. **Air:** There is commercial service to New London. **Private boat** (canoes and kayaks are most suitable; see camping section).

HISTORY AND DESCRIPTION Selden Island is the location of Selden Island State Park. It is the largest island in the Connecticut River, and is quite picturesque, with high cliffs and old hemlocks. Purchases of portions of the island for a park began in 1917.

A 1918 report on Connecticut's parks to the state governor cited a portion of a description of the island by one of its former owners, Professor H. P. Johnston, of the College of the City of New York, and summer resident of Hadlyme:

> This site represents, in part, one of the oldest colonial settlements on the lower Connecticut River. Its original name, with lands adjoining, was the "Twelve Mile Island Farm," so called as being distant twelve miles from the River's mouth and including the island now lying off Deep River landing.

Johnston goes on to summarize the history of the island, which was first granted to John Cullick in 1650 by the General Court of Hartford. The Indians in the vicinity were of the Mohegan tribe and were peaceful. Cullick sold the grant to John Leveret, son of the Governor of Massachusetts and later president of Harvard College. Leveret sold it to Mr. Joseph Selden of Hadley, Massachusetts, in 1695; this is the source of the name, "Selden's Neck." Joseph Selden was the son of Thomas Selden of Kent, England, who was one of the company that settled Hartford in 1636. Selden descendants occupied the principal portions of the original grant well into the twentieth century.

The island was originally part of the mainland, as is clear from its name; it is believed to have been separated from the mainland in the 1850s by an extra high spring freshet which cut a shallow channel across the low meadows at the northern end. There is little water on the bar at the north end of the island, especially at low tide.

Canoeists with Selden Island in Background

POINTS OF INTEREST   Observatory Hill, 200 feet high, is of interest.
The Connecticut Valley Granite and Mining Company was formed in 1890, and paving blocks were quarried at several sites on the island. The paving blocks were loaded onto schooners from the wharves on the island and taken to New York, where they were used to pave the streets. The remains of the wharves and quarries can be seen today and are an added attraction to hikers or campers visiting on the island.

SIGHTSEEING TOURS   None on the island, but North American Canoe Tours, Inc., 65 Black Point Rd., Niantic, CT 06357 (203/739-0791), run by David Harraden, offers guided canoe getaways for families and groups which go to Selden Neck. The summer weekend trips begin on Friday evening and last until Sunday afternoon; the first night is spent at the Gillette Castle outpost and the second on Selden Island. Trips are scheduled on weekends from July to October.

PARKS, BEACHES   **Parks:** The entire island is a state park (see
AND CAMPING   History and Description). There are hiking trails.
Beaches: The beaches are small and sandy, but not extensive. **Camping:** There are primitive riverside campsites available from May 1 through September 30. Stays are limited to one night. Sites are located at Cedars, Hogback, Springledge, and Quarry Knob. There are tent ground sites, outhouses, fireplaces, and drinking water. A nightly camping fee is charged. For camping permit, write or apply in person two weeks prior to intended stay to Mr. Donald Grant, Manager, Gillette Castle State Park, 67 River Rd., East Haddam, CT 06423 (203/526-2336). You should state the camp area, camping date, name and address of leader, number and ages of people in group, type of boat, intended launch and take-out points, and payment (at time of writing, $2 per person per night). The number of people is limited (Cedars, 20; Hogback, 6;

Springledge, 8, and Quarry Knob, 12). No open fires are allowed. The U-Paddle Service at Gillette Castle State Park, run by North American Canoe Tours, Inc. of Niantic, CT, offers complete outfitting with transportation to other launch sites if desired (203/739-0791). Minors under 18 must be accompanied by an adult.

MARINAS   There are no mooring or docking facilities available; the island is principally suited to canoeists and kayakers.

RESTAURANTS   There are no restaurants or concessions.

LODGING   There is no lodging.

RENTALS   There are no rentals.

CONTACT   State of Connecticut, Dept. of Environmental Protection, Office of State Parks and Recreation, 165 Capitol Ave., Hartford, CT 06106 (203/566-2304).
(See Camping for details about obtaining a camping permit). Also, Mr. Donald Grant, Manager, Gillette Castle State Park, 67 River Rd., East Haddam, CT 06423 (203/526-2336).

SHEFFIELD ISLAND

Area Code 203
LOCATION   Off the coast of Norwalk.

SIZE   3 acres.

Sheffield Island Lighthouse

ACCESS

Ferry: The Sheffield Island Ferry from Hope Dock (I-95 Ex. 15 or 16); it runs from mid-May to Oct. (838-9003). **Air:** There is commercial service to New York. **Private boat**.

HISTORY AND DESCRIPTION

The island is named for Captain Robert Sheffield, the first owner and a Revolutionary War veteran. His daughter Temperance married Gersham Smith, and the couple worked a dairy farm on the island, keeping cattle and sheep. Smith herded the rams onto a smaller island to separate them from the ewes; that is how Ram Island, nearby, got its name. In 1868, the U.S. Coast Guard built the lighthouse, and Smith served as its first keeper. The beacon warned sailors until 1902 when Green's Ledge Light was built. In 1912, Alfred Mestre built a palatial estate, but it later burned; the ruins still exist and you can hike to them. In 1914, Thorsten O. Stabell of Norwalk bought the island. His two sons, Anton ("Duck") and Thorsten ("Tut") and their families still own and maintain the summer cottage on the island, living in Norwalk in winter. "Tut" told a local newspaper reporter, Mike Smith, of the Hurricane of 1938: "Lord, that was something . . . It took us over three months just to roll all the boulders back into the Sound!"

A portion of the island has now been set aside as a wildlife refuge; the Norwalk Seaport Association bought the lighthouse and three acres of land. The Association has been renovating the lighthouse, and has built a sturdy dock. The present lighthouse keeper is Norwalk high school teacher Patrick O'Shaughnessy, who lives on the island during the summer.

POINTS OF INTEREST

The Sheffield Island Lighthouse was built in 1868; it has 2 stories and 10 rooms open to the public for exploration. The inside is clean, but unfinished. Clam rakes are in one corner, and old furniture is stored in other rooms. The octagonal tower is well worth climbing; from the top, there is a good view of the ocean and sailboats.

The Maritime Center, adjacent to the ferry dock on Water St. in South Norwalk is of interest, a 5-acre restored nineteenth-century factory focusing on the maritime history and marine life of Long Island Sound. There is an IMAX theater showing films on a 6-story screen and Maritime Hall, exhibiting nautical artifacts.

SIGHTSEEING TOURS

Tours are given of the lighthouse, but, at present, renovations are still underway. From Norwalk, the *Lady Joan*, which is a replica of a Mississippi River paddlewheeler, offers narrated cruises of Norwalk Harbor and Norwalk Islands daily July 1 to Labor Day. Departs from Norwalk Cove Marina, East Norwalk, 838-9003.

PARKS, BEACHES AND CAMPING

Parks: The island is a city park, and is adjacent to the U.S. Fish and Wildlife Sanctuary. **Beaches:** The beaches are rocky, but swimming is allowed. **Camping:** No camping is allowed.

MARINAS

None, but boaters may dock and come ashore for a small fee.

Volsunga III preparing to cruise the Thimble Islands, Connecticut

RESTAURANTS   None, but bring a picnic; there are picnic tables.
                        Soft drinks are available.

LODGING   None on the island.

RENTALS   None on the island.

CONTACT   Norwalk Seaport Association, 92 Washington St.,
                        South Norwalk, CT 06854 (203/838-9444).

THIMBLE ISLANDS

Area Code 203
LOCATION   In Long Island Sound, off Branford.

SIZE   They range from 20 acres down to $1/5$ acre at high
                        tide.

ACCESS   The islands are private, but there are summer
                        sightseeing ships, the *Volsunga III* (Capt. Robert
                        Milne, 481-3345 or 488-9978) and the *Sea Mist II*
(Capt. Mike Infantino, Jr., 481-4841), operating from the shore village of Stony
Creek, near Branford. They leave from the town dock (take Exit 56 from I-95; turn
left, go 2 mi.) The narrated cruises run from Memorial Day through Labor Day
and take from 30-45 mins. In the summer season there are also moonlight
cruises.

HISTORY AND DESCRIPTION   The Thimbles consist of about 33 rocky islets in Long Island Sound between Branford and Guilford. They are the largest group of islands on Long Island Sound. Some are mere specks of rock on which a single house perches; most are high out of the water. About half of the residents choose to have no telephone or electricity. When utilities were proposed for the two most populous islands, Governor's and Money, the people voted against it. Even the children and teenagers opposed it, not wanting, they said, "to ruin the island." About 112 families live on the Thimbles in warm weather; during the winter, there is one resident on Rogers (Phelps) Island, a caretaker. Most of the islanders have their own boats, but they rely on the *Volsunga III* and *Sea Mist II* for mail delivery and groceries as well as ordinary transportation. The service is continuous during the summer season. If islanders have an emergency, they fly an American flag upside down, for which the ferry captains keep an alert eye. Early on, some of the islands were used for sheep farming. East and West Crib islands were known for shipbuilding, and some of the smaller ones were used for oystering, fishing, and the gathering of seaweed for fertilizer. Captain Kidd, fleeing from authorities, is known to have sailed around the Thimbles, trying desperately to find a safe hiding place for his treasure. It is thought that he may have hidden treasure on some of the islands, such as Money, and that he may have hidden his ships between the cliffs of High Island.

Before the turn of the century, Stony Creek was a fashionable resort and was even called the "Newport of Connecticut." The Thimbles, at that time, had two hotels and some elegant boarding houses. An excursion steamer carrying as many as 1,000 passengers plied the waters between the mainland and the islands, and there were moonlight sailing parties, bands, dancing, picnics, and athletic events. Some of the islands have whimsical names, even for islands. Charles C. Kingsley, a lawyer from New Haven, owns East Stooping Bush Island. "In evenings, I can be completely away from the world," he says. The family of Captain Dwight Carter, who formerly ran one of the ferries, have inhabited the Thimbles longer than any other; some members are the seventh generation to spend summers on Jepson Island. The islands have long been a favorite summer retreat for celebrities; at present cartoonist Garry Trudeau and his wife, television celebrity Jane Pauley, television actor Frank Converse, and playwright Muriel Resnick all have summer homes on the Thimbles.

The showpiece of 7.6-acre Rogers Island is the 27-room Tudor mansion built in 1902 by John J. Phelps. Phelps, a financier, also built a submarine chaser in which he patrolled the islands during World War I.

Properties seldom come on the market here. Often, islands or houses are conveyed to family members. If they are sold to outsiders, it is usually handled through word-of-mouth and not advertised. Most owners want buyers who will value the Thimbles' way of life. Prices also are high; $500,000 is not unusual and asking prices are sometimes much more.

POINTS OF INTEREST   The homes, cliffs, rocky coves which are visible from the sightseeing boats.

SIGHTSEEING TOURS   None on the islands (see Access).

PARKS, BEACHES   None.
AND CAMPING

MARINAS   The Thimbles have many anchorages, but no
                     facilities or services. In the summer, a barge may
                     be anchored north of Pot Island selling hot dogs
and cold drinks to the many boaters who throng the waters around the islands.

RESTAURANTS   None on the islands, but the America's Cup Res-
                         taurant (481-8481) is across from the Stony Creek
                         ferry dock and is open all year (closed Mon. off
season), and serves lunch and dinner. It has a snack bar and gazebo. Parking is
sometimes a problem; you may have to park on a side street and walk to the
restaurant and boat landing.$$

LODGING   None.

RENTALS   None.

CONTACT   Branford Chamber of Commerce, 209 Mon-
                     towese St., Box 375, Branford, CT (488-5500).

MAINE

"Adam had no more in Eden," wrote James Russell Lowell of Maine, when, on an excursion up the Penobscot River, he saw sunset and moonrise simultaneously. Maine is still considered an Eden by those who know it well, by "summer people" hoping they will eventually be considered assimilated, as well as by natives. Maine is the largest and, with its rugged coastline, one of the most beautiful of the New England states. Its area exceeds that of New Hampshire, Vermont, Rhode Island, and Connecticut combined. It is known to have been visited by Sebastian Cabot as early as 1497; the first settlement was at the mouth of the Kennebec in 1607, where Popham now stands.

Literary chroniclers of Maine are legion—E. B. White, Louise Dickinson Rich, F. Marion Crawford, Nathaniel Hawthorne, Theodore Roosevelt, Henry Wadsworth Longfellow, Edna St. Vincent Millay, Rachel Field, John Greenleaf Whittier, Harriet Beecher Stowe, Edwin Arlington Robinson, and Sarah Orne Jewett, to name only a few. Artists such as Thomas Cole, Frederic Church, and Andrew and James Wyeth have depicted the scenic riches of many of the Maine islands.

Lawrence Durrell has said that everyone has a "home landscape" in his memory, a place within the circuits of the mind which evokes recurring dreams and images, and to which, ideally, he will return someday. The islands of Maine are a composite "home landscape" for island lovers, with rocky promontories and ledges set against hills covered with dark spruce, lobster traps piled near harbors, lighthouses of many shapes and sizes, and swooping sea birds. There are thousands in number, forming what the *W.P.A. Guide* calls "a long fringe of interdependent but individual units."

Though the islands share some physical similarities and all are rich in scenery, they are very different in features and personality. The wooded islands dotting Casco Bay are less isolated than most of the others; Peaks is close enough to Portland for daily commuting. Mount Desert Island, the northernmost discussed, is the home of the country's second most visited National Park, Acadia. The islands not accessible by bridge are invisibly tethered to the ports from which the ferries come, bringing mail and a variety of necessities and luxuries. The Cranberry Isles are connected thus to Northeast Harbor; the Isle au Haut to Stonington; Frenchboro and Swans to Bass Harbor; Matinicus, North Haven, and Vinalhaven to Rockland; Islesboro to Lincolnville; Monhegan to Port Clyde; Squirrel (summer only) to Boothbay Harbor, from which there is also summer service to Monhegan. Many of the islands also have air strips. The natives are invariably helpful and polite, patiently answering questions from off-islanders, no matter how feeble their understanding of what year-round life on an island entails. Lobstering is still a leading occupation on a number of islands.

This book only deals with those islands which are accessible by car or ferry, though many others, some owned by the state, are available for recreational use and may be reached by boat (especially by sea kayak). The Maine Island Trail, as it has been designated, includes about 65 islands scattered over 325 miles of coastline stretching from Yarmouth to Machias. (For details, contact the Maine Island Trail Assocation, 60 Ocean St., Rockland, ME 04841; 207/594-9209).

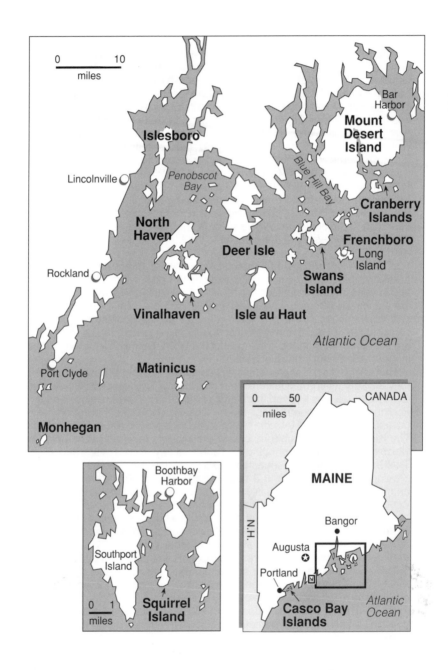

MAINE

CASCO BAY ISLANDS
(Bailey and Orr's, Cliff, Eagle, House, Little and Great Chebeague, Little and Great Diamond, Jewell, Long, Peaks).

Area Code 207

LOCATION   Scattered in Casco Bay off Portland; the bay stretches about 20 miles from Cape Elizabeth to Cape Small and is 12 miles in width.

SIZE   Great Chebeague (often called Chebeague) is the largest, about 5 miles long with an average width of 1 mile; Peaks is about 2 miles by 3 miles; Cliff is about 2 miles long and less than 1 mile wide (300 acres). Long Island is 3 miles by 1 mile. The others discussed range in size, with Little Diamond, 73 acres, being the smallest.

ACCESS   Ferry: From Portland; Casco Bay Lines, Custom House Wharf, Portland, Maine, 04101 (774-7871). Casco Bay services Peaks, Cliff, Chebeague, Long, Little and Great Diamond. Chebeague Transportation Co. (846-3700) runs a water taxi from Cousins Island (connected to the mainland by a bridge) to Chebeague. Capt. Wayne Selberg (774-6498 or 846-9592) runs a boat from Portland to Eagle Island. Hilda Cushing Dudley (799-8188), owner of House Island, offers group tours of the fort, by reservation, on the 60-ft. *Buccaneer*; they leave from Portland. The Bay Express Water Taxi (766-2508) picks up at a float on Commercial St. in Portland, carries six people, and for about $40 will go to most of the inner islands in the Bay. Bailey and Orr's are reached by bridge. *Air:* There is commercial service to Portland. *Private boat.* (Access to Jewell Island is only by private boat).

HISTORY AND DESCRIPTION   As the American work week began to decline in the last decade of the nineteenth century and the standard of living began to rise, annual vacations became the rule rather than the exception. The widely advertised islands of Casco Bay were a popular destination. In 1893, the popular periodical *The*

Outlook: A Family Paper, edited by Henry Ward Beecher, carried an advertise-
ment for Peak's and Cushing's as premier island resorts of the coast of Maine. A
large display ad in the June 1895 edition of the *Christian Union* (founded by
Beecher), entitled "On an Island for Your Summer Vacation," began,
"Numerous are the island resorts of the coast of Maine — Peak's, Cushing's, Mt.
Desert, Gerrish Islands, etc." The islands of Casco Bay are equally popular
today, both for year-round living and summer visiting. At the turn of the century,
nearly every city of note in Maine had an amusement park; that for Portland was
Greenwood Park, on Peaks Island (see Points of Interest). Visitors attended the
island's theaters to see summer stock productions. For many years Peaks and
Cushing were the only two islands served by steamers.

Casco Bay was named by a sixteenth-century explorer, Esteban Gomez, who
named it Bahia de Casco (Bay of the Helmet or Skull). It is thought that the
Vikings may have explored the islands around A.D. 1000. The islands are known
as the "Calendar Islands," so-named when an early explorer reported back to
his superiors that the bay near Portland "had as many islands as there are days
in the year." The actual count is about 136, more than any other coastal bay in
Maine. Many are privately owned. They link the rocky upper coast of Maine with
the lower one, which has sandy beaches. Running parallel to each other from
northeast to southwest, these islands are long and thin with striated ledges.

Bailey and Orr's: These islands are both accessible from the mainland by
bridge, and there are pleasant dinner cruises to Bailey Island from Portland in
the summer. Orr's is a large lobster-shaped island. Harriet Beecher Stowe
summered here in a small white cottage near the bridge from Great Island. Bailey
Island lies over a famous 1200-ft. cribstone bridge, constructed of granite blocks
arranged in a honeycomb pattern, without mortar, allowing heavy tides and
spring thaws to surge through freely. Bailey Island is known for the pirate
treasure found on the island, when John Wilson, an impecunious farmer, was out
hunting one day and the bird he shot fell on a rocky ledge. As he tried to retrieve
it, he fell in a crevasse between two rocks which contained a heavy iron pot filled
with Spanish gold. He took the gold to Boston, exchanged it for $12,000, sailed
home in a fine yacht, bought an expensive farm, raised a family, and became a
respected member of the community; the tale of how he obtained his wealth was
not known for many years. Bailey Island is now noted for its annual Tuna
Tournament which takes place in late July; sometimes tuna weighing as much as
700 pounds are displayed. Mackerel Cove is well known to fishermen and to the
yachting community. The dock here has a restaurant and coffee shop and good
views of the cove, with its many boats floating at anchor. Orr's and Bailey are
quiet, very pleasant islands, popular retreats for many retired couples and
families, who stay on the island and take day trips to Freeport, Bath, and other
destinations.

Cliff: This is a rocky island which is part of the City of Portland; it has about 80
year-round residents and, in summer, almost four times as many. It is said that
the pirate Captain Keiff once lured unsuspecting ships toward the island by
hanging a lantern around a horse's neck and driving it up and down the shore as
a decoy. It is largely private, but it is possible to take the ferry here, and wander
along the scenic roads and out on The Bluff (which may be slippery). There is no
inn and no restaurant, but hot dogs and lobster rolls are available at in the
building next to the ferry landing. Miss Johanna Von Tiling, a retired teacher and
opera singer, is one of the better known citizens of Cliff Island; she used to give
concerts in Portland. Both she and Paul McVane, who cares for many of the
lawns on the island and is its unofficial historian, are concerned about the
increasing summer population and decreasing number of winter residents,

which for a time threatened to close the school for lack of the required number of children. Islanders pooled their resources, refurbished a vacant house, and invited a Portland welfare family with three children to settle on the island. They were delighted, and the school was saved. In July and August island olympics are held, and there is an Old Timer's Day in late August. In 1986, the acclaimed film *The Whales of August,* adapted by David Berry from his play, was made on the island. It starred Lillian Gish, Bette Davis, and Vincent Price.

Eagle: Once named Sawungun and, later, Heron Island, it was finally called Eagle Island after the eagle inhabitants. In 1903, Admiral Robert Peary built a house here with island stone and wood; it was here that he drew up the plans which would lead him to the North Pole. It is maintained as a museum by the state.

House: This island was possibly occupied in 1623 by Christopher Levett, the first settler in Casco Bay. In 1907, the Public Health Service built three dwellings here, used as a U. S. Quarantine and Immigration Station until the 1930s. The island is now owned by Hilda Cushing Dudley, who offers tours of the fort (see Access and Points of Interest).

Jewell Island is not occupied and has no ferry, but you may reach it by private boat; there is an anchorage on the island's northern tip and a pier on the western shore. The Maine Audubon Society takes bird-watching groups to the island several times a year. Legend has it that the island was a bastion of smuggling; Captain Chase, a suspected smuggler, was supposed to have been murdered here. Captain Kidd's hoard may well lie buried somewhere on the island's southern tip (and few visitors can resist searching into rocky crannies and nooks in search of his treasure chest). During World War II, two fire-control towers and several guns defended the island. The island also features the Punchbowl — a semicircular cove where the swimming is good.

Little Chebeague and Great Chebeague (*the latter is also called Chebeague Island*) The smaller island, *Little Chebeague,* is now owned by the state of Maine (which turned down a chance to buy the island for $1 in 1950 and then spent $155,000 to buy it in 1972). Today there are few vestiges of human habitation other than some old stone foundations. The island has a small sandy beach. At low tide a sandbar connects Little and Great Chebeague; you can walk between them and explore the beaches. There was once a small community here. *Great Chebeague* is the largest and hilliest of the Casco Bay islands, and one of the few with accommodations. There are about 300 year-round residents and an additional 2,500 in the summer. The island was a favorite camping spot for many Indian tribes; Indian bands camped on the island well into the twentieth century. In the 1930s the Attean Indians lived in tents on the island, selling baskets and beaded moccasins. Sir Ferdinando Gorges, known as the father of Maine, was the first white man to own Chebeague. In 1760, Ambrose Hamilton settled on a 100-acre estate on the island; he had 14 children and 71 grandchildren. Many of his descendants still inhabit the island. He began the granite industry on Chebeague, transporting granite in sloops from New England quarries (one was on Vinalhaven) to eastern cities such as Boston and Philadelphia. At one time there were as many as 30 sloops known along the Atlantic seaboard as the "Hamilton stone fleet." Nearly all the forts, breakwaters, and lighthouses from Eastport, Maine, to Delaware contained Maine rock furnished by this fleet during the 1850s.

Tourism began in 1870, the first year summer visitors were accommodated at one of the farmhouses. The fame of the island as an ideal summer resort began to grow and, at the turn of the century, there were a number of summer hotels, including the Summit House, the East Inn Hotel, and the Hamilton Hotel; guests arrived in style by steamer. Today, shops include Eva's Gift Shop and the Island Market. There is a golf course.

Little Diamond and Great Diamond: There are no public facilities, no restaurants, and no public beaches on these islands. On Little Diamond even the roads are private, and the public is discouraged from visiting it. At low tide, Little Diamond is connected by a narrow sand spit to Great Diamond. The latter island has a select summer colony, a golf course, and varied topography, including deep ravines and green slopes going down to the Bay. It was named "Hog Island" until the 1880s, when resort homeowners renamed it after the quartz crystals found in Diamond Cove.

Long Island: This is one of the largest and most scenic of the islands. It has a year-round population of about 125, which grows to about 2,000 in the summer. There are good roads, and shady paths. Once there were a number of grand summer hotels here. Long Island is known for its beautiful state beaches; Andrews and Singing Beach are especially popular. Big Sandy Beach is a "primitive" beach with no facilities. The old schoolhouse contains a gift shop and library.

Peaks Island: This is the closest island to Portland. The island's 1,500 year-round population increases to about 6,000 in the summer. It has become a commuting suburb of Portland; one young lawyer pointed out that the 17-minute ferry commute was far more convenient than coping with traffic on expressways. Despite its large commuter population, Peaks remains spiritually an island. By 7 a.m. the commuters are walking down to the ferry, a diverse group — construction workers, professional people with briefcases, and gas station attendants. The ferry usually has its share of shopping carts packed with groceries and other wares from Portland stores; they are rolled right off the boat, up the wharf, and into Peaks homes. Many residents have their own boats, zipping across to Portland for the symphony and other events. Island children use the ferry as their school bus. Peaks has been "discovered" by Portland residents as the ideal suburb, bringing about increases in land values and taxes. There is a developing sentiment for forming a separate municipality of the Casco Bay Islands, as some residents feel Portland does not provide enough services for them.

In 1869, the *Helen Eliza* was wrecked on Peaks Island rocks; Longfellow based his ballad "The Wreck of the Hesperus" on its destruction. Longfellow's childhood home in Portland is open to the public.

POINTS OF INTEREST   *Bailey and Orr's:* There is a very pretty harbor on Bailey, site of the annual Casco Bay Tuna Tournament. Access to Bailey is via the world's only cribstone bridge. The Giant Staircase on Washington St., Bailey, is a natural rock formation dropping 200 ft. in steps to the ocean; this is a scenic overlook area.

Cliff: The cove on the southeastern side of the island is where most of the fishermen live. The island has reefs, coves, sandbars, and pine groves; there is no museum, but there is a nature preserve. The pirate Captain Keiff supposedly buried dead sailors from the ships he lured toward the island in what is called "Keiff's Garden," a grassy knoll above the island road.

Eagle: The Peary House, on the National Register of Historic Landmarks, is open from June 1 to Labor Day. The home of Admiral Peary and his family, it is maintained as a museum by the state and has many of Peary's possessions, such as his boyhood seabird-egg collection and an Eskimo kayak paddle. A visit here might be combined with the Peary-MacMillan Arctic Museum in Brunswick,

Peaks Island, Casco Bay

operated by Bowdoin College, of which Peary was an alumnus.

House: Fort Scammell, a Civil War-era fort, has tunnels and large stone rooms. Shots were never fired here, and the fort was retired soon after the Civil War. The island owner, Hilda Cushing Dudley, runs tours and operates a charter service here.

Jewell Island: has two World War II-vintage towers; take a flashlight to climb up and down the tunnels and see the gun slits. The Punchbowl is a semicircular cove where the swimming is good.

Little and Great Chebeague: Visitors approaching Great Chebeague are shown the only "palm tree" in Casco Bay—actually a well-pruned oak.

Little and Great Diamond: The Diamonds are privately owned and have no public recreational facilities. Fort McKinley, on the east side of Great Diamond, can be seen from the water; it once served as a subpost for Portland Harbor defenses.

Long: The island has a large World War II refueling base, now deserted. Long Cove, on the eastern end of the island, is scenic, with lobster traps on its wharf. Big Sandy Beach is wide and curving, popular with swimmers and sunbathers; you may bicycle there or walk (it is about a mile from the ferry).

Peaks Island: Greenwood Gardens was the scene of America's first Summer Stock Theater, in 1868. For twenty-five cents, you could have a round-trip boat trip and a good seat. Lobster bakes, auctions, dances, and plays are now held here. Battery Steele is a World War II fort and favorite picnicking site for islands and visitors. Whaleback Rock, with its breakers and seaspray, is an excellent vantage point for artists and photographers. Other scenic spots are Hadlock's Cove and City Point. The Avenue House (Island Ave.) was once an inn where such summer stock stars as Diana Barrymore, Rod Steiger, and Jean Stapleton stayed. Brackett Cemetery is the oldest on the island, with stones dating from the 1700s.

SIGHTSEEING TOURS   From Portland, Casco Bay Lines offers a mail boat cruise to Cliff, Great Chebeague, Long, Little and Great Diamond, a Bailey Island cruise, and a variety of other cruises (see Access).

The *Kristy K.* and the *Fish Hawk* also take passengers around Casco Bay; contact Eagle Tours, Long Wharf, Portland 04101 (799-2201 or 774-6498).

The *Longfellow II,* a steamboat replica, has a variety of cruises; Longfellow Cruise Line, Long Wharf, Portland 04101 (774-3578).

Devil's Den Charters at DiMillo's Marina in Portland (761-4466) has a 38-ft. sport fisherman available for charter. (Dimillo's restaurant, adjacent, is in a grand old paneled Chesapeake Bay ferry, *The Newport,* formerly *The Richmond.*)

Dolphin Marina, Basin Point, S. Harpswell 04079 (833-6000) will arrange trips to Eagle Island.

On Peaks Island, a taxi (766-2777) will meet boats and take visitors anywhere on the island at a modest charge.

On Chebeague Island, Atlantic Seal Cruises (865-6112) offers sightseeing cruises of Casco Bay, excursions to Eagle Island, and service to Freeport for a shopping spree at L.L. Bean and the factory outlet stores which abound there.

PARKS, BEACHES   **Parks and beaches:** *Peaks Island* has nature
AND CAMPING   trails and a trout pond (which has no fish but offers good ice skating). Ice House Pond is a popular skating spot. Bicycles are available for touring the island's 720 acres. Sandy Beach near the landing and another beach beside the Trefethen Evergreen Improvement Association Clubhouse both have public access. *Great Chebeague* has a small pebbly beach called the Nubble, which has good views of the bay and mainland. Other swimming spots include Deer Point and Hamilton Beach. Little Chebeague and Long Island both have state beaches.
Camping: There is no camping on Great and Little Chebeague, Cliff, Peaks, Great and Little Diamond, Eagle, and House. It is permitted on Jewell but bring water and all food. On Orr's there is the Orr's Island Campground, Orr's Island 04066 (833-5595).

MARINAS   **Bailey Island:** The Mackerel Cove Marina offers full service for boaters, with moorings as well as dockside space for rent. There are ample slips as a rule; the only crowded time may be during the tuna tournament. There is a seafood restaurant as well as a lounge adjacent to the marina; dockside electricity is provided.

Eagle Island: Floats, moorings, and dinghies are available.

Great Chebeague: The stone pier on the north end has floats; 30-minute anchoring allowed. There are moorings at the Chebeague Island Inn (and they will lend yachtsmen a dinghy for getting to shore). The Bounty Pub is particularly popular.

Little Chebeague: There are anchorages off the island south of Indian Point.

Little Diamond: Ted Rand operates a fuel dock and has moorings here, but the public is not welcome on the island itself.

Peaks Island: Lionel Plante Associates has a float and moorings (766-2508), and the Jones Landing Restaurant (see Restaurants) has space for boaters who wish to dine in the restaurant.

RESTAURANTS   *Bailey and Orr's* Rock Ovens, at the Bailey Island Motel (see Lodging) is a cheerful dining room in country decor.$$

The Mackerel Cove Restaurant and Marina (833-6656) has a nice dining room overlooking the water, with a good view of Mackerel Cove.**$$**

Eagle Island: There are no restaurants, but you may picnic on the beach near the Peary home.

Great Chebeague The Chebeague Island Inn (see Lodging) serves breakfast, lunch, and dinner. Lobster is a specialty. The menu changes biweekly; sometimes there is broiled swordfish with raspberry hollandaise or stuffed sole with scallop and crab stuffing. Homemade soups and breads accompany each meal. The Bounty Pub, with its handmade teak bar, is a popular gathering spot, particularly for boating people.**$$**

Long Island: The Spar serves lobster dinners (summer only) and Clarke's store carries lunch fixings.**$**

Peaks Island The Cockeyed Gull Restaurant is quite popular (commuters often take along their muffins on the ferry to work). The Dockside, Island Ave., serves light meals and sandwiches; it is open year-round for breakfast and lunch.**$** The Jones Landing Restaurant, Welch St., near the ferry landing, is open year-round for lunch and dinner, with a good water view.**$** Their drinks are under the heading "Attitude Adjustment."**$**

LODGING   **Bailey and Orr's:** The Bailey Island Motel, Bailey Island 04003 (833-2886) is open early May through October. It is just across the bridge to the island, and has very pleasant lawns, with inviting chairs, leading down to a rocky shore.**$$**

Little Island: Orr's Island 04066 (833-2392) is open mid-May through Oct; it offers a free continental breakfast, rowboats, a gift shop, bicycles, and a dock, wharf, and float. Rooms have refrigerators, oversize beds and private decks. Mrs. Jo Atlass is the innkeeper.**$$**

Chebeague Island: The Chebeague Island Inn, Chebeague Island 04017 (846-5155) is open May through October. This 3-story inn, built in 1926, is on a hilltop. It has a wide veranda overlooking the bay. It has 21 rooms, 14 of which have water views; there is a great room with books and games; it is a good inn for families and will supply cots or cribs, but does not accept pets. Amenities also include tennis and golf.**$$**

Long Island: Write Beach Avenue House, Long Island, ME 04050; here there are 3 apartments for rent, sometimes by the weekend.**$**

Peaks Island: The Moonshell Inn, Island Ave., Peaks Island, 04108 (766-2331), owned by Elinor (Bunny) Clark, is open year round. There are 6 guest rooms, 4 of which have water views; guests share 3 full baths. There is an airy breakfast room and a sitting room.**$**

Ms. Clark can also arrange accommodation with a neighbor, who has 3 rooms, at a reduced rate.**$**

RENTALS   **Cliff Island:** Contact Mrs. Eleanor Cushing, at the Post Office (Cliff Island 04019).

Long Island: Mark and Linda Greene rent a house; write 3 Kendall Hill Rd., Sterling Junction, MA 01565 (508/422-6293).

CONTACT   Portland Chamber of Commerce, 142 Free St., Portland, ME 04101 (772-2811).

Great Cranberry Island

CRANBERRY ISLES:

Little* and Great Cranberry, Baker Island, Sutton and Bear — (*Islesford is the postal address for Little Cranberry Island, and the island is locally called Islesford).

Area Code 207

LOCATION Off Mount Desert Island in the Great Harbor of Mount Desert (Coastal Atlantic).

SIZE Great Cranberry is 2 miles by 1 mile (900 acres); Little Cranberry is 1¹/₂ miles by ³/₄ miles; Baker is 123 acres, Sutton is 174, and Bear is about 20 acres.

ACCESS *Ferry:* From Northeast Harbor (Beal and Bunker, Inc., Cranberry Isles, ME 04625; 244-3575 or 276-5396. *Air:* There is commercial service to Bar Harbor and Trenton, ME. There is also a private water taxi run by John Dwelley from June 1 – October 15. *Private boat.*

HISTORY AND DESCRIPTION It has been said that big islands are always attended by small islands, like sharks with pilot fish. This is surely true of the Mount Desert, attended by the Cranberry Isles as well as a number of others. There are five islands in the group, Little and Great Cranberry, Sutton, Bear and Baker. They were named for a sizeable cranberry bog on Great Cranberry, the largest island of the group (though the bog was blighted when drained for mosquito control a few years ago). Lobstering and boatbuilding are the principal occupations now . Only Great and Little Cranberry have year-round residents. The first known visitor was Samuel de Champlain in 1604. Once Maine passed from the French to the English, after Wolfe's victory at Quebec in 1759, the islands were given to Sir Francis Bernard, governor of Massachusetts, who controlled them until the Revolution.

The first permanent settler was Ben Bunker (1762). He was followed by John Stanley, Benjamin Spurling, and John Hadlock; there are still descendants of these families on the islands, and, of course, the visitor's first introduction to the island is via the Beal and Bunker ferry. In 1830, the original Cranberry Isles, along with Bear Island, were incorporated into a town called Cranberry Isles.

Great Cranberry has about 75 year-round residents, increasing to 300-400 during the summer. Great Cranberry and Little Cranberry each have a one-room school (K-8), though they share a school board and selectmen. The ferry *Sea Queen* docks here. Nearby businesses include the Pine Tree Market, the post office, Spurling Cove grocery store, the Whale's Rib gift shop, the Granite Napkin, (a restaurant), the school and the attached library, and 2 boatyards. One of the boatyards was recently bought by Barbie and David Stainton, who are building a home on the island and have come to love life there despite what some people might consider inconveniences as far as shopping and other services go. There is some fear on the part of local people that they may gradually be forced out by the high prices commanded for property sold to summer people and that Great Cranberry will be, like Sutton, mainly an island of vacation homes. At the same time, newcomers feel included in the local social and civic life, taking part in town meetings and being invited to potluck dinners and social occasions. There is also a church which has summer services with different visiting ministers in July and August. The fire house doubles as a meeting/social hall. The Ladies Aid building, next to the church, is the site of potluck suppers and the focus of the annual August Ladies Aid Fair. The island now has 15 students, 2 teachers, and 2 rooms in the school.

The main road on Great Cranberry goes from Spurling Cove 2 miles to the eastern end of the island. Three paved streets run off this road. Most of the houses are spread along either side of this road or the side roads. Summer visitors are not discouraged from walking along the shore in front of residents' houses. Great Cranberry, says islander Barbie Stainton, has a large resident deer herd. They roam freely all over the island, feasting on fall apples from the numerous wild apple trees or on flowers and vegetables in unfenced gardens. Serious gardeners have invested in 6–8-foot deer fences. The islands have wild cranberries, blueberries, masses of lupine in May and June, and many old apple trees grown wild. There are herons, gulls, crows, ravens, eagles, and owls.

Little Cranberry, or Islesford, is also a ferry stop, with an historical museum and the Blue Duck Ships' Store (see Points of Interest), Puddles Restaurant, a market, a church, Heirloom Weavers, and a bed-and-breakfast inn. There are about 90–100 year-round inhabitants, which increases to about 400 in summer. However, because the museum and Blue Duck Ships' Store are part of Acadia National Park, the island attracts as many as 20,000 daytrippers per year. There is a fishermen's co-op on the island, selling lobsters.

Most of Baker Island is part of Acadia National Park; visitors should take the cruise boat from Northeast Harbor. Sights on the cruise include the osprey nest on Sutton Island and the seals on East Bunker Ledge.

Sutton (once the home of Rachel Field, author of *Time Out of Mind* and *God's Pocket*), is private. It was named by Eben Sutton, who reputedly bought it from the chief of the Indians at what is now Southwest Harbor for two quarts of rum (a larger island would have cost a gallon). He was a companion of Abraham Somes, who later founded Somesville at the top of Somes Sound, a natural fiord on Mount Desert Island.

Bear Island has an old lighthouse. The lighthouse is being restored, and was relighted during the summer of 1989. The National Park Service has plans to lease the house. One family has a summer residence on the island.

POINTS OF INTEREST   On Little Cranberry Island, at Islesford, there is the Islesford Historic Museum, operated by the National Park Service. It has exhibits on local island history from 1604, and is open daily mid-June to mid-September. The displays depict the era when area boats and ships sailed the fishing banks, coastal routes, and distant seas, and focus on the hardy and industrious people whose coastal culture is an important part of maritime New England.

The Blue Duck Ships' Store, also on Islesford (so named because a blue wooden duck in profile is mounted on the door frame), is of interest. It was built about 1850 by Edwin Hadlock, who, with his sons Gilbert and William, operated it as a ship's chandlery for about 25 years. About 1912 it was purchased by Dr. William Otis Sawtelle, a Haverford College professor, who became interested in maritime New England history and founded the Islesford Historical Society. The Blue Duck and the Islesford Historical Museum became part of Acadia National Park in 1948. The Museum, housed in a brick and granite building, is open from late June to mid-September. Neighborhood House, built with the aid of summer residents, has social activities and theatrical performances. In 1989 the residents of Islesford added a small library to the Neighborhood House.

Great Cranberry has a large peat bog in the interior, the Heath (pronounced "Hathe" by locals); it is pretty and peaceful, with good views.

Baker Island is part of Acadia National Park. Sights of interest here include a large lighthouse, run by the U.S. Coast Guard, and the "Dance Floor," which is actually a large flat ledge, also called Dance Hall Rock or the Dancing Rocks. The island's early inhabitants are vividly described in Charles W. Eliot's 1899 book (available from Acadia National Park) *John Gilley of Baker's Island.*

SIGHTSEEING TOURS   The Islesford Ferry Company operates a 2-hour Nature Cruise and a 4½-hour Baker Island Cruise from Northeast Harbor's Sea Street Pier, from mid-June to Labor Day, visiting osprey and seal habitats. (For these cruises, call the Islesford Ferry Co., Box 451, R.F.D. 2, Ellsworth, Maine, 04605; 244-3366; office hours 9-5:30 p.m.; off-season 422-6815). There is also a dinner cruise to Puddles Restaurant (call the restaurant for reservations and ferry schedule, 244-3177). Beal and Bunker run an Islesford Historical Cruise aboard the *Sea Princess,* from Northeast Harbor to Islesford (244-3575). The morning cruise passes the Bear Island Light Station; Sutton Island for a glimpse of a rare Osprey nesting site; East Bunker where there are seals, black back gulls, and other wildlife on the ledges; and Little Cranberry, where there is time for a visit to the historical museum. The boat then traverses Somes Sound to Valley Cove, and passes by the St. Sauveur Jesuit Mission on Fernald Point. The tour runs every day from late June to early September. There is also an afternoon cruise following the same route, and a late afternoon cruise which does not stop at Little Cranberry.

PARKS, BEACHES AND CAMPING   ***Parks:*** Most of Baker Island is part of Acadia National Park, as well as the Islesford Historical Museum and the Blue Duck Ships' Store on Little Cranberry island. The rare bird Leach's Petrel (seldom seen except far out at sea) nests here, and gulls and terns breed prolifically. ***Beaches:*** On Little Cranberry there are Sand Beach, Gilley Beach, and the Coast Guard Beach; access is only via public roads and visitors are asked to respect private property rights. Hardy souls swim on the island, when it gets really hot, but usually it is too cold. ***Camping:*** No camping is allowed on the Cranberry Isles, but on nearby Mt. Desert Island there are campgrounds.

MARINAS   Little Cranberry Harbor (Islesford) is a good choice if Northeast Harbor is crowded. Here there are moorings, fuel, and groceries, as well as a small hardware store. Islesford Dock (244-3177) is also the site of the restaurant; 4 transient slips; maximum length 40 ft.; approach depth 9 ft.; dockside depth 9 ft.; electric power — no; restaurant within walking distance — yes. The Islesford Yacht Club clubhouse is a room on the same pier as the Islesford Dock.

RESTAURANTS   Food service is available at Puddles Restaurant on Islesford and the Granite Napkin on Great Cranberry. Puddles has a rustic dining room and a smaller brightly decorated lounge; both have a good view of Mount Desert Island. The restaurant is so popular it is the destination of a dinner cruise from Northeast Harbor in summer. It has a full menu with a bar.$$ The Granite Napkin serves a continental breakfast and lunch only, 5 days per week, and has muffins, salads, soups, and desserts, but no alcohol.$ Both Cranberry and Little Cranberry have small grocery stores and gift shops.

LODGING   The Island Bed-and-Breakfast on Little Cranberry is run by Sue Jones (Islesford, ME 04646; 244-9283), whose family has been on the island since the late 1700s. The inn has several guest rooms, including a two-room suite.$

There is now a bed-and-breakfast inn on Great Cranberry, the Red House, owned by John and Dot Towns (244-5297); open summer only.$

RENTALS   There are no house rentals unless privately arranged.

CONTACT   For information about the Acadia National Park section of the Cranberry Isles, contact the U.S. Dept. of the Interior, Box 177, Bar Harbor, ME 04609 or the Superintendent, Acadia National Park, Bar Harbor, ME 04609 (207/288-3338). For information about the Cranberry Isles as a whole, contact Beal and Bunker Boats, Cranberry Isles, ME 04646 (207/244-3575) or the Bar Harbor Chamber of Commerce, Box 158, Bar Harbor 04609 (207/288-3393).

The *Mink* and the *Miss Lizzie*, Deer Isle

DEER ISLE
(Big and Little Deer Isle)

Area Code 207

LOCATION In Penobscot Bay, south of Bangor; Deer Isle, Bucksport, and Ellsworth form a triangle.

SIZE Little Deer Island is 3 miles long; Big Deer Island is 9 miles long; width is about 5 miles.

ACCESS ***Car:*** Toll-free bridge over Eggemoggin Reach. ***Air:*** Bangor is the closest major airport; there is also commercial service to Trenton (midway between Ellsworth and Bar Harbor), Ellsworth, and Bar Harbor. Flying to Bangor and renting a car there is the most economical connection overall. There is also charter air service from Owls Head, near Rockland (Penobscot Air Service, 596-6211), and charter air service from Belfast (Ace Aviation, 338-2970). See Sightseeing Tours for island taxi service from the airport. ***Private boat.***

HISTORY AND DESCRIPTION A local historian, Vernal Hutchinson, has stated that Deer Isle proper looks like "a figure eight drawn by a very shaky hand." As you drive over the high iron Sedgewick Bridge over Eggemoggin Reach, it is clear that you are arriving on an island; should you be in doubt, you then weave along a causeway edged by a serpentine stone wall which connects Little Deer Isle and Big Deer Isle. Rt. 15 loops through rural countryside to the towns of Deer Isle, Sunset, and Stonington; the town of Sunshine is off to the east. Beyond the southern end of Deer Isle lies a maze of out islands, scattered in the Deer Island Thorofare all the way to the Isle au Haut. The granite headlands, covered with spruce, are a dominant feature of the scenery on Deer Isle. The islands are, in fact, the peaks of what once were ancient mountains sculpted and drowned by glaciation. Deer Isle proper, the township containing Big Deer Isle and Little Deer Isle, has two principal towns, Deer Isle and Stonington.

The island was charted by Samuel de Champlain in 1604, and, like many of the Maine islands, claimed for France. Until 1696, it was owned by the Penobscot Indians, but in 1696 it was given to the fur trader Cotton Mather Olmstead by the Penobscot chief, who had been mauled by a bear, in exchange for medical treatment. By the end of the French and Indian Wars in the 1760s, the island had about 20 families, which had increased to about 100 by 1775.

The island's fortunes have risen and fallen; by the mid-1800s, Deer Isle was a thriving fishing port second only to Gloucester, Massachusetts, and had "three hundred sail of vessel," but the profits of vessel fishing declined. The granite quarrying industry also prospered, then went down, though some quarrying is still done. The granite for New York's Triborough Bridge came from Deer Isle (200 men worked two years to quarry and cut the granite). The island is famous for shipbuilding (the America's Cup winners *Columbia* and *Defender* were built here), and the island's skilled boatmen have manned island boats in international races. Until 1939, when the Sedgewick Bridge was built, the island was connected to the mainland by ferry; Capt. Scott's ferry celebrated its fiftieth anniversary in 1889. In this century, the residents' livelihood has come principally from fishing (there is a sardine cannery in Stonington), lobstering, and shipbuilding. Today lobstering is much in evidence; brightly-colored lobster traps hang from tree limbs and the walls of barns, and every harbor has its share of lobster boats. Much of the island is not inhabited, and visitors can sometimes sight seals, porpoises, cormorants, eiders, and ospreys.

John Steinbeck made Deer Isle one of the first stops in his 1961 odyssey *Travels with Charley,* declaring the island resists description. It "opens no door to words. . . But it stays with you afterward. . . Everything stood out separate from everything else, a rock, a rounded lump of sea-polished driftwood on a beach, a roof line. Each pine tree was itself and separate even if it was part of a forest." One still has the feeling of startling juxtaposition, of civilization making widely spaced, somewhat tentative imprints on the stark scenery. From granite hillsides, spruce forests part to reveal dark little islands in clear blue water; lobster traps are piled in tranquil harbors. The literary tradition is continued today by the writer Robert McCloskey, author of the children's book *Make Way for Ducklings,* who has a summer home on the island. Some pleasanter aspects of civilization have made inroads: there are well-stocked libraries at the Pilgrim's Inn and in each guest cottage at the Goose Cove Lodge; the Penobscot Bay Press occupies a building in Stonington. The Dockside bookstore has an excellent selection of material on Maine. In Sunshine, renowned craftspeople teach at the Haystack Mountain School of Crafts. Tucked discreetly here and there are galleries, along with special craft shops such as the Green Head Forge for sculptured metals and jewelry, William Mor Stoneware, the Eggemoggin Gallery and Stained Glass Studio, but these shops and galleries, along with Haystack, are so self-effacing they impose no "artsy" ambiance on the essentially primitive character of the island. The year-round inhabitants do not want to see the island overly developed. The Deer Isle Thorofare is, in summer, crowded with windjammers, ketches, and schooners, but there is a solid mix of seiners and lobster boats which remind the onlooker that Stonington is a working fishing village.

POINTS OF INTEREST   Ames Pond, on ME 15 in Stonington, has pink and white water lilies blooming in summer. Nearby is a Lilliputian village built by Everett Knowlton, with churches, houses, and stores on a miniature scale.

The Haystack Mountain School of Crafts campus in Sunshine, designed by Edward Larrabee Barnes, is of great architectural interest, with contemporary deck-connected studios and other buildings descending from the entrance down a hillside to the water. Master craftspeople from many places teach blacksmithing, metal-smithing, weaving, and crafts in other media to students who come for two- and three-week residential courses.

The 1836 Salome Sellers House, operated by the Deer Isle-Stonington Historical Society in Sunset (no telephone) is open from early July to early September, Wednesday, Saturday, and Sunday afternoons. The house is a repository of varied island memorabilia.

You may also tour the sardine cannery in Stonington, but it is not always open.

SIGHTSEEING TOURS   The *Palmer Day IV* offers 2-hour tours around the islands in Penobscot Bay (July 4–September 1); contact Capt. Reginald Greenlaw, Stonington (367-2207). Capt. Greenlaw promises that the excursions "are undoubtedly the best scenic tours and by far the most educational of all water trips offered in the State of Maine. I will feed mackerel or herring hopefully to my pet seal, and he will jump out of the water two or three feet." On Wednesdays, there is an excursion to Vinalhaven and North Haven, with stops at each. The Isle au Haut Boat Co. offers island tours on the *Miss Lizzie* from late June to early Sept. (The *Miss Lizzie* is also the mail boat to the Isle au Haut; she was named for a beloved island postmistress.) The mailboat to Eagle and Sprucehead Islands leaves from the Yacht Club wharf at Sylvester's Cove in Sunset; reservations are needed, but this is a delightful ride.

Sea Kayaking is offered by Explorers at Sea, Inc., Box 51, Stonington, ME 04681 (367-2356); trips range from 1–5 days.

Sailways, Burnt Cove, Stonington (348-2279) offers sailboat rentals and skipper service if desired.

A–Z Taxi and Tours, owned by Nancy Brooks, Box 184, Stonington (348-6186), offers tours of the island as well as airport pick-up.

PARKS, BEACHES AND CAMPING   **Parks:** Seven trails radiate from Goose Cove Lodge in Sunset; the trails are open to the public. If the tide is out, hikers can cross a sandbar to Barred Island, owned by the Nature Conservancy. **Beaches:** There are a number of beaches on the island; one is a sand beach near Fifield Point, Stonington. The water is usually cold. **Camping:** Small's Trailer & Campsites, Sunset (367-2497).

MARINAS   Billings Diesel and Marine Service, Inc., Stonington (357-2328), 15 transient slips; maximum length 120 ft.; approach depth 25 ft.; dockside depth 10 ft.; electric power — yes; restaurant within walking distance — no.

RESTAURANTS   Bayview, near the public wharf in Stonington (367-2274). This is in an 1880s building, and is the restaurant of the Captain's Quarters (see

Lodging), whose guests have a 10% discount. It has tablecloths, candlelight, fresh flowers, and good seafood specialties.**$$**

The Beachcomber Restaurant (see Lodging) serves excellent seafood.**$$**

Connie's, School St., Stonington, ME 04681 (367-2742), specializes in fish and homemade pies; diners may bring wine, beer, or liquor.**$$**

The Fisherman's Friend, School St., Stonington, ME 04681 (367-2442), offers a varied menu ranging from sandwiches to all-you-can-eat fried haddock dinners (the mini-platters are enormous). There is no liquor license, but you can buy wine or liquor along Rt. 15.**$$**

Goose Cove Lodge in Sunset (see Lodging) serves dinners during the season; the Friday night lobster feast is especially popular (bring your own wine or liquor). There is after-dinner entertainment in the form of slide shows, music, or lectures.**$$**

The Pilgrim's Inn (see Lodging) serves dinners every night but Thursday; reservations essential.**$$$**

LODGING

The Beachcomber Motel, Rt. 15, Little Deer Isle, ME 04650 (348-6115), is located just over the Deer Isle bridge. There are 20 rooms, just 100 feet from a private beach; they all have water views, carpets, and baths.**$**

Boyce's Motel, Box 94, Main St., Stonington (367-2421) has been on the island for many years; it has overnight accommodations plus kitchen units.**$-$$**.

The Captain's Quarters Inn Motel, Box 83, Stonington, ME 04681 (367-2420), is open all year, and has flower-filled sun decks overlooking the Harbor in Stonington. The buildings, which front on Main St., have been connected into unique lodging units. They date from the 1880s, and have in the past served various functions (barber shop, post office, telephone exchange, fish market, and food and clothing stores). There are now 15 rooms furnished with country pieces and, says Innkeeper Bob Dodge, "depending on help and circumstances, fresh garden flowers." Most of the rooms, some of them suites with fireplaces, overlook the harbor.**$-$$**.

Goose Cove Lodge, Sunset, Deer Isle, ME 04683 (348-2508) is set on 70 acres of scenic land. This lodge offers suites and comfortable cottages, many with fireplace, decks, and water views. The Pavloffs welcome hikers, non-guests as well as guests; "you can't really own Goose Cove," says George Pavloff. Wolffe Trail winds through a spruce forest and there are other trails as well. George and Elli Pavloff, who bought the Lodge in 1980, have a resident spaniel, Allegro, who is guaranteed to comfort guests afflicted with homesickness for their pets. The Pavloffs extended the main lodge living room with a pleasant many-windowed dining room. There is a minimum stay of one week in July and August. Rates include breakfast and dinner.**$$**

The Inn at Ferry Landing is a bed-and-breakfast inn at 108 Ferry Rd., Deer Isle, ME 04627 (348-7760). It is on Eggemoggin Reach, at the northern end of the island, converted from an 1850s New England farmhouse, at the landing where the ferry and steamboat once docked. In those days it housed Samuel Lowe's General Store and Livery Stable; once the bridge was built, the Lowe family continued to live here. Innkeepers Stephen and Donna Gormley have restored the house, which has many country antiques; the beds are adorned with patchwork quilts. Rates include a hearty breakfast with such delicacies as blueberry crumble and banana French toast.**$$**

The Pilgrim's Inn, Deer Isle, ME 04627 (348-6615), is a gambrel-roofed structure built in 1793 by Squire Ignatius Haskell, a wealthy sawmill owner. It was his daughter Rebeccah who first began offering rest and relaxation to the traveler and began the tradition of hospitality maintained today. Jean and Dud Hendrick are the innkeepers. Among the amenities of the inn are a wood-paneled Tap Room; a library adorned with studies of the Maine coast; gardens and lawn sweeping down to the water; and a Common Room with an 8-ft.-wide fireplace and bee-hive oven, where guests enjoy cocktails before dinner. Angela Lansbury has stayed here, welcoming the tranquility. The dining room is in a barn with hand-hewn beams and antique farm tools. The inn is open from late May through late October.**$$$**

Two bed-and-breakfast inns are Laphroaig (the word is Swedish for "Welcome"), Box 67, Deer Isle Village, ME 04627 (348-6088), run by John and Andrea Mayberry, ($) and the Deer Isle Village Inn, Box 456, Deer Isle, ME 04627 (348-2564), run by Paul and Bobbie Zierk.($) Both serve very good breakfasts.

RENTALS   Green's Landing Realty, Box 500, Stonington, ME
                         04681 (367-5140); Sea Breeze Real Estate,
                         Stonington (367-2305); Shepard's Select Proper-
ties, Inc., Stonington (367-2790).

CONTACT   Deer Isle-Stonington Chamber of Commerce,
                         Box 268, Little Deer Isle, ME 04681 (348-6124).

FRENCHBORO
(Long Island)

Area Code 207
LOCATION   Approximately 8 miles from Bass Harbor by ferry.

SIZE   3 miles by 3 miles.

ACCESS   **Ferry:** From Bass Harbor (Maine State Ferry
                         Service, Box 645, 517-A Main St., Rockland,
                         Maine, 04841; 207/594-5543; Bass Harbor office:
Bass Harbor, ME 04653; 207/244-3254). Note that the ferry only runs two days a week, in summer on Wednesday and Thursday. Mail comes six days a week, two on the ferry and four on the Frenchboro mail boat from Kent's Wharf, Swans Island Village, which makes a round trip. Call the Swans Island Village post office for times. **Air:** There is commercial service to Bangor. **Private boat.**

HISTORY AND   Frenchboro, the sole settlement on Long Island,
DESCRIPTION   is appealing, with its snug semicircular harbor,
                         ringed by weathered houses and a small white
church; there are piers and fishing shacks, alongside a harbor graced by lobster boats and occasional sailboats. The coastline is ragged, with pebbly beaches on the outer shores (such as Eastern Beach). Granite boulders are topped by tall spruce; there are pine groves and shady paths. Stone implements, flint arrowheads, and shell heaps suggest that the island was settled by the Abnaki Indians long before white men arrived. The island was long accessible to tourists via steamers from Portland. It once had as many as 200 people, and a good school. Much of the island is owned by the David Rockefeller family.

Congregational Christian Church, Frenchboro Elementary School, Parsonage

In her excellent history of Frenchboro, Vivian Lunt details the growth of the island. In a time when transience and mobility mark the lifestyles of many Americans, it is interesting to read the "Census," "Births," "Deaths," and "Marriages" sections of the book, and to find the names of families prominent in the twentieth century occurring in the earliest nineteenth-century records, especially Lunt, Davis, and Dalzell.

When fishing declined, however, so did the population until, a few years ago, only 51 year-round inhabitants remained — not even enough to support a grocery store. This meant residents had to shop on the mainland and stay in a motel (because the ferry only ran two days a week).

Islanders feared that the population would dwindle even further. Led by Jim Haskell, part-time town manager and apple grower, they formed a Future Development Corporation and applied for and received a grant for $336,000. The funds have been used to offer ten one-acre improved lots to new settlers (six were reserved for low-to-moderate income families). A 50-acre parcel of land was donated for the project by a nonresident, Margaret Rockefeller Dulany, daughter of David Rockefeller. This effort received national media attention; *Star* magazine headlined its article, "Come Live with Us on Fantasy Island," NBC did a film clip, and a story was published in *The New York Times.* The island was deluged by inquiries, including some from Dallas, Fort Lauderdale, Colorado, and France. "We don't want to burst the bubble," Dan Blaszczuk, then town treasurer, told the *National Geographic,* "maybe just deflate it a little. The town just can't afford to have a bunch of people arriving here lock, stock, and barrel saying, 'O.K., it's wonderful, now what do I do?' They need a working asset." Residents seem to agree that fishing, though uncertain, is the most natural prospective occupation, given the island's economy and resources. The sifting of applications is underway and 7 homesteads have been completed; the first one was designated for the teacher.

A previous effort of a different kind to increase the population had met with success; orphaned or abandoned children were, at one time, placed with foster island families by the Maine Department of Child Welfare. Charles Kuralt broadcast one of his "On the Road" television stories about the bringing of the foster children to the island, saying it was "bleached by the sun and weathered by time" and would be dying if it were not for the children. Some of them have returned to live there permanently.

The inhabitants of Frenchboro were mystified in 1988 when the town treasurer, Dan Blaszczuk, who had lived on the island for 8 years, apparently absconded with about $15,000 from the town treasury. His disappearance was reported in *The New York Times*. Neither he nor the money has ever been found. The money was repaid to the community from the company which had bonded Mr. Blaszcuk. His mother, Lillian, also sent $5,000 to the island to compensate for her son's mistake.

The island is a little difficult to visit on a day trip, though you can come out from Bass Harbor on the early morning Maine State ferry, spend about two hours, return on the early afternoon mail boat to Swans Island, and then go back to Bass Harbor on a Maine State ferry. One obstacle is that, once on Swans Island, you need to find a ride from Swans Island Village to the ferry terminal at Atlantic.

POINTS OF INTEREST The Frenchboro Historical Society and Museum, featuring island memorabilia, is in a building in back of the school; it has photographs and early furniture. Each summer, usually in August, an all-day fair is held to raise money for the society and the church; there are extra ferries laid on for the occasion. The island historian, Vivian Lunt, has lived on Frenchboro all her life and is President of the Frenchboro Historical Society. The museum was built in 1986 and ready for the summer season the same year.

Visitors might also enjoy shopping in the boutique which Rebecca Lunt runs in the basement of her home. She carries an unusual selection, including her own oil paintings, quilts, Christmas ornaments, crocheted slippers, pillows, and items made from rocks. She also carries fresh crabmeat and delicious home-made fudge.

Other sights of interest on the island include the Frenchboro Congregational Church, the elementary school, and the parsonage. Lunt's Harbor is very picturesque, with boats swinging at anchor and Swans Island visible in the distance.

SIGHTSEEING TOURS None.

PARKS, BEACHES *Parks:* None, but the island is a beautiful place for
AND CAMPING exploration on foot. *Beaches:* Eastern Beach offers swimming but only for the very hardy.
Camping: Camping is allowed at Eastern Beach.

MARINAS No marinas per se, but many people visit Frenchboro by mooring in the harbor and coming ashore. Lunt and Lunt pier has a float and a few moorings available for a small fee, along with fuel and water.

RESTAURANTS Lunt's Deli at the gas wharf is open from the middle of June until just before Labor Day.

LODGING	Rebecca Lunt, 34 Oceanview Rd., Frenchboro 04635 (334-2934) has an extra room with twin beds and will be glad to put up visitors overnight.
RENTALS	There are no rentals unless privately arranged.
CONTACT	Selectmen, Frenchboro, Bass Harbor, ME 04653.

ISLE AU HAUT

Area Code 207

LOCATION	6 miles south of Stonington.
SIZE	6 miles by about 2 miles.

ACCESS   ***Mail boat:*** From Stonington, on Deer Isle. The mail boat goes from here to the small village of Isle au Haut year-round and a tour boat goes to Duck Harbor, in the portion of the Island which is in the Acadia National Park, from late June to mid-Sept. (Isle au Haut Co., Isle au Haut, ME 04645; 207/367-5193). The *Miss Lizzie,* the mail boat, is named for the much loved former postmistress of Deer Isle. ***Air:*** Bangor is the closest major airport; there is also commercial service to Trenton (midway between Ellsworth and Bar Harbor), Ellsworth, and Bar Harbor. Flying to Bangor and renting a car there is the most economical connection overall. ***Private boat.***

HISTORY AND DESCRIPTION   The Isle au Haut is a beautiful, unspoiled island which has consciously discouraged tourist development; there is one inn on the island (see Lodging) and a portion of it is within the Acadia National Park. These provide the only, albeit limited and primitive, services for visitors.

The island was named by Samuel de Champlain and is variously called "eel a hoe" or "aisle a holt" by visitors but "aisle a hoe" by natives. Its highest point, Mt. Champlain, is 554 feet, the tallest on any offshore Maine island, but Duck Harbor Mountain, near the Acadia National Park boat landing, offers a better view. There are treacherous ledges surrounding the island, with heavy breakers in strong southerly winds.

The first settler is thought to have been Peletiah Barter of Boothbay, who came in 1792 with his brothers Henry and William. By 1880, there were 300 permanent residents. In 1879 Ernest Bowditch of Boston and a friend, Albert Otis of Belfast, established the first summer colony on the island. They founded the Point Lookout Club, a bachelor fishing club which eventually grew to include families. Over the years, the group built a clubhouse, cottages, and roads, and stocked the lake with game fish. Point Lookout is off-limits to visitors. Through the generosity of the Bowditch heirs, most of the land was eventually turned over to the Acadia National Park. The year-round population declined with the introduction of power fishing boats and the closing of the lobster canning industry. Today seals and protected deer inhabit the island along with a small number of permanent residents, mainly fishermen, and some summer residents. Each summer, several thousand people visit the Isle au Haut portion of Acadia National Park; to protect the fragile environment, park authorities limit the number to fifty per day.

One poet has pointed up the differing points of view between "summer people" and natives:

Says the summer man, when the fog hangs low,
"There's bridal wreath over Isle au Haut."
But the fisherman says when he launches his boat,
"It's gosh darn foggy off Isle au Haut."

Actually, however, it tends to be the other way around, with the summer visitor complaining about the fog and the year-rounder appreciating the beauties of the island in all weather.

A 12-mile road winds around the island, though most of it is unpaved. There are very few vehicles on the island; as there is no car ferry, they must be barged in, and, consequently, cars are patched and kept going as long as possible. Instead of telephones, islanders use ship-to-shore radios.

POINTS OF INTEREST   There is a tiny and unspoiled village consisting of a store, post office, church, library, and school.
The Isle au Haut Thorofare, running between Kimball Island and the island, is particularly scenic, with spruce-studded, softly contoured hills rising behind the high church steeple, the village of Isle au Haut, and the lighthouse.

Walking is the preferred mode of transportation (most of the roads are too rocky or sandy for satisfactory bicycling). There are more than 18 miles of trails, maintained by the National Park Service, on which hikers can explore the shore, lake, and marshes. Duck Harbor Trail offers access to Moore's Harbor, and there

Shoreline, Isle au Haut

are also Eben's Head, Western Head, Cliff, and Goat trails, all offering interesting prospects typical of Maine's rugged coast. There are good views between the stony shore of Duck Harbor and Western Head as well as from Duck Harbor Mountain.

Money Cove is where Captain Kidd is believed to have buried part of his fabulous pirate treasure; however, there has been no discovery to substantiate the legends.

The Isle au Haut lighthouse still stands and operates each night, its red light beaming a warning to wayward ships. The Coast Guard calls it the Robinson Point Light and it is so identified on charts, but most sources refer to it as the Isle au Haut Light and, more recently, as the Keeper's House (see Lodging). Most lighthouse properties are owned by the Federal government, but a few, including this one, were sold during the 1930s.

SIGHTSEEING TOURS   None on the island itself. If you visit Isle au Haut via the tour boat from Stonington, which goes to Duck Harbor (late June–mid- September only), you have six hours between boats in which to explore the Acadia National Park section of the island. (Be sure to take warm waterproof clothing, food, and drink; there are no shops, supplies, or shelter in the Park.) A ranger greets each Duck Harbor boat, hands out maps, and explains the park trail system, which has several loops of varying length and difficulty. A sightseeing boat from Stonington, the *Palmer Day IV,* also goes through the Isle au Haut Thorofare (July 4–September 1); call Capt. Reginald Greenlaw, 367-2207.

PARKS, BEACHES   ***Parks:*** About half of the island (48%) comprises
AND CAMPING   the wilderness area of Acadia National Park. (see History and Description section for discussion of trails). ***Beaches:*** The beaches are rocky, but there are picturesque coves and there is good swimming at a small sandy beach at the south end of Long Pond, an inland lake. The water is crystal clear but frigidly cold. ***Camping:*** There is camping at Duck Harbor, part of Acadia National Park (in 6 lean-to shelters; no tents permitted). For reservations, which must be made by mail, write for application form to Acadia National Park, Isle au Haut Reservations, Box 177, Bar Harbor, ME 04609. For information, call 288-3338. Advance reservations are mandatory; they are taken after April 1 and often fill by June. You will not be permitted to stay overnight without a reservation. Visitors are asked to help keep the island unspoiled by taking away their own trash, and any other trash they see.

MARINAS   None; yachtsmen may anchor in the Thorofare and explore the town by dinghy; dinghies may be tied to the float at the town wharf. There is no water hose and no dock-side fuel supply, but both are available in Stonington.

RESTAURANTS   None, but lodging at the Keeper's House includes meals. A typical dinner begins when the fog bell summons guests to dinner at sunset. Candlelight and gas lights provide evening illumination, as there is no electricity. Everything is homemade and fresh. Dinner might be Grace's spicy fresh mushroom soup, fresh garden salad with Island lettuce, native sauteed scallops in paprika, and seasonal lobster with lemon basil carrots and baked potatoes.

The meal is served with yogurt muffins and breads straight from the oven. For dessert there is usually a choice, such as raspberry peach tart or apple pie. Beverages might include sparkling cider, lime water, and coffee; guests bring their own wine.

LODGING

The Keeper's House, Box 26, Isle au Haut, ME 04645 (367-2261), is run by Jeffrey and Judi Burke. The mailboat brings guests directly to the

Isle au Haut Light

inn. It is open May 1 through October 30. The lighthouse station was built by the Coast Guard in 1907. The Burkes bought it in 1986 and have remodeled it as a living museum where guests can experience the beauty and solitude of an earlier period. The 4-room inn is unique on the East Coast. They have kept the way of life once led by the keeper intact, and there are no telephones or electric lights. There are, however, wood stoves providing hot water. There are 4 large bedrooms and 2 modern bathrooms in the main inn; the Oil House offers separate accommodation for one or two people, with an outdoor shower and "backhouse." The rates include all meals and taxes. Jeffrey Burke explains the reason for their project: "The lighthouse is symbolic of a whole era of American history. . . . The fact that they're threatened to some degree now strikes a chord in most people's hearts." Valerie Nelson, co-director of the Lighthouse Preservation Society, based in Rockport, Massachusetts, believes the Burkes' venture to be an ideal solution to the expense of restoring and maintaining lighthouse stations. The light is still maintained by the Coast Guard.

The island and surrounding waters are a delight for naturalists, with wild deer, seals, and porpoises; from the Keeper's House the hiking trails of Acadia National Park are easily accessible.$$$

RENTALS   Charles and Joanne Turner, Turner Cove duplex rental (5 persons max.; May-September), 11 Cricket Hill, Amherst, NH 03031; 603/673-1449.

CONTACT   For information about the portion of the island within the Acadia National Park, contact the Superintendent, Acadia National Park, Bar Harbor, ME 04609 (288-3338). For direct information about the island or about the Keeper's House, contact Jeff and Judi Burke (see Lodging).

ISLESBORO

Area Code 207
LOCATION   In Penobscot Bay, about 6 miles from Belfast and 3 miles from Lincolnville.

SIZE   10 miles by 1 mile or less in places.

ACCESS   **Ferry:** From Lincolnville Beach (Maine State Ferry Service, Box 645, 517-A Main St., Rockland, Maine, 04841 (594-5543); Lincolnville office: Lincolnville, ME 04849 (789-5611). **Air:** There is commercial service to Bangor. There is also charter air service from Owls Head, near Rockland (Penobscot Air Service, 596-6211; no taxi service on the island), and charter air service from Belfast (Ace Aviation, 338-2970). **Private boat.**

HISTORY AND   Islesboro (originally called Long Island) was not
DESCRIPTION   settled until about 1769, though it was visited in 1692 by the Benjamin Church expedition, which mounted a campaign against the Indians. In 1779, a large naval engagement occurred between Islesboro and Castine, when 22 American ships were destroyed by 5 British frigates. One of the houses at Pripet, at the upper end of the island, has a cannonball hole in its wall dating from this time. In 1780, an

Grindle   Point Lighthouse and Museum, Islesboro

academic expedition from Harvard was sent to observe the solar eclipse; they received permission to anchor in what were then British waters, and set up their instruments in the barn of one of Islesboro's first settlers, Shubael Williams. They made the first scientific notes about the astronomical phenomenon known as "Baily's Beads."

The town of Islesboro was incorporated in 1788. Winters were much more severe in the early nineteenth century, and Penobscot Bay sometimes froze as far out as the Isle au Haut; sleighs drawn by oxen often crossed to the mainland. At one time, there was steamer service to Castine, Belfast, and Camden as well as Lincolnville, but there is now only ferry service to Lincolnville. A new ferry has just replaced the beloved *Governor Muskie,* the *Margaret Chase Smith,* which is the largest vessel in the Maine State fleet and carries 30 cars. Cars were banned in 1913 but readmitted in the early 1930s, when they came by scow (the first car ferry dates from 1936).

Islesboro is the largest island on this section of the coast and the longtime home of an exclusive summer colony, but ordinary visitors will also find much of interest on the island. The summer colony developed in the latter part of the nineteenth century. Jeffrey Brackett, a Harvard student, sailed by the island, which he thought very beautiful, enroute to Bar Harbor, which was getting too staid for his taste. He purchased 200 acres on the island and, with Harvard friends, formed the Islesboro Land and Improvement Company of Philadelphia; in 1889 they purchased about 2,000 acres on the southern part of the island for $100,000. They sold it in lots to other wealthy families (the island had originally been settled by Indians and was a thriving farming and fishing community with some white settlers). Most of the large and elegant mansions, or "cottages" in the Newport sense, still stand, and are occupied by private families; there are about fifty, some with households of two dozen servants, including chauffeurs and boatmen. Most cannot be seen from the road but, from the water, they are clearly visible to yachtsmen. Islesboro may be one of the few American islands left where prospective visitors may encounter British butlers on the ferry enroute to service in these mansions. Among the prominent people who have had homes here are Douglas Dillon, Secretary of the Treasury under J. F. Kennedy; Hodding Carter; Lady Astor; the Rothschilds; the Biddles; the monologist Ruth Draper; Marshall Fields; and novelist Sidney Sheldon. His novel *Master of the Game* focuses on Islesboro, which he calls "the jealously-guarded colony of the super-rich." The illustrator Charles Dana Gibson built a mansion on Seven Hundred Acre Island, one of the small ones nearby. Louise Dickinson Rich, author of *We Took to the Woods* and *The Coast of Maine,* also lived on Islesboro at one time, writing that, on the ferry, she readjusted her thinking to "island tempo," watching the lighthouse draw nearer and searching for seals or porpoises playing in the water.

There are about 525 year-round residents, but no central village; the island is a long, low, tree-clad strip of land with several settlements. The post office, a garage, and a gift shop are in one cluster; the laundromat, bakery, and general shop in another, and the historical society and library are in yet another. There is little commercial development. There are stunning sunsets behind the Camden Hills, across Penobscot Bay; a good viewing spot is the ferry landing. The island has many pleasant coves bounded by evergreens and rocky beaches. Pendleton Point is the southernmost tip of the island, and Turtle Head the northernmost. You may drive up to Pripet, at the north end of the island, or down to Dark Harbor, where many grand old summer homes coexist with more modern ones. Dark Harbor is a popular stop for bikers; the Dark Harbor Shop, owned by realtor Bill Warren, has everything from books and gifts to ice cream. Here you can learn more about the island in an hour of mingling over a cup of coffee than in a whole day of driving about. There is also an art gallery, a golf course, and pleasant gift shops such as the Popcorn Tree and Islesboro Yarns, There are two antique shops, the Swallow's Nest and Beaver Dam Antiques.

Pedestrian ferry riders should realize it is a long walk from the ferry to anything except the Sailors' Memorial Museum in the Grindle Point Lighthouse; a car or a bike is necessary for getting around the island. According to Agatha Cabaniss, an Islesboro writer and publisher of the *Islesboro Island News* and *Purrr* newsletter, bikers have become a serious problem. Though the island is flat, the roads are narrow and twisting with sand shoulders. As a result, bikers ride down the middle of the lane, two and three abreast—an increasingly dangerous situation. Bikers are, therefore, discouraged from coming. Bringing vehicles, too, is difficult at certain times because of the limited ferry space. The solution may be not to come in the high season, and avoid weekends. Local families with several drivers sometimes maintain a small fleet of more or less aging cars, some parked in Lincolnville, to combat long ferry lines.

Remember that the last ferry leaves Islesboro at 4:30 p.m. (5:30 on August weekends); don't count on getting lodging reservations at the last minute.

POINTS OF INTEREST   The Grindle Point Lighthouse at the ferry landing is no longer in use, but you can visit the Sailors' Memorial Museum in the keeper's house, where there are artifacts of maritime history.

The Islesboro Historical Society, on West Road, in the former town hall, has photographs of former days.

The Alice L. Pendleton Memorial Library, at the corner of Main Road and Hewes Point Road, has interesting books about the history of the island.

SIGHTSEEING TOURS   The 45-foot schooner *Flying Fish* takes up to 6 passengers out for the day, an excellent way to view some of the island's mansions, most of which overlook the water. Meals are included. Contact Capt. Earl MacKenzie, Islesboro, ME 04848) (734-6714 or 734-6984).

PARKS, BEACHES   **Parks:** Warren Island State Park, reached only by
AND CAMPING   private boat, is at the tip of Islesboro. It is never crowded, and is a port of call for cruise schooners. There are good trails at Turtle Head on the northern tip of the island; it is private land, but the owners usually grant permission to visitors to walk there. **Beaches:** Pendleton Point, on the southern tip, has good beaches and coves for picnicking. **Camping:** For camping at Warren Island State Park, contact Camden Hills State Park, Belfast Rd., Belfast, ME 04843 (236-3109). There are no campgrounds on Islesboro; contact Town Manager (734-6445) for information about private land on which camping is permitted.

MARINAS   The Tarratine Yacht Club, Dark Harbor (767-3254), is private; 20 transient slips; maximum length 100 ft.; approach depth 10 ft.; dockside depth 10 ft.; electric power—no; restaurant within walking distance—no; its 9-hole course is open to the public for a fee. Pendleton Yacht Yard, Islesboro, ME 04848 (734-6728) has several moorings available for visiting yachtsmen; it is just across the cove from the yacht club. Occasionally it has small boats for rent. The Islesboro Inn, Islesboro, ME 04848, on Gilkey Harbor (734-2221) is a popular spot; 4 transient slips; maximum length 30 ft.; approach depth 20 ft.; dockside depth 6 ft.; electric power—yes; restaurant within walking distance—yes. Dark Harbor Boat Yard, Cradle Cove, off Seven Hundred Acre Island, Box 196, Islesboro, ME 04848 (734-2246) does not have transient slips. Warren Island State Park has heavy moorings, a dock and float, picnic tables, tent sites and shelters.

RESTAURANTS   The Dark Harbor House (see Lodging) opens Memorial Day and closes at the end of Oct. It serves a fixed-price 4-course meal with a choice of entree; guests have a copious full breakfast.**$$$**
Sandi's Pizza, a mobile home on the Dark Harbor road, offers crabmeat rolls. The Islesboro Bakery at Dark Harbor Village has tempting cookies, breads, and cakes, and also serves coffee. Leach's Village Market, Dark Harbor, has a tank with lobsters that can be cooked to order, hamburgers, and snack foods. There are good restaurants in Lincolnville, but the ferry schedule precludes dining there and returning the same evening.

LODGING   The Dark Harbor House, Box 185, Islesboro 04848 (734-6669), was built in 1896 in the Georgian revival style of the period as the summer "cottage" of a Philadelphia banker. It has 7 spacious, handsome rooms, all with private bath. Some have other amenities, such as a fireplace or balcony. Breakfast is included in the room rate. **$$$**

RENTALS   Warren Realty, Box 38, Islesboro, ME 04848
                                 (734-8857); Island Property, Box 300, Islesboro,
                                 ME 04848 (734-8809). Some fully furnished sum-
mer homes rent for as much as $12,000 per month; owners often ask how much
silver service will be needed.

CONTACT   Town Manager, Islesboro, ME 04848 (734-2253).

MATINICUS

Area Code 207
LOCATION   20 miles south of Rockland.

SIZE   1³/₄ miles by ³/₄ mile.

ACCESS   ***Ferry:*** Maine State Ferry Service, Box 645, 517-A
                                 Main St., Rockland, Maine, 04841; (594-5543).
                                 Call to find out when the boat is scheduled.
Captain Richard Moody offers service from Rockland aboard the *Mary and
Donna* (day 366-3700; night 366-3926). Other charter service is offered by
Captain Albert Bunker of Matinicus aboard the *Dorothy Diane* (366-3737)and by
Captain Mark Ames aboard the *Lori Ellen* (366-3067). ***Air:*** There is commercial
service to Bangor. There is charter air service from Knox County Regional
Airport, Rockland (Penobscot Air Service, Ash Point Rd., Owls Head, ME 04854;
596-6211); passengers can also ride the daily mail plane. The Knox County
Airport is served by Bar Harbor Airlines (Eastern Express) from Portland,
Boston, and New York City. For information about taxi service on the island, call
366-3700. ***Private boat.***

HISTORY AND   Matinicus Island is 15 miles east of Monhegan
DESCRIPTION   Island, and a destination irresistible to ferry
                                 lovers. For one thing, the trip takes 2 hours, 15
minutes — enough to give the sense of a real ocean voyage. For another thing,
one has a sense of achievement even catching the ferry, which runs only one day
a month and that day subject to availability of the vessel and weather conditions.
The mail and most supplies are flown to Matinicus; vehicles and freight wait for
the ferry.
    Norman Hall wrote in *Down East Magazine* of a trip to Matinicus. He and his
wife waited for the ferry in a Rockland motel: "our proposed trip to Matinicus
stamped us with prestige." The trip was foggy; we "listened our way" from one
"bobbing bell buoy to the next." Today many visitors and islanders have come to
rely on the air service from Rockland; there is a small airstrip of parched grass
among the spruces, a short distance from the village.
    The name is said to have meant "Place of Many Turkeys" or, alternately, to
have come from the Indian word "Manasquesicook," "A collection of grassy
islands." It is possible the Vikings landed on Matinicus, and it has been deduced
from the remains of stone huts that French fishermen visited the island in the
sixteenth century. In 1671, an English traveler, John Josselyn, wrote that the
island was "well supplied with homes, cattle, arable land, and marshes." By
1751, however, only one family lived on the island — that of Ebenezer Hall of
Portland. He was massacred by Indians, thought to be the Penobscots, who
were angry because he had burned the fields to improve the hay crop and had

tried to keep them from fishing and catching seals. (Four Indians had written the governor and received no reply). The rest of the Hall family escaped. After the Treaty of Paris, Hall's son, also Ebenezer, returned to the island and raised a family of 15 children. His in-laws, the Youngs, also settled on the island in large numbers, and there are many descendants of the Halls and the Youngs on Matinicus today. The Joseph Young homestead, a Cape Cod-style home, built in 1800, has doors with Biblical motifs and a rare piano with mother-of-pearl keys. A plaque on a rock by the harbor tells the story of the massacre. It has also been documented by the island historian, Charles A. E. Long, in *Matinicus Isle, Its Story and Its People.*

There are no farms now; lobstering and fishing are islanders' principal livelihood. Many children have boats and tend their own lobster traps. Residents of Matinicus do not solicit tourists; "there's nothing here for tourists," they say, and they do not want to be "another Monhegan." There are no facilities for visitors, such as inns, restaurants, gift shops, or rental bicycles. There is, however, a general store/post office. Matinicus is a close-knit island. During the winter, Matinicus has as few as 35 or 40 people. Islanders are proud, however, of their hardy, challenging life.

The island is relatively flat, with rocky headlands, two small ponds, sand beaches, and open fields. Most residents live along a central gravel road in gray shingled cottages, connected by boardwalks. The harbor is picturesque, with lobster boats and a granite pier where the ferry lands. Because of the 12-foot tides, fishing shacks, small houses, and piers cluster on stilts at one end of the harbor. There is a large wooden church and a one-room schoolhouse for grades K-8; high school students board with families on the mainland. The Maine Seacoast Missionary Society, operating the *Sunbeam* (called "God's Tugboat"), based on Mount Desert Island, provides a minister for Matinicus during the summer months. Services are held Sunday evenings in the island church.

Matinicus Rock, called The Rock, lies five miles south of Maticinus. Here the

Centennial Building and Wharf, Matinicus Island

wind is always blowing and the sea breaking in a wild spray; there are rare puffins of interest to ornithologists, along with arctic terns and gulls. The Maine Audubon Society calls Matinicus Rock "Maine's most famous sea bird colony." The first lighthouse — it was a cobblestone structure with a wooden tower — was built in 1827. It was replaced in 1847 by a granite lighthouse with two towers. The Rock rises 50 feet out of the sea where the light stands, bringing the total height of the structure to 95 feet above sea level. The light is visible for 15 miles. In 1856, when she was 17, Abbie Burgess (her name is given in some sources as Abby), eldest daughter of the lighthouse keeper, was left in charge of her invalid mother and four young sisters while her father went to Matinicus on a brief trip. A terrible storm arose. Abbie helped the family retreat to the lighthouse towers, saved the family's chickens, cared for her sisters and mother and kept the light going during her father's absence, which, because of high seas, stretched to four weeks. She has become a heroine for many New Englanders.

POINTS OF INTEREST   You may climb the path past gardens, over rocks, and around beaches; on a clear day, the granite headlands have good views of the sea. Bird-watching is a favorite pastime also; in May as many as 75 species may be visible.

SIGHTSEEING TOURS   All three boat captains, Captain Richard Moody, Captain Albert Bunker, and Captain Mark Ames offer sightseeing trips to Criehaven and Matinicus Rock (see Access).

PARKS, BEACHES AND CAMPING   *Parks:* There are no parks as such. *Beaches:* Beaches such as Markey Beach, Condon Cove, or South Sandy Beach provide scenic retreats. It is somewhat cold for swimming. *Camping:* No camping is allowed.

MARINAS   There is no yacht club or harbormaster, but there are guest moorings.

RESTAURANTS   The eating facilities are seasonal. Sunshine Lunch is a lunch wagon serving hamburgers and seafood rolls at outdoor tables. The store at the harbor sells lunch fixings. The Farmers' Market, open as a rule from 11 a.m.–1 p.m., a project of the Ladies Aid Society, is also a seasonal enterprise and may not be open every day. Members sell baked goods, crafts, paintings, fruits, vegetables, and second-hand paperbacks.

LODGING   There are no inns or bed-and-breakfast guest houses. Sometimes, however, accommodation can be arranged for a night or two. Write the Postmaster, Matinicus Island, ME 04851 (366-3755) to arrange a visit, or contact Harriet Williams (see Contact), at the Tourist Bureau; she keeps a list of people who will provide overnight accommodations.

RENTALS   A number of cottage rentals are available, usually by the week. Contact Nellie Blagden, Matinicus 04851 (366-3818); Tom Clough, Matinicus 04851 or, after September 1, 7 Stetson St., Lexington, MA 02173; Geoffrey Katz, 156 Francestown Road, New Boston, NH 03070 (603/487-3819); Sally Owen, Matinicus 04851 (366-3663), or, winter, 1 Judson Rd., Andover, MA 01810 (470-0850). Agents for other rentals are Donna Rogers, Matinicus 04851 (366-3011); Dick Moody, Matinicus 04851 (366-3700 or 366-3926; William P. Hoadley, Matinicus 04851 (366-3830); Denise Bray, Matinicus 04851 (366-3091).

CONTACT   Harriet Williams, Tourist Bureau, Matinicus Island, ME 04851 (366-3868).

MONHEGAN

Area Code 207
LOCATION   9 miles off the Maine coast.

SIZE   1³/₄ miles by ¹/₂ mile.

ACCESS   *Ferry:* Port Clyde (all year): Capt. James Barstow, Monhegan Boat Line, Box 238, Port Clyde, ME; 372-8848); Boothbay Harbor (summers only; Capt. Bob Campbell, Box 102, Boothbay Harbor, ME 04538; 633-2284); New Harbor (summers only, Capt. Vern Lewis, Hardy Boat, Small Bros. Wharf, New Harbor, ME 04554; 677-2026). All ferries are passenger, not vehicular. *Air:* There is commercial service to Bangor. *Private boat.*

HISTORY AND   Don't look for switchboards and microwaves on
DESCRIPTION   Monhegan. Don't even, in fact, look for much
                           electricity (at 10 p.m. the generators at the various
inns yield to kerosene lamps). Look, instead, on this idyllic island, for glowing warmth, even before you set foot ashore. It is evident on the dock, where everyone assembles each noon to meet the ferries and greet neighbors, arriving friends, and newcomers. Look for taxing, virtuous trails once you are there; for good, mostly simple, food; and, above all, for a wholesome narrowing of choices. You can shop at the Monhegan Store for groceries or at the Island Spa (which has gifts, snacks, and cards), and also visit the studios of artists. One noted artist, Fred Wiley, in fact, invites guests to view his paintings when he is absent, leaving a message pad and a sign, "out painting" ("Out painting a friend's windows this morning, I believe," suggested an island resident at the Trailing Yew dinner table). You can hike around the island to White Head, Gull Cove, Pebble Beach, Calf Cove, Pulpit Rock, Squeaker Cove, and other sites, but the trails may be rough in places, unless you are extremely agile; don't believe any guidebooks claiming you can walk around the whole perimeter several times in one day. (See Parks section for warnings about dangerous sites.)

You can also compose yourself by wandering along the few hundred yards of rocky road and sitting for a time in the grand heavy white Adirondack chairs outside the tiny library. If it's rainy you can, from your guest house or inn living room library, select from any number of worthy volumes and curl up and wait for meals. If it's sunny you can take one with you out to a rocky perch.

"Ah, Monhegan . . ." says Bill Cook to prospective visitors, with the faraway Monhegan gleam one learns to recognize, "I envy you." Cook owns the East Winds Inn at Tenants Harbor (a very good place to spend the night before taking the morning ferry from Port Clyde). "Sometimes," Cook observes, "people need to stay here again when they return, for a sort of decompression before they return to civilization."

"Jamie's already there," says the Port Clyde parking lot attendant in early June. But Jamie (Wyeth) has gone to the island on his own boat, though, once on Monhegan, you can view his home, formerly that of Rockwell Kent, from a respectful distance. Kent founded an artists' colony here in the early 1900s, and potters, illustrators, and painters still find inspiration on the island. It has been depicted by many artists, including Andrew and James Wyeth, Paul Henri, and Charles E. Martin (known for his *New Yorker* drawings). It is said that if you can only visit one Maine island, it should be Monhegan, with its jutting cliffs, brimming flowerboxes, slow pace, and freedom from traffic (no cars are allowed, though small trucks labor up and down the rocky hill between the ferry dock and the various inns and guest houses, carrying luggage).

It is possible that Leif Ericson landed on Monhegan about 1000 A.D.; runic figures are carved on the rocky ledges of Manana, the tiny island across the harbor. In 1498, John Cabot saw the island, and John Smith landed on it in 1614. It was called "Island of the Sea" by the Indians, and, over the years, it has echoed with the voices of Norse, Basque, Breton, Spanish, Portuguese, and English visitors. For a time, it was a pirate den. The first permanent settlement was begun in 1619; Monhegan was an important center of trade, the first port for many English ships. There was shipbuilding, fur trading, and fishing. In 1676, however, the settlement was disbanded because of Indian uprisings on the mainland, and the settlers set out for Salem and Boston. In 1770 the Bickford family of Beverly, Massachusetts, bought the island for £160; they sold it to Henry Trefethren, who brought his brothers-in-law, Francis Horn (Orne) and Josiah Starling, to the island. Their descendants still own land here. The home of Josiah Starling, Jr., was the Pink House, now incorporated in the Island Inn (the lobby is a room from the original house). Thomas Edison's son, Theodore, greatly furthered island conservation in 1956 by founding Monhegan Associates, a land trust.

Today, there is a winter population of just under 100, which increases in warm weather to about 2,000; there are many daytrippers in July and August. A good time to come is late June, before the crowds begin coming and when the winter residents are amenable to, and even yearning for, new faces. Though artists outnumber lobstermen, lobstering is one of the main occupations of the residents; trapping is only permitted from January to June, so that the lobsters will fatten during the other months. Trap Day, in January, when the lobster season opens, is a major event of the year (the island has a 15-vessel lobster fleet). During June, you will see more and more traps piled around the island as they are gradually removed from the water.

POINTS OF INTEREST   The Cathedral Woods, in the middle of the island, are deep and quiet, as the name implies. Look carefully along the trails here for the surprise fairy houses built of twigs and pebbles by island children to enable fairies to set up housekeeping. (Enhancement by living moss and plants or manmade materials is frowned upon by the "guardians of the woods.")

White Head, 160 ft., is the highest point on the island. Henry Thoreau, in *The Maine Woods,* mentions seeing Monhegan from the Boston to Bangor steamer; he remarks that "Whitehead, with its bare rocks and funereal bell, is interesting." Trail maps are widely available for twenty-five cents and are a must for comprehending their 17-mile layout.

The library is dedicated to two children, Jacqueline Stewart Barstow and

Edward Winslow Vaugh, who drowned in 1926 while playing on the shore.

The Lighthouse was built in 1824 but has not been manned since 1959. Visitors are not admitted, but from its base there is a good view.

The Monhegan Museum, displaying island memorabilia, is housed in the former keeper's house and outbuildings, which are on the Registry of American Historic Sites. It is open daily during the summer (but not until July 1).

Artists' galleries are worth a visit. (Some have posted hours).

You can visit Manana, across the harbor, if you have a boat; also, sometimes you can hire rowboats to take you across. This island had, at one time, a resident hermit, Ray Phillips, who served as the inspiration for Yolla Niclas' children's book *The Island Shepherd*.

SIGHTSEEING TOURS   None.

PARKS, BEACHES AND CAMPING   The entire island, while not an official park, is a fragile primitive environment and it is hoped that visitors will keep it as such and not pick any of the plants. With 100–200 visitors a day in season, if each person fancied a botanical specimen, there would soon be none left. Volunteer help to mark and maintain the trails is very welcome. Stout boots, heavy sweaters, and windbreakers are the coin of the realm; leave your dressy clothes and jewelry at home. Be very wary of the headlands on the back side of the island, where there are wet rocks covered with invisible moss; people have been swept into the sea. Do not climb about on the rocks alone. During and after large storms, sudden "combers" or huge waves come without warning and sweep away any thing or person on the rocks. No able walker, though, should miss taking one of the coastal trails; you may see all the way to Matinicus on a clear day. *Beaches:* There are several beaches, but they tend to be rocky with frigid water. Do not swim alone; the only safe swimming is at Middle and Pebble Beaches. The area from Green Point to Lobster Cove is especially dangerous because of undertows. *Camping:* No camping anywhere on the island is allowed, but there is camping on the mainland at Boothbay and New Harbor.

MARINAS   There are a few guest moorings available for short-term and overnight use; consult the harbormaster, Shermie Stanley. You should not tie up a boat at the dock when the ferries are arriving and leave it unattended. Anchorage is difficult because of the depth and the old schooner chains criss-crossing the bottom which foul anchors. If you are unable to moor overnight, consider anchoring out and retreating for the night to one of the island inns — escaping the ocean billows, rolls, and surges which afflict the harbor.

RESTAURANTS   The Island Inn and the Trailing Yew (see Lodging) serve meals to outside guests. As a rule, you can dine at these two inns even if you are not staying there. Guests may also order box lunches to take on the trails, but all trash must be brought back. Day trippers may lunch at the Island Inn (the Periwinkle Coffee Shop is closed). If you are picnicking, it is best not to lug heavy hampers but to bring a light lunch, or buy one at the Island Spa or the Monhegan Store, where you can get a sandwich, fruit, small can of fruit juice, and a candy bar, all of which can easily be carried in your pocket.

White Head, Monhegan Island

LODGING   The Hitchcock House, Barbara Hitchcock, Monhegan, ME 04852, is open year round but serves no meals (594-8137).$

The Island Inn, % Bob and Mary Burton, Monhegan, ME 04852 (596-0371), overlooks the harbor and has a restaurant. This is often the site of wedding receptions and other celebrations and is the island's grand hotel. In 1990, the Burtons will celebrate their twenty-fourth year as innkeepers at the Island Inn.$

Monhegan House, % Victor and Jean Lord, Monhegan, ME 04852 (594-7983), is located in the center of the village, and has 32 comfortable rooms (none with private bath). Its spacious lobby has a large stone fireplace. Breakfast is served from late May through early October; dinners do not begin until mid-June and end Labor Day.$

Shining Sails, % Amy Melenbacker and Bill Baker, Box 44, Monhegan, ME 04852 (596-0041) is a very pleasant guest house with efficiency apartments and rooms.$

The Trailing Yew (596-0440) was founded in 1926 by Josephine Day, who still presides over the kitchen. In 1989 she was 92 and still cooking. Two meals are included, but the inn has no private baths. It opens earlier in the season than most other lodging places. The inn is named for the rare shrub trailing yew or *prostrate savin* found on a few Maine islands.**$**

RENTALS   Tribler Cottages, Martha Yandle and Richard Far-
                                     rell, Monhegan, ME 04852 (594-2445) is open all
                                     year but offers no meals. Shining Sails has rental
listings for cottages (see above) and Hitchcock House (see above) has a cabin.

CONTACT   There is no Chamber of Commerce, but the
                                     various inn owners are most helpful.

MOUNT DESERT ISLAND

Area Code 207
LOCATION   Across the Mt. Desert Narrows from Trenton,
                                     about 10 miles S. of Ellsworth, 47 miles SE of
                                     Bangor; it is the largest rock-based island and the
third-largest island on the Atlantic Coast.

SIZE   About 12 miles x 12 miles, though it is bisected by
                                     Somes Sound.

ACCESS   *Car:* Bridge from Trenton (Rt. 3). *Ferry:* From
                                     Yarmouth, N.S., Canada (Marine Atlantic, 121
                                     Eden St., Bar Harbor, ME 04609; Continental US
800/341-7981; ME only 800/432-7344). *Air:* There is commercial service to Bar
Harbor. *Private boat*.

HISTORY AND   The island (pronounced locally duh-*zert*) was
DESCRIPTION   termed by the American clergyman and scholar
                                     Henry Van Dyke "the most beautiful island in the
world." It has been called a geologist's wonder, with the effects of glaciation
evident in its jutting peninsulas, cliffs, islands, bays, and mixture of granite,
forest, and flowers. Somes Sound, the only true fjord in North America, was
carved by glacial action. There are 18 hills, along with 26 lakes and ponds.

It is thought that Viking explorers discovered the island as early as the eleventh
century, but it was the French explorer Samuel de Champlain who named the
island, in 1604, "Isle des Monts Deserts" because of its bleak mountain tops.
"This island is very high and cleft into seven or eight mountains in a line," he
wrote; the same line of mountains is visible as one approaches Mount Desert
Island on Rt. 3 from Ellsworth. There was a short-lived French Jesuit settlement
on the island in the early 1600s, but it was destroyed by Capt. Samuel Argall,
acting on instructions from the governor of the Jamestown Colony. The colony
was ceded by Louis XIV to England in 1713, and in 1759 the deed was given to Sir
Francis Bernard, governor of the Massachusetts Bay Colony.

In 1836 the first bridge was built to the mainland, and in 1844 the artist Thomas
Cole came to the island, was greatly attracted to it, and began painting island
landscapes; he was followed by other artists, such as Frederic Church, Thomas
Birch, and FitzHugh Lane; they became known as the Hudson River School.
Wealthy people such as the J. P. Morgans, A. Atwater Kent, Joseph Pulitzer,
George W. Vanderbilt, and John D. Rockefeller, Jr., then arrived and and
"rusticated" in hotel-size "cottages" (local inhabitants called the newcomers
"rusticators").

Two summer residents, George B. Door and John D. Rockefeller, Jr., recognized the fragile beauty of the environment, and combined to buy up land for Acadia National Park and to persuade their friends to join them. Dorr lobbied Congress, successive Presidents, and Secretaries of the Interior, to establish and then improve the park. They were thus responsible for the creation of Acadia National Park, the first established east of the Mississippi. Today, with over four million visitors per year, it is the second most visited national park, after the Great Smokies. It preserves two-fifths of the island, including almost all the mountainous and scenic parts.

The island has been called a promised land for naturalists, as it is on a boundary line between two ornithological and botanical zones. John James Audubon and Louis Agassiz also came to the island to study the wildlife. The island suffered a devastating fire in 1947, which destroyed 67 estates, including that of novelist Mary Roberts Rinehart, much wildlife, and thousands of acres of woodland, as well as the records of a major cancer research facility, the Roscoe B. Jackson Memorial Laboratory. Today, however, the forest has grown back and all the resources of the park have been restored for the enjoyment of visitors.

POINTS OF INTEREST   Acadia National Park occupies nearly half the island (along with areas on Isle au Haut, Little Cranberry Island, Baker Island, Little Moose Island, and portions on the mainland at Schoodic Point). The Visitor's Center, which features a slide presentation, is an excellent place to start. Cadillac Mountain, 1,530 feet, is the highest point on the Atlantic coast and is a must for visitors (a particularly good time to visit it is at sunrise). Here the broad granite rocks have striated swirling patterns, as though a giant "ribbon" of pale pink icing had been spread over the top and frozen. In the (often misty) distance, the Cranberry Isles, Isle au Haut, and a number of others are visible. The park gift shop at the top of the mountain is guaranteed to make shoppers out of naturalists and naturalists out of shoppers. It has chimes and wind socks twirling on the porch, and cassettes such as "Seascape" playing inside.

The Park Loop Road, 27 miles long with many scenic overlooks, is a must. It is closed in winter except for a 2-mile section along the ocean. It provides access to Sand Beach and its shell fragments; Great Head, a high headland; Thunder Hole, a chasm where the surf creates a resounding boom at certain times; and Otter Cliffs, edged by a forest. At Sieur de Monts Spring, in the Park, is the Robert Abbe Museum, filled with Indian artifacts and local history exhibits. Next to this is the Wild Gardens of Acadia, one of three public gardens on the island. A Nature Center is also here, with a wildflower garden and natural history exhibits. (Sieur de Monts Spring, near Bar Harbor, is a memorial to the founder of Acadia National Park, George B. Dorr.) Jordan Pond; Bubble Pond, where the water rolls over stones; and Precipice Trail, a steep path overlooking the water, are also popular and well marked on Park Service maps.

There are also 50 miles of gravel woodland carriage roads suitable for bicycling, walking, horseback riding, jogging, and cross-country skiing. Built between 1917 and 1933, these were the inspiration of John D. Rockefeller, who, as early as 1917, foresaw the need for an antidote to motor vehicles with noisy combustion engines.

Schoodic Point, on the tip of Schoodic Peninsula across Frenchman Bay, has a 400-foot-high rocky headland rising beside it.

Mount Desert Rock Light is 27 miles from the island; it is only a half-acre in size and 17 feet above water. The rock, despite its size, ranks with Cape Hatteras and

Bass Harbor Head Light, Mt. Desert Island

Key West in the number of disasters caused before the light was erected in 1830. The Superintendent of Acadia National Park, Jack Hauptman, says, "There's nothing better than right here. You've got the mountains meeting the sea; you've got it all." Visitors will concur.

Outside the park, there are numerous towns of interest as well.

Bar Harbor: This is the largest town on the island, with a summer population of more than 20,000. The first hotel was opened here in 1855 and by 1888 there were 18 hotels. From the 1840s to the 1920s, the town became the elite resort of choice for generations of affluent Americans. During the 1890s, about 175 summer homes were built in Bar Harbor. F. Marion Crawford, in "High Season at Bar Harbor" (1894), described the scene on Main Street on a summer morning, with buckboards drawn up ready to be hired, "light private traps" driven by women on household errands, and the scene at the Post Office, with "grooms in undress livery with leather mailbags slung under one arm, who have ridden in from outlying cottages." Today, it is no longer quite so opulent, with souvenir and gift shops along Main St. instead of the branches of Madison and Fifth Ave. shops described in the 1937 WPA guide to Maine. At one end of Main St. is the village green, and at the other the Municipal Pier, jutting into Frenchman Bay, alluring with its outlying islands. The visitors are a mix of families, dropping in to see Bar Harbor before or after touring Acadia National Park, yachting people, retired couples, and folk musicians with guitars and dulcimers. Always there is the sense of the park nearby, which still offers the grandeur of the natural wonders for which the island first became renowned. Some of the cottages which survived the fire may be seen along West St. and in the vicinity of the Shore path leading south from the Municipal Pier. A number of them have been converted into bed-and-breakfast inns.

The Natural History Museum is on Rt. 3 a half-mile west of Bar Harbor; it is open year round (288-5051).

The Marine Atlantic ferry *Bluenose* runs from Bar Harbor to Yarmouth, N.S. (the terminal is not in the center of town but on SR3, near the Park entrance). The town is also regularly visited by cruise ships, as many as 14 per summer.

Bass Harbor: This is a tiny fishing village, with seafood restaurants and the landing for the Maine State ferries to Swans Island. Outside town, the Bass Harbor Head Lighthouse overlooks the entrance to Bass Harbor, but it actually stands on a hillside below the parking lot, and it is a rugged climb down to the rocks to view and photograph it. It is 56 feet above sea level.

Northeast Harbor: This is a very appealing harbor, and a well-known yachting center. Thuya Garden is open to visitors; the park was founded by Joseph Henry Curtis, a Boston landscape architect, enlarged by John D. Rockefeller, Jr., and is still growing.

Northeast Harbor makes a good lunch stop if you stay at Bar Harbor and visit Cadillac Mountain and the Loop Road in the morning. The Beal and Bunker ferries run from here to the Cranberry Isles, whose three spruce-clad cliffs rise a few miles offshore.

Seal Harbor: This is not a commercial center, but a quiet community graced by impressive cottages, including the summer homes of the Nelson Rockefellers and Edsel Fords.

Somesville: Somesville is at the head of Somes Sound, which is a dramatic waterway with small mountains of 600-700 feet dropping down to the water. It is so named because Governor Bernard, who came to inspect the island in 1762, found a man named Somes building a small cabin here. Today, the entire village is on the National Register of Historic Places. There are shops, restaurants, and the Acadia Repertory Theater.

Southwest Harbor: This community, on the western side of Mount Desert, has the Wendell Gilley Museum of Bird Carving (Main St.) and the Mount Desert Oceanarium on the waterfront.

SIGHTSEEING TOURS   **Acadia National Park:** There are nature walks and boat cruises in summer; details are posted at National Park Headquarters. The Park Service runs informative tours from Bar Harbor throughout the season for those who prefer not to drive, or do not have a car. The loop road, though it is easy driving, may be quite crowded in July and August.

Bar Harbor: The Frenchman Bay Co. (288-3322) offers a variety of trips, including deep-sea fishing, sightseeing, Windjammer, naturalist, and sunset cruises. The office is next to the Municipal Pier on the Bay. There are also whalewatching trips to view finbacks, humpbacks, and minkes.

Coastal Kayaking Tours, Box 405, 48 Cottage St., Bar Harbor (288-5483 or 288-9605) offer both expert and novice the opportunity to explore the waters around Mount Desert Island in a sea kayak.

The Golden Anchor Inn & Pier (800/242-1231) offers whale-watching tours and nature cruises to seal ledges. The *Golden Anchor,* a turn-of-the-century style Friendship sloop, sails several times daily.

Carriage and haywagon rides within the park are available; reserve at Wildwood Stable on Park Loop Road (276-3622).

Bass Harbor: Call Lobsta' Boat Rides (244-5667), to go along as a passenger as lobstermen check their traps.

Northeast Harbor: Maine Whalewatch offers all-day trips; call Capt. Bob Bowman (276-5803).

PARKS, BEACHES
AND CAMPING

Parks: Most of the island is in the Acadia National park. **Beaches:** Sand Beach is located off the Park Beach Road; it really consists of tiny shells finely crushed and spread by wave action onto the shore in spring and swept out to sea again during winter. This is Acadia's only salt water beach. The water is cold, but swimming here is permitted and there are lifeguards and changing facilities. **Camping:** There are two national park camps, Seawall (first-come, first served), and Blackwoods (reservations by Ticketron after June 15, 14-day max.). There are several private campgrounds also: Smuggler's Den Campground, Southwest Harbor, ME 04679; 244-3944; Barcadia Tent and Trailer Grounds, Bar Harbor, ME 04609; 288-3520; Bass Harbor Campground, Box 122, Bass Harbor, ME; 244-5857; Hadley's Point Campground, Bar Harbor, 04609; 288-4808; Mount Desert Campground, Mount Desert, 04660; 244-3710; Mt. Desert Narrows Camping Resort, Bar Harbor, ME 04609; 288-4782; and Somes Sound View, Mount Desert, ME 04660; 244-3890.

MARINAS

Bar Harbor: Very limited dockage. Bar Harbor Municipal Pier (288-5571); 6 transient slips; maximum length 120 ft.; approach depth 20 ft.; dockside depth 10 ft.; electric power — yes; restaurant within walking distance — yes. Frenchman Bay Boating Co. (288-3322) has a fuel dock but no transient slips. The Golden Anchor Inn (800/242-1231) has 3 transient slips for guests staying at the inn; maximum length 40 ft.; approach depth 4 ft.; dockside depth 6 ft.; electric power — no; restaurant within walking distance — yes. The Bar Harbor Yacht Club (288-3275) has no transient slips.

Bass Harbor: Bass Harbor Marine (244-5066) has no transient slips, but does have moorings. There is good anchorage in the harbor.

Bernard: (across Bass Harbor from the town): Bass Harbor Boat Corp. and Marina (244-3514); 6 transient slips; maximum length 50 ft.; approach depth 10 ft.; dockside depth 7 ft.; electric power — yes; restaurant within walking distance — no. F. W. Thurston Co. (244-3320) has no transient slips.

Manset: There are no transient slips, but moorings are sometimes available for a night or so from the boatyard of Henry R. Hinckley (244-5531) or the nearby gas dock.

Northeast Harbor: Reservations for dockage are taken as early as the previous summer, as reaching Northeast Harbor is the zenith of yachting for many boaters. Northeast Harbor Marina (276-5059); 50 transient slips; maximum length 160 ft.; approach depth 8 ft.; dockside depth 8 ft.; electric power — yes; restaurant within walking distance — yes. If you cannot get dockage, you can rent floating moorings, and there is a waiting list; names are called each evening at 5 p.m. on the VHF radio. The Mount Desert Yacht Yard (276-5114), next door, is essentially a boat yard for repairs. The Northeast Fleet Club (276-5101) and Clifton Dock (276-5308) have no transient slips.

Seal Harbor: Municipal Dock, no telephone or transient slips, but there is a dinghy landing and a broad sandy beach at the head of the harbor. Moorings are available.

RESTAURANTS

Acadia National Park: The Jordan Pond House, Park Loop Rd., 2 miles north of Seal Harbor on the grounds of Acadia National Park (276 3316) offers outdoor dining. **$$-$$$**

Bar Harbor: The Brick Oven Restaurant, 21 Cottage St., Bar Harbor, ME 04609 (288-3708) features turn-of-the century decor. **$$**

Duffy's Quarterdeck, One Main St., Bar Harbor, ME 04609 (288-5292) over-looks Frenchman Bay and has excellent seafood.**$$**

Galyn's Gallery, 17 Main St., Bar Harbor, ME 04609 (288-9706), on a busy shopping street, has an informal atmosphere. The upstairs bar is an "in" place for locals.**$**

George's, behind the First National Bank (288-4505) is in an old summer cottage and is a local favorite, with Greek dishes and Mississippi mud pie.**$$$**

The Parkside, corner of Main and Mount Desert Sts., Bar Harbor, ME 04609 (288-3700) features a shady outdoor seating area overlooking the park.**$**

The Reading Room Restaurant at the Bar Harbor Motor Inn is a gracious dining room with a circular windows offering superb view of Frenchman Bay.**$$$**

Rinehart Dining Pavilion at the Wonder View Motel (see lodging; 288-5663) is in a round building with a grand view of Frenchman Bay and Bar Harbor. It is on the former estate of mystery writer Mary Roberts Rinehart (the house was destroyed in the 1947 fire).**$$**

Bass Harbor: There are two restaurants, the Seafood Ketch (244-7463), which serves fresh seafood and homemade bread(**$$**), and Geary's. The Deck House is open in summer; college students put on floor shows.

Northeast Harbor: Main Sail (at Kimball Terrace Inn Motel;**$$**); Asticou Inn (see Lodging); view of harbor, very pleasant staff.**$$**

Somes Sound: Off Rt. 198, at the head of Somes Sound, is Abel's (276-5827), which has good lobster and steamers and home-made pies; you can eat at picnic tables overlooking the sound or in the dining room.**$**

Southwest Harbor: The Claremont (see Lodging) welcomes guests for lunch and dinner. Specialties include shrimp stuffed with crab meat, lobster, rack of lamb, and homemade breads and desserts.**$$$**

The Moorings, at Moorings Motor Sail Inn (see Lodging) has outdoor dining overlooking the harbor.**$$** Seawall Dining Room, Seawall Rd. (244-3020) is chef-owned.**$$**

LODGING   ***Bar Harbor:*** Atlantic Oakes By-the-Sea, SR 3, Bar Harbor 04609 (288-5801), on SR 3 adjacent to the *Bluenose* ferry landing, is a deluxe resort right on Frenchman Bay, but not in the center of town.**$$$**

Bar Harbor Inn, Box 7, Newport Dr., Bar Harbor 04609 (288-3351) is a beautiful choice, right on the bay. The main building was built during the town's heyday (President Taft once stayed here); it was completely redecorated in 1986. The inn has the flavor of a grand old hotel in the Lake District in England; there is a new lodge wing.**$$$**

Bayview Waterfront Resort, 111 Eden St., Bar Harbor 04609; 800/356-3585, former Georgian estate furnished with antiques.**$$$**

Bluenose Motor Inn, Eden St., Bar Harbor 04609 (800/445-4077) is on a cliff overlooking Frenchman Bay.**$$$**

Golden Anchor Inn and Pier, West St. Bar Harbor 04609 (800/242-1231) has waterfront rooms, many with balconies or terraces. This inn is an excellent choice because it is right on the waterfront, within easy walking distance of restaurants, shops, and cruises.**$$-$$$**

Ledgelawn Inn and Carriage House, 66 Mount Desert St., Bar Harbor 04609 (288-4596) was built in 1904. This Edwardian-style manor house has a graceful sweeping staircase, huge fireplace, and many antiques; some rooms have four-poster beds.**$$-$$$**

Manor House Inn, West Street, Bar Harbor 04609 (288-3759) is a spacious 22-room Victorian mansion in a residential district, with a pleasant veranda and former chauffeur's cottage; rates include continental breakfast.**$$**

Park Entrance Motel, SR 3 & Hamor Ave. Bar Harbor 04609 (288-9703) offers water views, patios, and balconies.**$$**

Wonder View Motor Lodge, Eden St., Bar Harbor 04609 (800/341-1553; in ME 288-3358); is on former estate of mystery novelist Mary Roberts Rinehart (see Restaurants).**$$**

Bass Harbor: The Bass Harbor Inn, Shore Road, Bass Harbor 04653; 244-5157. Rates include continental breakfast.**$**

Pointy-Head Inn and Antiques, Doris and Warren Townsend, Rt. 102A, Bass Harbor 04653 (244-7261). This is an old sea captain's house, now a bed-and-breakfast inn. Rates include full breakfast.**$**

Northeast Harbor: Asticou Inn, Northeast Harbor 04662 (276-3344), 1 mile NE of Northeast Harbor on ME 3, 198, is at the head of the harbor, adjacent to the public dock. This renovated grand old country inn was built in 1902.**$$$**

The Harborside Inn, Northeast Harbor 04662 (276-3272) on Rt. 198, going into Northeast Harbor, has delightful rooms with antiques; some have kitchenettes.**$$-$$$**

Kimball Terrace Inn, Box 1030, Huntington Rd., Northeast Harbor 04662 (276-3383) overlooks the harbor.

Southwest Harbor: The Claremont Hotel, Box 137, Southwest Harbor 04679 (244-5036) is a first-rate former summer hotel, founded in 1884. It has wooden chairs on the sloping lawn overlooking the water, and offers croquet games. **$$$**

The Inn at Southwest, Kathy Combs, Southwest Harbor 04679 (244-3835); overlooks harbor.**$$**.

The Island House, The Gills, Box 1006, Southwest Harbor 04679 (244-5180) is a bed-and-breakfast inn. Rates include full breakfast.**$**

Island Watch Bed and Breakfast, Maxine C. Clark, Freeman Ridge, Southwest Harbor 04679 (244-7229) is on the ridge overlooking the harbor; a full breakfast is served.**$$**

Kingsleigh Bed and Breakfast Inn, James and Kathy King, Southwest Harbor 04679 (244-5302) overlooks the harbor.**$$**

Moorings Motor Sail Inn, Shore Rd., Southwest Harbor 04679 (244-5523) is an inn and motel with adjoining cottages; built in 1784, this is the oldest house in town.**$$**

RENTALS   **Bar Harbor:** There are many realtors in Bar Harbor; the Chamber of Commerce will send a complete listing. One is L. S. Robinson Co. Real Estate, 61 Cottage St., Bar Harbor 04609 (288-9784), which has rentals on both sides of the island, Bar Harbor and Southwest Harbor. Another realtor is Fred C. Lynam & Co., 194 Main St., Bar Harbor (288-3334).

Bass Harbor: Bass Harbor Cottages, Mel and Connie Atherton, Rt. 102A, Bass Harbor 04653 (244-3460) is a bed-and-breakfast inn with housekeeping cottages, which come with rowboats.

Southwest Harbor: Harbour Woods Cottages, Box 1214, Southwest Harbor 04679 (244-5388).

The Harbor View, Box 701, Southwest Harbor 04679 (244-5031).

CONTACT   **Acadia National Park:** Superintendent, Acadia National Park, Bar Harbor 04609; 288-3338.

Bar Harbor: Bar Harbor Chamber of Commerce, Box 158, Bar Harbor 04609; 288-3393.

Southwest Harbor: Southwest Harbor-Tremont Chamber of Commerce, Southwest Harbor 04679; 244-3333.

NORTH HAVEN

Area Code 207
LOCATION   12 miles east of Rockland in Penobscot Bay.

SIZE   8 miles by 3 miles.

ACCESS   **Ferry:** The *North Haven* runs from Rockland
                    (Maine State Ferry Service, Box 645, 517-A Main
                    St., Rockland, Maine, 04841; 594-5543). There is
a water taxi between North Haven Village and a small landing on the Fox Island
Thorofare at Vinalhaven, 7 miles from Carver's Harbor (867-4621). **Air:** There is
commercial service to Bangor. Penobscot Air Service, Ltd., Ash Point Rd., Owls
Head, ME 04854 (596-6211) runs a charter service; passengers can also ride the
daily mail plane. There is Tiny Taxi service on the island (867-2076). **Private
boat.**

HISTORY AND   North Haven, a resort island, is less commercial
DESCRIPTION   than its sister island, Vinalhaven, though for a
                    time the former had a larger population. In 1784,
there were 68 taxpayers on the island (versus 42 on Vinalhaven). It was largely
settled by natives of Massachusetts. In 1846, North Haven was incorporated as a
separate township from Vinalhaven. Islanders have occupied themselves principally with fishing, farming, boat-building, and, more recently, tourism.

North Haven, ferry in background

In the late nineteenth century summer people began coming to the island, including families of substantial, though unostentatious, wealth, such as the Saltonstalls and the Cabots, and many summer estates were built in the early 1900s. One home, on Crabtree Point, was that of Dwight Morrow, Ambassador to Mexico; his daughter, Anne Morrow Lindbergh, devotes one chapter of *North to the Orient* to North Haven. She describes her flight across the top of the world, saying that its "knotted end is held fast in North Haven." The Morrow house, where Charles Lindbergh often landed his light plane on the front lawn, still stands. Among the U.S. presidents who have stayed on North Haven are Ulysses S. Grant and Franklin Delano Roosevelt.

The island has a population of fewer than 400 during the winter; the number triples during the summer season. There are unusual shops in the village, such as North Island Yarn. Owners Chellie Pingree and Debbie Anderson, her partner, have made a great success of sweater knit kits with Maine designs and yarns spun in Maine and New Brunswick, an outgrowth of a business which for many years employed island women during the winter months to make sweaters sold in the shop in the summer. Calderwood-Hall is an art gallery selling model ships made by local people, paintings, photographs, and other crafts of high quality. The North Haven Gift Shop and the North Haven Gallery are of interest (all three are open seasonally). There are rental bicycles in the village also.

North Haven Village has always been popular with boating people, as it fronts on the Fox Islands Thorofare, the principal passage across Penobscot Bay. During the summer the harbor is filled with yachts, sloops, dinghies, sardine carriers, windjammers, and other vessels. The North Haven dinghies (small wooden boats with bluff bows and gaff-rigged sails) originated here; they form the oldest one-design sailboat racing class in America. Pulpit Harbor, on the northern end of the island, has also long attracted yachting enthusiasts and has been visited by U.S. presidents. In the village is an Episcopal Church which is Baptist in winter.

POINTS OF INTEREST   Ames Knob, a mile from North Haven Village, gives a good view of the Fox Islands Thorofare. The Historical Society, in a room off the Town Office, has photographs of early life on the island, along with books. It is open Thursday afternoons, 2–4, July and August.

SIGHTSEEING TOURS   None on the island, but there are sailing trips from Rockland on schooners which go out into the bay. Call the Maine Windjammer Association, Box 317-B, Rockport 04856 (800/624-6380). Among the vessels are the schooners *Isaac H. Evans, Lewis R. French,* and the *Heritage.*

There are harbor cruises departing from the Black Pearl Restaurant in Rockland aboard the schooner *Memory* (594-2044) and the M/V *Lively Lady* (863-4461).

PARKS, BEACHES   **Parks:** Mullen Head Park, 4 miles from the vil-
AND CAMPING   lage, has hiking trails and picnic tables.
Beaches: There is swimming at Mullen Head Park, but the water is cold. Other beaches are Bartlett Harbor Beach and Narrow Place Beach. The island's 9-hole golf course is open to the public for a small fee. *Camping:* Haskell Village Camps, Bartlett's Harbor, North Haven 04853; weekly reservations requested. Mullen Head Park Camping Area, Town Offices, North Haven 04853 (867-4433); prior reservations necessary.

MARINAS   The North Haven Casino is a yacht club, one of the oldest in Maine; it is in the village on the Fox Islands Thorofare. It has two guest moorings, a wharf, and several floats. There are two town moorings; for information, contact the Harbormaster, Foy Brown (through J. O. Brown & Son). J. O. Brown & Son (867-4621) is a boatyard established over a century ago, in 1888 and operated by Jim Brown, grandson of J. O. Brown; 10 transient slips; maximum length 45 ft.; approach depth 25 ft.; dockside depth 8 ft.; electric power—yes; restaurant within walking distance—yes.

Pulpit Harbor, on the northwest shore of North Haven, at Pulpit Rock, is extremely popular; there are narrow coves opening from the harbor entrance providing ample anchorage. Boating people are warned, however, not to go ashore without an invitation.

RESTAURANTS   Brown's Coal Wharf Restaurant (867-4739) is open seasonally. Lobsters are a specialty.**$**
The Landing, a take-out window in North Haven Village, is open seasonally.**$**

The Pulpit Harbor Inn (see Lodging) has excellent food; it is open to the public at breakfast and dinner, and offers a fixed-price meal. Christie and Barney Hallowell own the inn, and Christie does the cooking.**$$**

LODGING   Currently, there is only one inn, the Pulpit Harbor Inn, Box 704, North Haven 04853 (867-2219; open year round), owned by Christie and Barney Hallowell. This is a two-mile walk from the village of North Haven, but, if you opt not to bring a car, the Hallowells will meet you at the ferry landing. The inn is a classic nineteenth-century farmhouse recently renovated; it is nestled amid pastures (with sheep grazing), fruit trees, gardens, and evergreens. It has 6 rooms. The kitchen is closed Mondays. The inn is open February through mid-November.**$$**

RENTALS   See Contact for cottage listings.

CONTACT   Rockland Area Chamber of Commerce, Public Landing, Rockland, ME 08481 (596-0376) serves as an information source for North Haven and also has cottage listings.

SQUIRREL ISLAND

Area Code 207
LOCATION   3 miles from Boothbay Harbor, in the outer harbor, between Southport Island and Ocean Point.

SIZE   1 mile by 1/2 mile.

ACCESS   **Ferry:** From Boothbay Harbor, Captain Bob Campbell, Box 102, Boothbay Harbor 04538 (633-2284). The *Maranbo II,* serving Squirrel Island, is an institution on the island (summer only). **Air:** There is commercial service to Portland. **Private boat.** Note that day trips only are allowed, as there are no public accommodations on the island.

Squirrel Island

HISTORY AND
DESCRIPTION

Squirrel Island was the first organized summer resort in Maine. In 1870, two families, the Hams and the Dingleys, hired a fisherman who took them out to Squirrel Island for a picnic. They became enamored of the island, and Mr. Ham then bought it from the owner at that time, William Greenleaf ("Squire" Greenleaf). Mr. Ham, with several other proprietors, including Ethan Allen Chase, began developing the island as a resort. They took a party out from Bath to inspect the property and dine at the former Greenleaf house, the only one on the island. After the meal, they held an auction, with lots going for just a few dollars each.

In 1871, the Maine Legislature allowed incorporation of the Squirrel Island Association, with 22 members. It was decreed that houses be plain, that there be no Sunday boating, and no intoxicating liquors or "spooning." When Ethan Allen Chase, one of the original proprietors, had his lumber planed, Frank Dingley accused him of being "too much of an exquisite for the colony." In 1900 Dingley founded a newspaper, *The Squid,* which, because of its wit, became known throughout the state.

During the 1890s, the Kennebec Steamboat Company steamers *Kennebec* and *Sagadahoc* ran between Boston and Bath, Maine, among other places, connecting with steamers for Boothbay, Mouse Island, Squirrel Island, and other "watering places" in Boothbay Harbor. These outings were advertised in the *Outlook,* founded by Henry Ward Beecher; the company claimed passengers could circumvent the "dust and noise attendant upon railway travel and enjoy the scenery on the North Shore and the Kennebec River, which is second to none in this country."

The Squirrel Island Association still controls the island, with annual meetings at which every property owner can vote. With about a hundred cottages, the island has been summer home to some families for as many as six generations; it is only occupied during the summer (there are winter caretakers). Many college professors and literary figures, including Theodore Roethke, Anne Sexton, and

Robert Penn Warren, have resided here. Summers here speak of childhood outdoors, of Arthur Ransom and Enid Blyton, of children sprawled with books in their grandmothers' porch swings, and of home-grown pageantry in the annual Masquerade mounted by islanders (each summer has a different theme, such as Squirrel Island Characters, Past, Present, and Future).

The Campbell family's ferry *Maranbo II,* much loved on the island, makes several trips daily, loaded with everything from champagne to lumber. Libby Lovatt, writing in the *Boothbay Register,* commended the *Maranbo* crew, who, on the May 1986 rainy Memorial Day weekend, "gallantly loaded more and more boxes and bags and covered them with tarpaulins. Islanders brought more and more bags and boxes — and dogs, and more dogs, leading to the first of this season's quotable quotes, 'There is an increasing smell of wet dog.'" Libby Lovatt's dog Spike is known to wait for the boat on Squirrel Island enjoying an ice-cream cone, standing on his hind legs and waving a salute when he hears the word "Maranbo." There is electricity, but there are no private telephones, no cars, and no bikes. People trundle home groceries and supplies, purchased on the mainland, along the five miles of cement sidewalks, using the special long, cylindrical wheeled baskets made for the island; sometimes they are transported on the ferry to the mainland for further shopping. On Sunday morning the ferry makes a trip to the island for services in the century-old chapel (as well as to All Saints by the Sea Episcopal Church on Southport Island). The movie *Carousel* was filmed on Squirrel Island.

POINTS OF INTEREST   There are no accommodations or restaurants; the ferry schedule allows several hours on the island, however. There is a Tea Shop (for members only) and there are two small gift shops, Acorn Hollow and the Indian Basket. The latter is run by Sadie Ranco Mitchell, a descendant of the Penobscot tribe who summered on Squirrel Island in the 1600s.

Several nearby islands passed by the *Maranbo II* also have rich cultural associations. Harry Emerson Fosdick lived on Mouse Island, the former home of Rachel Carson is on Southport Island, and Cape Island boasts the home of Margaret Hamilton, who played the Wicked Witch of the West in *The Wizard of Oz.*

It is thought that the island's name comes from the 1583 shipwreck of a vessel called the *Little Squirrel.* Although a white settlement was known to be on the island in 1622, residents may have fled at the time of the Indian Wars. The first recorded owner of the island was an Englishman, Colonel Samuel Ball, who arrived soon after the Revolution. The next owner was Samuel Greenleaf, called "King William," who ultimately sold the island to Mr. Ham.

On the east coast is Kidd's Cove, a tunnel-like cavern extending over 100 feet back into the rock; it is thought Captain Kidd may have used it to hide his loot.

SIGHTSEEING TOURS   None, but, from Boothbay Harbor there is a popular nightlights cruise in summer past six lighthouses, navigational buoys, and cottage lights; contact Captain Bob Campbell (see Access). There are also trips covering the region by Argo Cruises, Pier 6, Fisherman's Wharf (633-4925). One trip offers dining in a 1900 lodge on Cabbage Island (633-6222).

PARKS, BEACHES AND CAMPING   **Parks:** There are no public parks. Day visitors may picnic but should be very careful to remove all litter. **Beaches:** All property on the island is private and there are no public recreational beaches. **Camping:** None, but you may camp on the mainland at Boothbay.

MARINAS   None, but there are ample moorings and transient slips at Boothbay Harbor, including 5 slips at Cap'n Fish's Motel & Marina (633-4033) and 20 at the Boothbay Harbor Marina (633-6003).

RESTAURANTS   None; if you come for the day, bring a picnic lunch.

LODGING   None; visitors may come for the day only.

RENTALS   If any, only arranged on a private basis.

CONTACT   Boothbay Harbor Chamber of Commerce, Box 356, Boothbay Harbor, ME 04538 (633-2353).

SWANS ISLAND

Area Code 207
LOCATION   5 miles southwest of Mount Desert Island.

SIZE   12 miles by 6 miles.

ACCESS   **Ferry:** From Bass Harbor (40 mins.): Maine State Ferry Service, Box 645, Rockland, ME 04841; 594-5543. **Air:** There is commercial service to Bar Harbor. **Private boat.**

HISTORY AND DESCRIPTION   The island is somewhat hilly, with many deep coves along the shoreline, a forested interior, and many scenic sea vistas. The terrain is somewhat hilly; Goose Pond Mountain is 240 ft. and Big Mountain is 210 ft. There are three villages, with separate post offices, making up one township: Atlantic (where the ferry lands), Minturn (which has a quarry with warm, clear water for swimming) and Swans Island Village (a fishing settlement with Victorian cottages). A narrow isthmus between the eastern and western parts of the island, the Carrying Place, was once used by the Indians as a canoe portage. There are about 12 miles of paved roads, and 15 miles of unpaved roads. Among the scenic highlights are Fine Sand Beach and the lighthouse overlooking Burnt Coat Harbor. The island is a popular yachting center; boaters are attracted by the many coves, and windjammer schooners call here. There is no taxi service on the island, but bicycles may be rented.

It is known that Indians camped on the island and buried their dead not far from Hocomock Point, and it is thought that many fishing vessels passed near here and that fishermen established temporary camps on this and other Maine islands. The island was named *Brûle-Côte* by Samuel Champlain, or "Burnt Hill," possibly because the top of one of its low hills appeared to be burned. It is

Swans Island

possible that Burnt Coat Harbor may have been Old Harbor. There were early colonists, who had bitter disputes with the Indians (there was a raid by the Indians in 1750, when they captured most of the family of Capt. James Whidden and sold them into slavery in French Canada). Colonel James Swan, born in Fifeshire, Scotland, settled in America in 1765. He bought the "Burnt Coat" group of islands (Swans Island and some smaller ones) in 1784, and tried to encourage settlement by exchanging deeds to 1,100-acre tracts for seven years of land improvement. He built a lumber mill, a gristmill, and a mansion. In 1808, he was arrested by the French government and confined in the St. Pelagie debtor's prison; he remained there for 22 years rather than pay debts for which he claimed not to be responsible. After the French Revolution of 1830, Swan was released, but had nowhere to go. It is said that he fulfilled his main wish, to embrace Lafayette, and started back to prison, but died on the street. Other settlers staked out land on Swans Island and moved there. The influential "King" David Smith, who had arrived in 1791, is considered the first permament inhabitant; he had three wives, 24 children, and many grandchildren. Boat building and fishing were islanders' main occupations after lumbering died out. Lobstering is now the principal economic base.

About 350 people live on Swans Island year round; that figure doubles in the summer. There is a school for grades K-8; high school students commute to Mount Desert Island by ferry. There are also growing residential developments which is unusual on most Maine islands (and which worries some residents, who do not want the island to become too populated). Three are the Island Retreat on Back Cove, nearly 300 acres; Red Point; and West Point. Among the more interesting residents is Jim Bock, once a Larchmont lawyer, who builds reproductions of French harpsichords in his spare time.

You will need a car or a bicycle, as the sights are quite spread out around the island. Remember, though, that the *Everett Libby* only handles 12 cars and you may have difficulty getting off the island. There are 3 guaranteed reservation spots for each crossing, which can be secured for a small fee; if your schedule is tight, contact the Maine State ferry service up to 30 days in advance. Southwest

Cycle, at Southwest Harbor, on the mainland, has rental bicycles (244-3254).

POINTS OF INTEREST   *Atlantic:* Swans Island Museum and Library, next to the ferry landing, has a collection of memorabilia and a bedroom furnished as it would have been in the island's early days. It is open, as a rule, Saturday afternoons as well as certain other days.

Minturn: Quarry Pond offers swimming in a former granite quarry.

The Carrying Place: The Natural History Museum and Gift Shop is filled with marine exhibits and other items.

Hockamock Head has a Coast Guard lighthouse, now automated.

SIGHTSEEING TOURS   None.

PARKS, BEACHES AND CAMPING   *Parks:* No parks as such, but the island has many trails. Much of the shoreline is private property; walkers are asked to be careful and build no fires. *Beaches:* Fine Sand Beach is popular with residents and visitors. *Camping:* Camping is not allowed.

MARINAS   Mackerel Cove, where the ferry lands, is popular with yachtsmen; there is a dinghy float here. Boaters also flock to Buckle Island Harbor, Seal Cove, and Burnt Coat Harbor. At the latter, there is the Swans Island Boatshop/ Bridge Restaurant, Swans Island Village (526-4368); no transient slips; maximum length 65 ft.; approach depth 5 ft.; dockside depth 5 ft.; electric power — yes; restaurant within walking distance — yes.

RESTAURANTS   Note that some of these businesses are seasonal.

The General Store, Minturn, has a lunch counter.$

Harbor Cash Market, Swans Island Village, sells hot dogs, sandwiches, pizza, and lunch fixings.$

Odd Fellows Hall, Swans Island Village, has all-you-can-eat Sunday breakfasts during the summer season.

The Old Salt Restaurant, Minturn (526-4171) is open seasonally.$ Tozier Take-Out, Atlantic, is open seasonally.$

LODGING   Alberta Buswell's Guest House, Long Cove, Minturn 04685 (526-4127) is run by Alberta and Ted Buswell, who rent rooms in their home and run a bed and breakfast; they house summer policemen and have had members of the Kennedy family as guests.$

RENTALS   Peg Bailey, Realtor, at Knowles Realtors, Swans Island, ME 04685 (526-4122) is very knowledgeable about the island and handles weekly rentals. Maili Currier, Minturn (526-4350) also has cottages for rent.

CONTACT   Alberta Buswell, Long Cove, Minturn 04685 (526-4127) will gladly answer questions about the island.

Vinalhaven

VINALHAVEN

Area Code 207
LOCATION   15 miles east of Rockland in Penobscot Bay.

SIZE   7 miles by 5 miles.

ACCESS   **Ferry:** From Rockland; Maine State Ferry Service, Box 645, Rockland, ME 04841; 594-5543.
There is a water taxi between a small landing on the Fox Island Thorofare (7 miles from Carver's Harbor) and North Haven Village (867-4621). **Air:** There is commercial service to Bangor. Penobscot Air Service, Ltd., Ash Point Rd., Owls Head, ME 04854 (596-6211), runs a charter service; passengers can also ride the daily mail plane. **Private boat.**

HISTORY AND   The island is the largest of the Penobscot Bay Fox
DESCRIPTION   Islands and the third largest on the Maine coast.
The Fox Islands are so called because the explorer Martin Pring, who visited the islands in 1603, was intrigued by the many silver foxes. It was settled in 1789 and incorporated 14 years later. No point on the island is more than a mile from salt water, as Vinalhaven, with its ragged shoreline, has innumerable inlets and bays. Most of the island is wooded with spruce or other coniferous trees; it is largely flat, with a few hills. Fox Rocks, at 215 feet, is the highest point on the island. The village of Vinalhaven is on Carver's Harbor; this is the commercial, residential, and resort center.
As was the case on a number of Maine islands, early settlers on Vinalhaven

were set upon by raiding Indians during the French and Indian wars. One early settler was Thaddeus Carver, for whom Carver's Harbor, the island's only town, is named; he came to the island about 1765 to work for Francis Coggswell, who ran a sawmill. After the war, islanders' legal affairs were handled by a Mr. John Vinal of Boston; his son William (known as William Vinal, Esq.), was one of the assessors chosen at the first town meeting. He was so prominent that when North and South Fox Islands were incorporated, they were named Vinal Haven or Vinalhaven.

Vinalhaven was for many years unique among the Maine islands in providing a very high quality of granite, used for the columns of the Cathedral of St. John the Divine in New York, the Boston Museum of Fine Arts, and for many famous public buildings. When the granite industry was at its peak, in 1880, the island had over 2,800 people. At the July 4 parade in 1872, the Vinalhaven band was carried in chariots drawn by 72 yoke of oxen. An authentic galamander, a wagon which once hauled granite blocks from the quarry to the wharf, stands in the middle of the village green. It is painted "Littlefield blue," after the Rev. W. H. Littlefield, a local pastor, who invented the contraption and first painted it blue. The rear wheels are over nine feet in diameter. Now two abandoned quarries, Booth ($2^1/_2$ miles from the village) and Lawson (1 mile from the ferry), spring-fed and filled with fish, are popular swimming holes with warm, clean water.

Today Vinalhaven is an island with a population of more than 1,250 with stores, gift shops, restaurants, and picnic areas. Don't miss the Island Gift Shop, whose proprietor, Mrs. Amy B. Durant, has lived in a number of other states but eagerly returned to her native Vinalhaven. Most of the year-round residents live in or near the hilly shores of Carver's Harbor. With its miles of paved roads, Vinalhaven is an ideal destination for cyclists. Local shops sell a Bicycle Route and Street Map charting a bike route taking $2^1/_2$ hours.

The ferry is the lifeline to the mainland; the *Governor Curtis* threads its way through the passage between Greens Island and Vinalhaven, marked with red "nun" and green "can" buoys. Residents who live on the northern part of the island, on the Fox Island Thorofare, are likely to do some of their shopping on North Haven (by motorboat or water taxi) rather than take the ferry to Rockland. Fishing and lobstering constitute the primary economic base, supplemented by income from summer people and tourists. The island has a fleet of over 200 boats. Harold Vinal, a descendant of John Vinal and a native of the island, has embodied the beauty of Vinalhaven in his poetry: "My mother bore me in an island town — I wear the sea like others wear a crown," he once wrote.

Vinalhaven is a popular destination for daytrippers, who enjoy the wildlife preserves, beaches, parks, and hiking trails. If you are a day visitor, you will have about five hours on the island, enough to wander through the village, see Lane's Island Preserve, climb to the top of Armbrust Hill and look out over Carver's Harbor, and perhaps go out to the swimming hole at Booth Quarry. Unless you plan a long stay, it is best not to bring a car over, especially during August weekends. You may have to keep the car in the return ferry line all day to get a spot and keep moving it up. Carver's Harbor, where the ferry docks, is small and the places of interest are within walking distance. There are bike and moped rentals.

POINTS OF INTEREST   The Vinalhaven Historical Society Museum (863-4969) is open mid-June through Labor Day. It has quilts, old photographs, and a display of quarrying tools.

The Carnegie Library has books written about the island.

Among the natural beauties of the island are Tip Toe Mountain and Isle-au-Haut Mountain, both with trails and excellent views. Tip Toe Mountain is an easy climb; it has picnic tables and, from the top, an excellent view of Crockett's Cove and Dogfish Island.

Brown's Head Light, on the western tip of the island, has a panoramic view of the Camden Hills and an osprey nest atop the Microwave Tower; the lighthouse overlooks the Fox Island Thorofare, North Haven Island, Penobscot Bay, and the Camden Hills. It is automated, as is Heron Neck Light, on the outer side of Green's Island.

Hurricane Island, just offshore, has an Outward Bound Sea School offering year-round courses in sailing, rock climbing, sea kayaking, and other outdoor activities to persons aged 16$\frac{1}{2}$ through 60. During the summer school season, visitors in private boats are welcome and, if time permits, a member of the staff will conduct a tour (Box 429, Rockland, ME 04841; 800/341-1744 or, in Maine, 594-5548).

SIGHTSEEING TOURS   Bob Noonan has a taxi service (863-4378) and will guide visitors to some of the principal sights, time permitting. There are sailing trips from Rockland on schooners which go out into the bay. Call the Maine Windjammer Association, Box 317-B, Rockport 04856 (800/624-6380). Among the vessels are the schooners *Isaac H. Evans, Lewis R. French,* and the *Heritage.*

There are harbor cruises departing from the Black Pearl Restaurant in Rockland aboard the schooner *Memory* (594-2044) and the M/V *Lively Lady* (863-4461).

PARKS, BEACHES AND CAMPING   *Parks:* Grimes Park, next to the ferry terminal, is located to the left of the State Ferry Terminal. The oxen and horses which once hauled granite used to drink at the watering trough here. It was given to the Woodcock-Cassie-Coombs Post of the American Legion, which generously allows the public to use it. Narrows Park is located behind Booth's Quarry. Armbrust Hill, where in 1840 William Kittredge began Vinalhaven's first quarrying of commercial building stone, is a park with trails and a children's playground $\frac{1}{4}$ mile from the village. It is a wildlife reservation, mostly for birds and plants. The Vinalhaven brochure has a good map of the reservation, with main trails marked with a double dotted line and others ("goat trails for the agile and wary only" marked with a single dotted line). Lane's Island Preserve, 45 acres, is a half mile from town, over a bridge; visitors are asked to remove trash and not to light fires or hunt here. (The area was threatened in 1968 by developers but saved by the Nature Conservancy.) Booth Quarry Town Park is located on the south side of the Pequot Road, 2.7 miles from the Post Office (on the site of the former Booth Bros. Granite Quarry). Arey's Neck Woods has a trail going to Arey's Cove. *Beaches:* There is a sandy beach in Lane's Island Preserve and there is a popular freshwater swimming hole, with a parking lot, at the Booth Quarry Town Park. Visitors are asked not to bring soaps or animals. Grimes Park has two small beaches. *Camping:* None is permitted on Vinalhaven, but there is camping on the mainland at Thomaston and Rockport, both near Rockland.

MARINAS   There are 3 guest moorings in the harbor. Contact the Harbormaster, Harold Chilles, Vinalhaven, ME 04683 (863-2216; Channel 6 VHF). To anchor, ask his advice. Three floats are available also; dinghies may be tied to them. Calderwood's, the fuel dock, and Hopkins Boat Yard do not have transient slips. There are also anchorages in the island's many coves, especially at Old Harbor, at the north end of The Reach.

RESTAURANTS   Sands Cove Lobster and Clambake, on the shore, is popular; meals are served outside on picnic tables (Memorial Day through Labor Day; closed Tuesdays).**$**

The Haven is across from the Post Office; it serves muffins and coffee at 9:30 a.m., lunch, and dinner (call 863-4969 for reservations and for information about winter hours).**$**

The Millrace serves three meals daily, but no dinner on Thursday.**$**

The Sand Dollar on Main St. is open year round and serves breakfast, lunch, and dinner.**$**

LODGING   The Fox Island Inn, Carver St., Vinalhaven 04683 (863-2122) is run by Peter Sandefur and Anita Kellogg. This is a newly decorated Victorian inn, formerly the home of a midwife; it is open summer only.**$$**

The Tidewater Motel, Phillip and Elaine Crossman, Vinalhaven, ME 04863; 863-4618; this is in the center of the village and was once a blacksmith shop for the quarries. Some units have sundecks built over the harbor. No meals are served, but it is near restaurants. Open year round; reservations are recommended.**$$**

RENTALS   Peterson's Camps has 2 equipped cabins and is open June through October; contact Winona Peterson, Vinalhaven 04863 (863-4836). Also see Contact for cottage listings.

CONTACT   The Rockland Area Chamber of Commerce, Public Landing, Rockland, ME 08481 (596-0376) serves as an information source for Vinalhaven and also has cottage listings.

MASSACHUSETTS

Bernard DeVoto once stated that New England was a "finished place," the first "old civilization, the first permanent civilization in America." The linchpin of that civilization is surely Massachusetts, with its sense of mission — missions not just conceived but carried out and made manifest. The hardy Pilgrims fell on their knees at Provincetown in November 1620 and "blessed ye God of heaven, who had brought them over ye vast & furious ocean," proceeding to establish one of the strictest theocracies ever known. The state was a hotbed of sedition when resentment of British taxes brought about the Boston Tea Party and, later, the Boston Massacre and Paul Revere's ride. Yet Massachusetts was capable of shifting, with many citizens discarding what historian Perry Miller calls the "husks of Puritanism" to embrace the Transcendentalist philosophy which, under the impetus of Emerson, fused God and nature and elevated the intuitive and mystical. The dual strains of orthodoxy and individualism are still much in evidence today.

Thomas Hamilton, author of *Men and Manners in America*, remembers his period of residence in Boston with "peculiar pleasure." He declares, "Nowhere in the United States will the feelings, and even prejudices of a stranger, meet with such forbearance as in the circle to which I allude. Nowhere are the true delicacies of social intercourse more scrupulously observed, and nowhere will a traveller mingle in society, where his errors of opinion will be more rigidly detected or more charitably excused."

John Gunther once observed he had never run into anything in Albania "quite so exotic as Boston . . . infinitely complex and variegated," with its juxtaposition of "entrenched Puritan conscience" and "influx of the foreign born." Boston was called by Henry James "the city of character and genius," and is still a place where eccentricity is not only tolerated but cherished; it is literate, rational, and industrious.

One of the operative missions in Massachusetts today is preservation; citizens have realized, with the increasing pressure of an expanding population, that islands are particularly vulnerable. Thacher Island is now protected, as is the portion of Plum Island contained within the Parker River National Wildlife Refuge. Nantucket sets aside 2 percent of all land sales for the acquisition of public lands (those outside the state have sometimes called this procedure the "Nantucket Land Grab," but residents of Nantucket accept it with equanimity). Many of the Boston Harbor Islands are managed by the Department of the Environment and the Metropolitan District Commission. Martha's Vineyard and Nantucket are the most famous of the islands of Massachusetts; both have a firmly traditional flavor combined with a cosmopolitan flair (imparted to some extent by the many celebrities who reside on each island), along with surprisingly deserted beaches. They are accessible by air and ferry. Contact their respective tourist bureaus about new summer service from Boston. Martha's Vineyard was visited by Bartholomew Gosnold and perhaps by Leif Ericson. Nantucket was included in the royal grant to the Plymouth Company in 1621. Both have been celebrated since whaling days. Cuttyhunk, in the Elizabeth Islands, is less well known to tourists than to yachtsmen, but it is a rewarding, quiet island on which to stay.

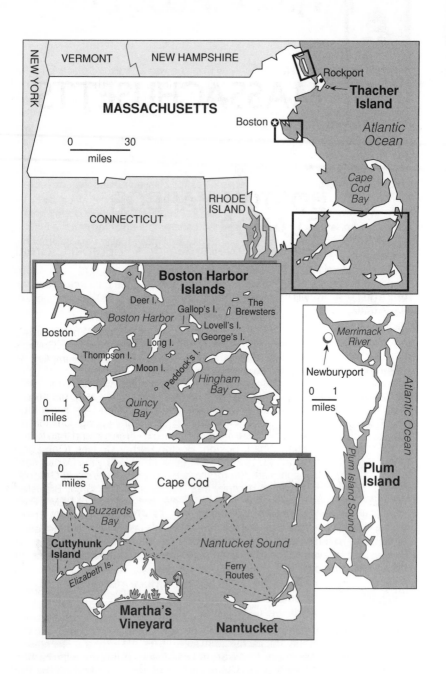

NEW YORK

VERMONT   NEW HAMPSHIRE

MASSACHUSETTS

Rockport

Thacher Island

Boston

Atlantic Ocean

0   30
miles

RHODE ISLAND

CONNECTICUT

Cape Cod Bay

Boston Harbor Islands

Deer I.

Gallop's I.

The Brewsters

Boston Harbor

Lovell's I.

Boston

George's I.

Long I.

Thompson I.

Peddock's I.

Moon I.

Hingham Bay

Quincy Bay

0   1
miles

Merrimack River

Newburyport

0   1
miles

Atlantic Ocean

Plum Island Sound

Plum Island

0   5
miles

Cape Cod

Buzzards Bay

Cuttyhunk Island

Nantucket Sound

Ferry Routes

Elizabeth Is.

Martha's Vineyard

Nantucket

MASSACHUSETTS

BOSTON HARBOR ISLANDS

(George's, Lovell's, Gallop's, Bumpkin, Great Brewster, Peddock's, Grape).

Area Code 617

LOCATION

Boston Harbor.

SIZE

Peddock's is the largest (188 acres) but George's (30 acres) is the most readily accessible. Gallop's has 16 acres; Lovell's 62 acres; Bumpkin 35 acres; Grape 50 acres; and Great Brewster 23 acres.

ACCESS

Ferry: The service is seasonal; as a rule only in effect from June through Labor Day; some trips begin on weekends in early spring. Call for the schedules to various islands. There are more trips to George's Island than to any of the others. From Long Wharf, Boston: Boston Harbor Cruises (One Long Wharf, Boston, 02110; 227-4321). Free water taxis, provided by the Department of Environmental Management, run regularly between George's and Gallop's, Lovell's, Peddock's, Bumpkin, Grape, and (occasionally) to Great Brewster. There are also ferries from Hewitt's Cove in Hingham, location of DEM's Park Headquarters (parking is available). Contact Mass Bay Lines (542-8000). There is service from Lynn, MA also, aboard the *M/V Irene* (598-1974). For information about other services to the islands, contact Boston Harbor Association, 51 Sleeper St., Boston 02210 (330-1134). **Air:** There is commercial service to Boston. **Private boat**.

HISTORY AND DESCRIPTION

Almost four centuries after Captain John Smith first spotted them on the horizon, the Boston Harbor Islands still remain largely undiscovered, even by the natives. It was not until 1979 that they became very accessible to the tourist public, when the Massachusetts Department of Parks and Recreation annexed them as a state park. There are approximately 30 islands in the harbor. Seven are managed as a unique state park, operated cooperatively by the Department of Environmental Management (DEM) and the Metropolitan District Commission (MDC).

Gallop's Island, Boston Harbor Islands

Most of the islands have no permanent residents, and none have hotel facilities. Overnight campers are welcome, but must register for a permit (for a nominal fee) with the Parks Department (see Camping). The islands are only 45 minutes away by ferry from the Boston wharfs. A full day's visit can comfortably allow stops at two or three islands. The park is maintained by Department staffers and by a supplementary crew of volunteers who belong to the Friends of the Boston Harbor, an organization some 600 strong. Each volunteer donates at least six days a season to island projects, manning information booths, guiding walking tours, or organizing a constantly shifting schedule of special events and novelty tours (see Sightseeing Tours). The acknowledged bard of the islands was the late Edward Rowe Snow, who spent years guiding visitors around the islands on foot and introducing the public to their heritage with his fanciful breed of homespun history. Each year George's Island salutes Snow with a special day dedicated to his memory. Another patron is former Representative Tip O'Neill, for whom one of the Park Service boats is named.

POINTS OF INTEREST   **George's Island:** The closest thing to a central island in the cluster, George's is the starting point for any excursion to the Harbor Islands. The island is almost wholly dominated by Fort Warren, a two-century old fortress so embedded in the landscape that it seems to have taken root. It was built between 1834 and 1860 of massive blocks of Quincy granite. Among the points of interest in the fort are the demi-lune, the exterior granite bulding guarding the landward side of the fort; the sallyport, or main entrance; the exterior coverface and ditch; the signal tower; the ramparts, where long-ranged cannons were placed; and the powder magazine, where gunpowder for the cannons was stored. The fort has fulfilled a number of diverse roles in its career: not just as a military embattlement, but also as a Civil War prison, a World War II barracks, and, lately, as an historical tourist attraction. Historians have given Fort Warren partial credit for launching the "Battle Hymn of the Republic," a song whose tune was adapted from a barracks number first made popular at the fort, "The John Brown Song." The most well-worn bit of fort lore is the tale of the "Black Lady," an oft-depicted local ghost said to belong to the tormented fiancée of a Confederate prisoner. According to the tale, the woman managed to sneak ashore one night to help her lover escape. She had costumed herself as a Union soldier. When guards caught the lady and her lover in mid-escape, she drew a hidden pistol on her would-be arrestors, only to watch it explode by accident, killing her lover instead. The fort's commander had the lady executed as a spy, dressed up in a makeshift black gown — since there were no ready-made dresses available on the island. Her ghost is occasionally resurrected for the benefit of island tourists.

Lovell's Island: The island was named for Captain William Lovell, an early Dorchester settler. Today, it is one of the very few places near Boston where anyone can still lay claim to his or her own patch of coastline on a summer afternoon. Beachfront encircles most of the waterfront, giving way to a bouldered sea-wall in places (but swimmers are cautioned that there are strong currents on the west side of the island; it is better to swim on the south side). The flow of tourists is constant but slow. A few campers perch their tents among the old Fort Standish fortifications, watching the daytrippers come and go. The fort was built in 1900, and named for Myles Standish. Today the bunkers, gun batteries, and guardhouse remain. After the Civil War, a tunnel was constructed under the channel between Lovell's Island and Gallop's Island; enemy ships could, it was thought, be sunk with explosives set off from within the tunnel.

Gallop's Island: Formerly a burial ground for captured pirates in the eighteenth century, Gallop's today enjoys a more peaceable crowd. It has also served, at times, as a Civil War encampment, a private farm, a popular nineteenth-century resort, and an early twentieth-century immigration station. Its main attractions are sandy beaches and unobstructed views of the mainland and surrounding islands.

Peddock's Island: One of the few islands with year-round inhabitants, Peddock's is the largest and most self-sufficient of the Harbor Islands. During the summer it is home to some 40 cottage owners, but during the rest of the year the island's populace consists of a single family, the McDevitts, who are the island's officially designated caretakers. They live year round with no electricity or telephone service, ferrying their children across the bay and off to school during the week.

Middle Head, on the island, is the site of a summer colony first established by Portuguese fishermen in the 1800s. West Head is a wildlife sanctuary. East Head is the site of Fort Andrews, the predominant structure on the island, which was built in the aftermath of the Spanish-American War as an added assurance of safety for Boston Harbor. Initially used as a garrison for coastal artillery and antiaircraft outfits, during World War II the fort served as a prison for captured Italian soldiers. Most of the structure is now in ruins, largely destroyed by a series of vicious hurricanes in the late 1940s. Island staff conduct guided tours during the summer season. Visitors are welcome, but their island travel is restricted to the fort and to designated picnic areas. Access beyond these areas is permitted by guided tour only.

Grape Island: One of the few Harbor Islands with no history of military fortification, Grape retains the most pristine natural environment of all the islands. It was named for the grapes which flourished here during the Colonial period. Blackberry and raspberry bushes and assorted shrubs punctuate the expanse of wild grasses. The land has been farmed continuously for centuries, starting with Indian settlers, whose traces had remained long buried until recently, when archeologists began excavating on the island. A famous hermit, Amos Pendleton, lived on Grape during the nineteenth century. He was, according to legend, a slave-runner who became a smuggler after the Civil War, and who then fled to Grape to live a reclusive life, fending off intruders with a gun.

Bumpkin Island: The island was once a farm; then it was the property of Harvard College from 1682 until 1900, when it was purchased by a wealthy local benefactor. He built a hospital for paraplegic children on the island, but it was destroyed by fire in 1945. The island's only structural feature is the crumbling ruin of the hospital. The island is now a regular tourist stop on the water-taxi route. Privacy is easy to come by here; the island is ideal for camping or picnics. It was used briefly as a Navy barracks during World War I. Seclusion and spaciousness make Bumpkin a peaceful place for retreat.

Great Brewster Island: The Brewsters are also known as the islands of the outer harbor. There are eight: Great Brewster, Little Brewster, Middle Brewster, Calf, Little Calf, Green Shag Rocks, and the Graves. They were named for Elder William Brewster, the Plymouth preacher who, with Captain Myles Standish, explored the harbor in 1621. In the late seventeenth century, the islands belonged to the town of Hull, and then were sold to private citizens; they have once again become public lands. Eventually it is planned to develop these islands into the Boston Outer Harbor Sanctuary. The most outstanding geological feature of Great Brewster is a large drumlin, an elongated hill of glacial drift. Access to Great Brewster is limited, but from the island there are outstanding views of Boston Light and the outer harbor.

Thompson Island, though open on a limited basis, is also of interest. It covers 157 acres, and is owned by the Thompson Island Education Center. The Center offers educational programs and conference facilities, and provides boat transportation to the island. The island has about 50 acres of salt marsh; trees, wildflowers, and open fields cover the remainder and there is an excellent beach on the northeastern end.

Webb, while not an island, is part of the park. This is a 36-acre peninsula in Weymouth, featuring scenic walking trails, harbor vistas, and tables and grills for picnicking, as well as a group picnic pavilion. It is accessible by car.

Among the other islands open to the visiting public are **Moon, Long**, and **Nut** (all accessible by road).

SIGHTSEEING TOURS   George's Island has tours of Fort Warren. There are guided tours on Peddock's Island. On Lovell's Island, there is a "Living History Tour," in which re-created characters from the island's past spring back to life for an afternoon: sword-wielding pirates, musketeered Union soldiers, and decked-out WWII GIs are all fully garbed in period costume.

PARKS, BEACHES   **Parks:** The islands are contained in the Boston
AND CAMPING   Harbor Islands State Park. There are trails and picnic areas on all the islands. Note that fresh water is not available on Gallop's, Lovell's, Bumpkin, Grape, or Great Brewster; visitors should bring sufficient supplies for their own use. **Beaches:** The only supervised swimming beach is on Lovell's Island, but the rocky beach on

Bumpkin Island is popular for fishing. **Camping:** There are campsites on Lovell's, Peddock's, Bumpkin, Grape, and Great Brewster. Permits are required; for Grape, Bumpkin, and Great Brewster contact the Department of Environmental Management at 740-1605. For Lovell's and Peddock's, contact the Metropolitan District Commission at 727-5290. No alcoholic beverages are allowed on any of the islands.

MARINAS   There are boating piers on all the islands. Private boats may offload passengers at the docks, but must moor offshore.

RESTAURANTS   There are refreshment stands on George's and Thompson.

LODGING   There is no lodging on any of the islands.

RENTALS   There are no rentals.

CONTACT   Island Park Headquarters (740-1605) or the Massachusetts Department of Environmental Management, Division of Forests and Parks, 100 Cambridge St., Boston, MA 02202 (740-1605). For camping permits you may also telephone the Metropolitan District Commission (727-5290).

CUTTYHUNK ISLAND

Area Code 508
LOCATION   About 14 miles off the Massachusetts coast, near New Bedford.

SIZE   Approximately 2 miles by ³/₄ mile.

ACCESS   **Ferry:** From New Bedford (the *Alert,* Cuttyhunk Boat Lines, Inc., Pier 3, New Bedford, MA, 02741; 508/992-1432). **Air:** There is commercial service to New Bedford. From New Bedford, Island Shuttle (508/997-4095) flies to Cuttyhunk. **Private boat.**

HISTORY AND   Cuttyhunk Island is the southernmost island in
DESCRIPTION   the Elizabeth Islands archipelago, between Martha's Vineyard and the mainland. There are about 16 islands in all, most privately owned. Cuttyhunk, the only one officially open to the public, was the site of the first English settlement in Massachusetts; Bartholomew Gosnold built a stockade here in 1602. The island is washed on one side by the waters of Vineyard Sound and on the other by the waters of Buzzards Bay; David Yeadon has called the island "a tiny patch of sand and sumac." Today, the children and grandchildren of earlier summer settlers come back, forming convivial groups.

The island was discovered in 1602 by Gosnold, who christened it Elizabeth Island (whether for his queen or his sister has been disputed). The Indian name, meaning "land's end," prevailed. Most of the other Elizabeth Islands also have Indian names, such as Nashon or Uncatena.

Walter Teller has described the islands: " . . . each link rises clean and abrupt like a chain of low mountains with watery rifts between. Rolling or hilly, some hillsides furrowed with valleys, the islands present sun-bleached concave faces, cliffs of pale yellow clay and sand. . . . Settlement never gained much of a hold on these islands." The terrain is hilly and the beaches somewhat rocky. The atmosphere on Cuttyhunk is of primitive beauty, and much of the island is privately owned, but respectful hikers are permitted to wander along most of the island.

Cuttyhunk has seen its share of shipwrecks; it is estimated that since November 1854, over 200 ships have been wrecked in the vicinity of the Elizabeth islands. Ninety-three were on the shores of Cuttyhunk, especially on the rocky islets known as the "Sow and Pigs."

For the two centuries prior to 1864 the Elizabeth Islands were tied to the town of Chilmark on Martha's Vineyard; they then became the Town of Gosnold. Many of the navigational pilots who guided ships into New Bedford during the whaling days of the nineteenth century made their headquarters at Cuttyhunk. In 1864, an exclusive men's fishing club, the Cuttyhunk Club, was founded for bass fishing (one prerequisite was that you had to be a millionaire). Bass stands were placed around the island and members drew lots to determine who would use them the next day. Those who lost stayed at the club, played cards, and talked of business, money, and politics. It has been said that the blessing of the Cuttyhunk Club members was essential for a candidate's success. The harbor often contained 5 or 6 millionaires' yachts from Newport and New York, belonging to John D. Rockefeller, J. P. Morgan, Andrew Carnegie, Andrew William Mellon, and others.

Bass fishing still lures sports anglers as well as yachting folk; all summer Cuttyhunk Pond is filled with ketches, yachts, and other craft, and most have fishing gear. The world's record striped bass (73 pounds) was caught here. Fishing boats, with tackle, can be rented by the hour or by the "tide." Sometimes visiting boaters radio the boat *Half-Shell* and place orders with Seth and Dorothy Garfield for cherrystone and littleneck clams, and Belon (*Bay*-lon) oysters they raise on their Shellfish Farm. Deer come down to the edge of the pond at dawn; there is the sweet smell of honeysuckle and bay.

The winter population is about 40 people, many of whom are related. In summer, it increases to about 400, with a good number of visitors sleeping aboard their boats. There are a number of summer daytrippers also, though nothing like the crowds on Martha's Vineyard or Nantucket. The trip from New Bedford takes about an hour and a half; visitors often enjoy chatting with the affable Capt. Ray Hopps, who owns the ferry and has been piloting it since 1974. Gosnold Village, with its small gray and white houses on Lookout Hill, is visible from the Harbor. Overlooking the ferry landing are imposing white houses perched on nearby hills, with red roofs. As on Catalina, golf carts are a popular form of transportation. Biking is limited because of the scarcity of paved roads (the only motor road is 3 miles long), but footpaths lead to other parts of the island. There is a town hall, Gosnold church, general store, schoolhouse, and library, as well as a computerized wind-powered generator, similar to those in use on Block Island (not used because people fear it is uncontrollable in strong winds). There are public beaches and two restaurants. Shops include Dot's Gifts and Cuttyhunk Crafts. A big event each day is the arrival of the scarlet and cream ferry *Alert* from New Bedford, as it is also the mail and supply boat.

POINTS OF INTEREST   The Captain Bartholomew Gosnold Memorial Tower is at the west end of Cuttyhunk Island, on Gosnold Island, in Gosnold Pond. This is the island's highest point, and is good for viewing the other Elizabeth islands as well as Martha's Vineyard. Built in 1903, it marks the site of the first English habitation on the coast of New England. The Coast Guard Light is also on the west end of the island. Otherwise, visitors can take their cue from the Allen House brochure: "Cuttyhunk is very much a do-it-yourself island. . . . Bring books, games, fishing equipment and walking shoes. . . . Everything else for a perfect vacation is here in abundance."

SIGHTSEEING TOURS   None; charter boats are for hire (call the Allen House; see Lodging) or the Cuttyhunk Wharfinger (996-9215).

PARKS, BEACHES AND CAMPING   **Parks:** There are no formal parks, but the island itself is undeveloped, covered by wildflowers, green shrubs, and open meadows. **Beaches:** There are high cliffs on the southern shore and on portions of the northern shore. There is a beach at the southwest corner of the island. **Camping:** Camping is not allowed.

MARINAS   The island is extremely popular with New England yachtsmen. Cuttyhunk Pond has a square anchorage area with moorings marked "Town of Gosnold." There are also rental moorings. Make marina reservations for July and August as far in advance as possible. Cuttyhunk Town Marina (996-9293; this is a pay phone, so be persistent); 20 transient slips; maximum length 100 ft.; approach depth 10 ft.; dockside depth 10 ft.; electric power—yes; restaurant within walking distance—yes. Frog Pond Moorings (475-0502) accepts vessels up to 50 ft. in length; approach depth 12 ft.; dockside depth 12 ft.

RESTAURANTS   The Vineyard View Bakery and Restaurant has good lunches (including a delicious chowder).$ The Allen House (see Lodging). The food here is considered very good. Bring your own liquor or wine; Cuttyhunk is a dry island.$$

LODGING   Allen House, Cuttyhunk Island, MA 02713 (996-9292). This overlooks the ferry landing, and the enclosed front verandah offers a good view of the docking. It is open from late May to early October.$$

RENTALS   The Allen House (see Lodging) has private cottages with shower available.

CONTACT   There is no Chamber of Commerce, but prospective visitors can call the Allen House (see Lodging) or Cuttyhunk Boat Lines (see Access).

MARTHA'S VINEYARD

Area Code 508
LOCATION   7 miles from the Southwest point of Cape Cod.

SIZE   10 miles by 20 miles.

ACCESS   **Ferry:** From Woods Hole (Steamship Authority, Box 284, Woods Hole, MA, 02543; for information and advance reservations (508/540-2022); from Falmouth (Island Queen Corporation, Dillingham Ave., Falmouth, MA 02540; 508/ 548-4800); from Hyannis (Hy-Line, Ocean St. Dock, Hyannis, MA 02601; 508/775-7185); from New Bedford (Cape Island Express Lines, Box J-4095, New Bedford, MA, 02741; 508/997-1688). **Air:** Continental Express (formerly PBA; 800/525-0280), flies to the island from Boston, Newark, Providence, and other New England locations. **Private boat.**

HISTORY AND DESCRIPTION   *"L'ile chic,"* the chic island, is what the magazine *Paris Match* calls Martha's Vineyard, and the epithet, even though it seems an unlikely accolade for the French to award any American destination, is surely appropriate. The triangular island is off Cape Cod, its lower and outer edges tattered with inlets, bays, and ponds. The island tends to be a little haphazard, unlike Nantucket, which by comparison is homogeneous and highly controlled. The Vineyard has a wide variety of cottages (some shingled and some with scrollwork and gingerbread), landscapes (ranging from heath to surf-beaten beaches, rural roads, high cliffs, and scrubby oaks), simple fishing villages and bustling harbors crowded with white sails. There are, thankfully, no high-rise hotels or condos. It seems almost a composite of the perfect island, with a balance between deserted and unspoiled beaches and such cosmopolitan places as Edgartown.

The island's summer inhabitants are a lexicon of notables, including Walker Cronkite, Art Buchwald, Katharine Graham, Carly Simon, William Styron, Beverly Sills, John Hershey, and Jacqueline Onassis. Each August, Art Buchwald acts as auctioneer at the "celebrity auction," where there is lively bidding for such prizes as an afternoon with Kay Graham or a boating trip with Walter Cronkite. The proceeds are used to provide island services for those who cannot afford them.

During World War II, Martha's Vineyard was a haven for writers and theater people. Somerset Maugham spent summers at the Colonial Inn in Edgartown. Katharine Cornell had a home called "Chip Chop" because it stood between East Chop and West Chop; she would meet guests in Vineyard Haven with a horse and buggy, and she coped with rationing by making her own butter in the garage. The late actress Ruth Gordon, who was first taken to the island at the age of two, later had a home in Edgartown. She once wrote that it was a million miles from the world in which she did her work, but if the saying were true that "home is where you keep your scrapbooks," her home was really on Cottage Street in Edgartown.

The Vineyard has odd touches of elegance; along the most rural road you may discover, not a car wash, but a small rather heraldic announcement of an Auto Bath, with gold letters on a blue field. There is still no neon and there are no large signs. The Scottish Bakehouse, run by Isabella White, a Scotswoman who arrived on the island 20 years ago with a suitcase of recipes, is also tucked away on a country road; people flock in for bread and shortbread.

There are six towns on the island, the largest of which are Edgartown, Vineyard Haven, and Oak Bluffs. The others are Gay Head, Chilmark, and West Tisbury. You will hear the terms "Up Island" and "Down Island"; the former refers to the hilly western end, away from Edgartown, Oak Bluffs, and Vineyard Haven. The remainder is Down Island. (The expression are a holdover from the days of the seafarers; as you travel west you move up the scale of longitude.)

Edgartown, which causes visitors to have a sense of *déjà vu,* because it was once reproduced in a Hollywood film set, is an elegant port and yachting center,

Edgartown Harbor, Martha's Vineyard

and is the island's oldest town. There are grand white Greek Revival ship captain's houses, with fan lights and widows' walks; North Water St. is especially known for its row of captains' houses. There are curving tree-lined streets with small specialty shops and restaurants. The aura of the tall square-rigged ships which once left the island to sail the world's oceans still lingers in the bustling harbor, with its plethora of yachts, continually criss-crossed by the Chappaquiddick ferry. It is said that the contrast between Edgartown and Vineyard Haven is apparent in the two yacht clubs. In the Edgartown Yacht Club, coats and ties are worn, reflecting the town's conservative, WASP-ish climate. Shorts and T-shirts can be worn in the Vineyard Haven Yacht Club, however, as the town tends to be more liberal and casual. Nearby is Katama, or South Beach, where Thornton Wilder lived and worked. Edgartown has many interesting shops, including the Fligors', a very pleasant bookstore. The *Vineyard Gazette* is the vintage newspaper here; on Friday mornings, it even offers free rolls of newsprint for painting and other projects. On display in the office is an old hand press, dated 1840. The paper has been published without interruption since 1846; Henry Beetle Hough was editor for over 50 years.

Vineyard Haven is much plainer than Edgartown; it suffered from a devastating fire in 1883, which destroyed the town center; as a result, the harbor and buildings are not so imposing. The shopping street is interesting, and there is a superb two-story bookstore, the Bunch of Grapes, which rivals, in variety of selection and pleasant ambiance, any in Boston or New York. The *Martha's Vineyard Times* is published here, a paper with a large off-island subscription list. Between Vineyard Haven and Oak Bluffs is East Chop, with a lighthouse; this route is a beautiful drive.

Oak Bluffs served, in 1835, as the site for Methodist annual summer camp meetings. Wesleyan Grove, the Oak Bluffs Camp Ground, began with communal tents, advanced to family tents, then to wooden cottages, and then to cottages ornamented with gingerbread trim and bright colors (which have been compared to a stage production of *Hansel and Gretel* or the *Wizard of Oz*). They may still be seen surrounding the pretty town green. (Oak Bluffs had a counterpart in Craigville, near Hyannis, which also began as a summer church conference ground). The original Camp Ground may still be seen, with a wrought iron Tabernacle. On Illumination Night, in mid-August, the electric lights are turned off and the cottages are graced with Japanese lanterns hung under their eaves. Oak Bluffs is the home of the State Lobster Hatchery. Chilmark, which includes Menemsha, has rolling hills, a beautiful beach, and old stone fences which once marked sheep farms. It has been called an "intellectual compound of psychiatrists, analysts, and academics." At the end of the North Road is Menemsha Creek, which is a small fishing village; there are two seafood shops here, and private yachts are anchored in the harbor.

West Tisbury has a white Congregational church, general store, post office, old mill, farms and ponds. Daniel Webster once stayed at the West Tisbury house next to the store. Music Street, where descendants of the ship captains still live in large houses, was so named because several of its families used whaling profits to purchase pianos.

Gay Head occupies a corner of the island about equidistant from Vineyard Haven and Edgartown. It was once the home of the Wampanoag Indians, many of whose descendants still live and work here; they were also in demand in the whaling industry. One of the first revolving lighthouses in the country was erected in Gay Head in 1799. Jacqueline Onassis has an estate here; she reputedly has garnered a fortune in land on Martha's Vineyard. Bartholomew Gosnold was the first white man known to have visited the island, though Leif Ericson may have done so earlier. It was colonized in 1640, when a shipload of settlers bound for Virginia ran short of supplies, put in to what is now Edgartown, found the Indians friendly, and decided to stay where they were.

The winter population of about 10,000 grows after Memorial Day to about 60,000, plus daytrippers (in fact, they say the island sinks three inches a day when the ferries unload). You can easily escape to the beaches, though and find isolation and solitude. The island is bigger than it looks, and it is well worth bringing a car (though this is discouraged) or renting one for thorough exploration. Reserve car space on the ferry or rental cars as far in advance as possible. Bicycles and mopeds are also available. Parking in the towns is a problem, but the sightseeing tours do not cover the entire island, and public transportation is limited.

POINTS OF INTEREST   **Edgartown:** The Dukes County Historical Society on Cooke St. in Edgartown has relics of the Vineyard's whaling days, including scrimshaw and other artifacts. Chappaquiddick Island, just across from Edgartown, is accessible via the "Chappy Ferry" *On Time.* (The first *On Time* is now a floating seafood market moored north of the ferry docks). Here there are some houses and several wildlife refuges, including Cape Poge (501 acres), Mytoi (14 acres), and Wasque Reservation (200 acres). It has dunes, salt marsh, tidal flats, and a barrier beach. It has a very good view of Edgartown and the lighthouse. There is very little that is commercial, but a visit here makes a nice excursion (it is popular with cyclists), and there are beaches for picnicking. The island was the scene of the drowning incident involving Senator Edward Kennedy in 1969. The famous Old Whaling Church, on Main St., was built in 1840; it now houses the Performing Arts Center. The Vincent House, Main and Church Sts., is considered the oldest on the island (1672); it is open Monday through Friday, 10:a.m. to 2:00 p.m., late June through late August.

Vineyard Haven: Seaman's Bethel Museum and Chapel, dating from 1893, was once a place of rest and refuge for sailors. The Old Schoolhouse Museum, 110 Main St., houses artifacts depicting early Island life. The Tisbury Museum is in the Ritter House, Beach Road; eight rooms in this 1796 house depict life in the town from 1800–1900. On the Vineyard Haven-Edgartown Road, is the Windfarm Museum, with both historic and modern windmills and a solar-heated, wind-powered house.

Oak Bluffs: The Flying Horses Carousel, carved in New York City in 1876, is a National Historic Landmark. It is maintained by the Martha's Vineyard Historical Preservation Society.

Gay Head: The spectacular ochre and gray Gay Head Cliffs have been suffering from erosion, so you are no longer allowed to climb on them. Lillian Hellman once had a shack with beach chairs at Gay Head, where she used to picnic.

SIGHTSEEING TOURS Sightseeing buses leave the ferry terminal areas in Vineyard Haven and Oak Bluffs almost hourly during the summer. Four companies, Gay Head Sightseeing, Island Transport, Edgartown-Katama Stagelines, Inc., and Martha's Vineyard Sightseeing operate. Most of the taxi companies will arrange private guided tours.

The *Shenandoah,* a 152-ft. square-rigged vessel, takes about 29 guests on 6-day cruises, providing a sense of what it was like during the sailing days before steam. Call Captain Robert S. Douglas, Coastwise Packet Co., Vineyard Haven, MA 02568 (693-1699).

PARKS, BEACHES AND CAMPING **Parks:** There are two wildlife refuges on the island, Long Point Wildlife Refuge at West Tisbury (586 acres) and Menemsha Hills Reservation (158 acres). The island has over 125 miles of bike trails. **Beaches:** There are four public beaches: Katama, or South Beach, on the ocean two miles south of Edgartown; State Beach, on Nantucket Sound between Edgartown and Oak Bluffs (some scenes in *Jaws* were filmed here); Menemsha, on Vineyard Sound, and the Cape Poge Refuge-Wasque Point Reserve, on Chappaquiddick Island off Edgartown. Parking is free. There are also town beaches, which are restricted to local residents who pay a seasonal fee to use them. However, summer tenants and visitors staying at island lodging houses are regarded as residents. Owen Park is the Vineyard Haven Town Beach. Others are the Oak Bluffs Beach, the Edgartown Town Beach, Lighthouse Beach at Edgartown, South Beach south of Edgartown, and East Beach on Chappaquiddick. **Camping:** There are two campgrounds (no pets or motorcycles allowed): Martha's Vineyard Campground, Edgartown Rd., Vineyard Haven (693-3772) and Webb's Camping Area, Barnes Rd., Oak Bluffs (693-0233).

MARINAS There are four harbors taking transient vessels. Edgartown is the most elegant, and has many moorings, most owned by Edgartown Marine (627-4388), which has unlimited launch service. Edgartown Marine has 2 transient slips; maximum length 60 ft.; approach depth 25 ft.; dockside depth 25 ft.; electric power—yes; restaurant within walking distance—yes.

Vineyard Haven is the chief port, with moorings and marinas, but it has heavy ferry traffic. The Harbormaster's no. is 693-0474; he may know of moorings belonging to boaters who are away. Vineyard Haven Municipal Dock (693-0474); 6 transient slips; maximum length 30 ft.; electric power—no; restaurant within walking distance—yes. Coastwise Wharf Co. (693-3854); 1 transient slip;

maximum length 100 ft.; approach depth 12 ft.; dockside depth 9 ft.; electric power—yes; restaurant within walking distance—yes. The Pilot House Marina (693-0720); 2 transient slips; maximum length 100 ft.; approach depth 15 ft.; dockside depth 12 ft.; electric power—yes; restaurant within walking distance—yes.

Oak Bluffs is the most crowded haven for boaters, and is also besieged by ferries; but it is very friendly and does not turn yachtsmen away. Oak Bluffs Harbor Marina (the Town Dock, 693-5511); 92 transient slips; maximum length 60 ft.; approach depth 11 ft.; dockside depth 10 ft.; electric power—yes; restaurant within walking distance—yes. Church's Pier (693-2679); 2 transient slips; maximum length 60 ft.; approach depth 11 ft.; dockside depth 11 ft.; electric power—yes; restaurant within walking distance—yes. Dockside Market Place and Marina (693-3393); 2 transient slips; maximum length 40 ft.; approach depth 11 ft.; dockside depth 10 ft.; electric power—yes; restaurant within walking distance—yes. The town itself has 30 moorings, marked Town of Oak Bluffs.

Menemsha is a working fishing port; the Menemsha Basin has some transient moorings and slips, but they are much in demand. Menemsha Town Dock (645-2846); 20 transient slips; maximum length 60 ft.; approach depth 10 ft.; dockside depth 10 ft.; electric power—yes; restaurant within walking distance—yes. Menemsha Texaco (645-2846); 1 transient slip; maximum length 60 ft.; approach depth 10 ft.; dockside depth 10 ft.; electric power—yes; restaurant within walking distance—yes.

RESTAURANTS Alcohol can be ordered in restaurants only in Oak Bluffs and Edgartown. There are many restaurants on the island; the following list is a necessarily brief selection.

Edgartown: L'étoile, in the Charlotte Inn, S. Summer St. (627-5187) is considered the best on the island by some people; it is known also for its appealing decor. Specialties are lobster pernod and braised quail (see Lodging).$$$

Gay Head Cliffs, Martha's Vineyard

Warriners, Post Office Square (627-4488) is panelled in dark wood; it has an excellent wine list and is known for fine food.**$$$**

Vineyard Haven: The Black Dog Tavern, Beach Road (693-9223) has a varying menu and nautical atmosphere; bring wine or liquor.**$$**

Le Grenier, Main St. (693-4906), is known for good country French food. Bring wine or liquor.**$$$**

Louis' Tisbury Cafe, 102 State Rd. (693-3255) is an Italian restaurant known for its pasta and salad bar. Bring wine or liquor.**$$**

Menemsha: The Beach Plum Inn, on a hill above Menemsha (see Lodging) is a country inn known for its fine food and desserts.**$$$**

The Homeport, on the water in Menemsha (645-2679), has fresh seafood and an excellent view; bring wine or liquor. They have half-price "back-door dinners" which were often served to Lillian Hellman and her friends, who would take them out on the dunes at sunset.**$$**

Oak Bluffs: Linda Jean's, Circuit Ave. (693-4093) has received much attention for the quality and variety of its food.**$**

The Ocean View, Chapman Ave. (693-2207) is popular with island residents and has daily fresh seafood specials.**$$**

For nightlife, try the nightclub Hot Tin Roof, located at the Airport off the Edgartown-West Tisbury Road, is the best place to go; there may be jazz, comedy acts, or live rock bands, and this is where the "beautiful people" gather.

LODGING   ***Edgartown:*** The Chadwick Inn, owned by Peter and Jurate Antioco, Box 1035, Pease's Point Way, 02539 (627-4435), was built in 1840. The original house has high ceilings, fireplaces, and canopy beds; there is a newer Garden Wing also. In the late afternoon, ship's bells ring in the library and guests can enjoy a before-dinner drink before the fireplace amid Federal antiques.**$$$**

The Charlotte Inn, 27 S. Summer St., 02534 (627-4751), is usually considered the best hotel on the island. It is owned by Gerret and Paula Conover and is filled with antiques; some suites have fireplaces, and there is an art gallery.**$$$**

The Daggett House, 59 N. Water St., 02539 (627-4600), is a traditional inn with gardens and a private pier. Rates include a continental breakfast, served in a breakfast room which was once part of a seventeenth-century tavern; it has an open hearth and is filled with antiques.**$$$**

The Harborside Inn, Main and Water Sts. 02539 (627-4321) is a collection of whaling captain's homes overlooking Edgartown Harbor; it has a heated swimming pool and saunas.**$$$**

The Harbor View Hotel, North Water St., 02539 (627-4333), was built in 1891 and is a landmark on the Edgartown waterfront.**$$$**

Vineyard Haven: The Captain Dexter House, 100 Main St., 02568 (693-6564) is a small inn with a garden; it was once a sea captain's home, and was built in 1843. There are no room telephones or elevator, but there is a complimentary continental breakfast and a library; the inn has many antiques.**$$-$$$**

Hanover House, Marc and Linda Jean Hanover, Box 2107, 10 Edgartown Rd., 02568 (693-1066) is a gracious small inn, recently renovated with fine bedcoverings and a wealth of pillows. Some of the rooms have large sofas and coffee tables; others open onto spacious sundecks. A continental breakfast is served on the sunny enclosed porch, which has interesting books to read and comfortable wicker furniture; you could cheerfully spend the day there if it were not for seeing more of the island. Marc Hanover's mother, Barbara, manages the inn during the summer, and is an informative and gracious hostess.**$$**

The Ocean Side Inn, 107 Main St., 02568 (693-1296) is so close to the ferry landing the owners say you almost need a boarding pass to check in. The inn is on two acres of waterfront property and overlooks the harbor.**$$$**

Menemsha: The Beach Plum Inn, North Road, 02552 (645-9454) is a deluxe country inn on a hill above Menemsha; it has a cozy living room and relaxed, secluded atmosphere.**$$$**

Oak Bluffs: The Wesley Hotel, 1 Lake Ave., 02557 (693-6611) was built in 1879 and has recently been restored. The lobby is a gracious large room filled with Victorian antiques, and Paul Chase, the genial owner, will let guests choose an alarm clock from a shoebox if they need to get up early.**$$**

RENTALS There are several dozen real estate agencies which handle rental property on a seasonal, monthly, and weekly basis. For a full list, write the Chamber of Commerce. Four realtors are: Martha's Vineyard Real Estate, Edgartown (627-4737); Hughes & Associates, Vineyard Haven (693-0208); Ocean Park Realty, Oak Bluffs (693-4210); Up Island Real Estate, Chilmark (645-2632).

CONTACT Martha's Vineyard Chamber of Commerce, Box 1698, Beach Road, Vineyard Haven, MA 02568 (693-0085).

NANTUCKET

Area Code 508
LOCATION 30 miles from the south shore of Cape Cod.

SIZE 14 miles by 3¹/₂ miles.

Brant Point Light, Nantucket

ACCESS   **Ferry:** From Woods Hole (Steamship Authority,
                              Box 284, Woods Hole, MA, 02543; for information
                              and advance reservations 508/540-2022); from
Hyannis (Hy-Line, Ocean St. Dock, Hyannis, MA 02601; 508/775-7185). **Air:**
There is service from various Northeastern points, including Boston; call Conti-
nental Express (formerly PBA), 800/525-0280. **Private boat.**

HISTORY AND   Who could not love Nantucket? Wilder and more
DESCRIPTION   primitive than Martha's Vineyard, yet, at the same
                              time, more homogeneous and controlled, the
island is one of the most sought-after retreats in New England. It has been
accused of having a surplus of tourists and a surplus of perfection, of "dripping
with quaintness" as though the shady cobblestone streets, substantial ship
captains' homes, absence of neon, manicured hedges, grey shingled cottages
behind picket fences, tidy shops with tubs of flowering plants, hilly moors,
windswept beaches and sturdy lighthouses were somehow a mantle fashioned
for visitors.

In fact, Nantucket has always been appealing; there are few places so
evocative of an entire era. It was a long-established whaling center when
Melville's Ishmael made his way there: "For my mind was made up to sail in no
other than a Nantucket craft, because there was a fine, boisterous something
about everything connected with that famous old island which amazingly
pleased me." There is, among the well-proportioned buildings, walkable streets,
and fashionable shops with posh names like "the Toggery" a sense of homespun, ships' chandlers, and oilskins; it is a living museum, but an accessible
one. The series of children's books by Brinton Turkle centering on a child named
Obadiah Starbuck is set on Nantucket, and gives a faithful depiction of a child's
life during the days of whaling and ship captains. The Coffins and Starbucks
accounted for 13 of the handsome houses on Main St. The Starbucks were
descended from one of the first settlers, Edward Starbuck; the Ships Inn on Fair
Street was built in 1812 by Captain Obed Starbuck.

A law requires that all houses on the island must be built of cedar shingles, in
the style of 1840. Any non-shingled houses must be shingled when they change
hands. This gives the island a decidedly uniform look. New shingles gradually
fade to the typical gray within a few years and after a decade or so are almost
indistinguishable from the earlier homes. Outside of town, there are moors (the
island looks much like the flatter reaches of Scotland and England's North
Country). They are covered with bayberry and cranberry vines and border many
lonely stretches of beach.

The name "Nantucket" is a corruption of the Indian word *Nanticut,* or "far-away
land"; another Indian name for it was *Canopache,* "the place of peace." Because
it is frequently shrouded in mist, it has also been called "the gray lady." The
island was part of the royal grant to the Plymouth Company in 1621. It was then
sold in 1641 to Thomas Mayhew of Watertown, Massachusetts, who wanted the
island for sheep pasturage. He decided against this use, and, in 1659, it was sold
to the "Ten Original Purchasers," who included Edward Starbuck and Thomas
Macy (who established the department store with money made from whaling).
As early as 1673, inhabitants turned from farming and sheep raising to whaling,
since they had observed the Indians catching whales. A century later there were
70 ships and by 1768 the town possessed 125 whaling ships, and virtually every
man over 15 on the island worked in whaling.

The French writer Hector St. John Crevecoeur wrote of Nantucket in *Letters from an American Farmer.* He commented on the taste for neatness, prudence, softness of diction, and frugality with which island children were reared. He doubted that "the common follies of society" could "take root in so despicable a soil."

In the early 1800s, the island was a port-of-call for transatlantic packets and coastal vessels, and was a major port. Graceful old steamers then began bringing "summer people" to the island; they built cottages and summer houses, advertising them in the Boston and New York newspapers. The tourist business then began in earnest.

Nantucket, like Martha's Vineyard, has long been a magnet for writers and others in the arts. Peter Benchley, author of *Jaws,* had a home here. Lillian Russell once had a small cottage in the charming village of Siasconset (pronounced "Sconset"), where there was a prominent summer colony for theater people. Siasconset is an appealing village with tiny shingled cottages, covered with rambler roses. They were once single-room fishermen's shacks, enlarged by wives who came out to visit. The Nantucket Railroad was extended here in the 1880s and ran until 1917.

Between Cliff Beach and the Bathing Beach is the spot where Frank B. Gilbreth, the efficiency expert, summered with his family of twelve children. He bought two lighthouses abandoned by the government and a cottage. Island tour guides say that six boys were in one lighthouse and six girls were in the other, but in fact, according to *Cheaper by the Dozen* (the book about the family written by Frank B. Gilbreth, Jr., and Ernestine Gilbreth Carey), the parents used one lighthouse as an office and den and three of the children used the second as a bedroom. The Gilbreths' book gives a memorable picture of Nantucket just after World War I and during the 1920s; they began going to the island before cars were allowed.

Today there is a virtual mania for preservation. The island is managing valiantly, with the help of the Conservation Foundation and the Land Bank, to protect its natural beauty and stave off overdevelopment. Twenty-nine percent of the land is now owned by the Conservation Foundation and the Land Bank assesses 2 percent of all real estate sales for the purpose of further conservation.

Beach, Nantucket

The island has over 50 guest houses, and nearly 20 hotels, along with a variety of clothing, gift, and basket shops; these could not be sustained without a high number of visitors. There is even a honeymoon planning service on the island, Heaven Can Wait, run by Dorothy Vollans (257-4000); she specializes in recommending inns, tours, and beaches. One Nantucket hotel owner is unsympathetic to complaints about the tourist invasion by college students, who come in droves in late May and early June to work in the inns and guest houses and even take temporary jobs in supermarkets awaiting hotel positions. "Without the tourists, this island would be like the Falklands. . . . Maybe the college kids could learn to raise a few sheep."

In winter, there are 6,000–7,000 people, but, beginning in June, there are about 45,000 summer residents (and many more daytrippers). If you come in July or August, you must have advance reservations. Unless you plan a long stay, it is best *not* to bring a car. Bringing cars on the ferry is very expensive, and parking is a formidable problem near the main streets and harbor. There are sightseeing buses which meet morning arrivals, shuttles to the beach, and rental mopeds, bicycles, and cars. Public transportation around the island is not very good, so you might consider renting a bicycle, moped or car for extensive exploration (the island tours are excellent for an overall glimpse of the island, but do not allow time for photography, beach walks, or swimming). An alternative is to fly to the island, taxi downtown and take an island tour; the parking problem downtown means that a car is something of a liability, though very good for seeing the outlying areas. If you decide to rent a car on the island, make the reservation very far ahead in summer. If you take a car over without a return reservation, there are a few last-minute reservations kept open, but you may have to get in the ferry line the night before to secure one. High season, therefore, is the worst time to come if you can avoid it.

POINTS OF INTEREST   The Whaling Museum,, Broad St., is a must; it includes a whaling boat, a whale skeleton, a sail loft, and a room full of scrimshaw.

The Peter Foulger Museum, Broad St. (next to the whaling museum) is a "folk museum" with a reference library. This museum traces the history of islanders from the Indians to the present, with information about the Great Fire, Nantucket's railroad, and the sheep industry.

The Hadwen-Satler Memorial House, Upper Main St. is a Greek Revival mansion built in 1844; its elegant interior reflects the prosperity of Nantucket in its whaling days. There are Italian carved marble fireplaces, silver doorknobs, and gardens in authentic 1850s design.

The Lightship *Nantucket,* Straight Wharf, once served as the harbor light.

The Jethro Coffin House, built in 1686, is the oldest on the island. On Oct. 1, 1987, a bolt of lightning exploded inside the house, causing extensive damage, but no fire. The interior is at present under reconstruction, and visitors are not permitted, though donations toward the cost of the work are much needed and very welcome.

The Three Bricks are famous; they are three identical imposing town houses built by Joseph Starbuck, a prosperous shipowner, for his three sons, George, Matthew, and William; they were built in the 1830s and are a landmark on Main Street. Another Starbuck house, belonging to Christopher Starbuck, is at 105 Main St.

The Old Mill, on Mill Hill, built in 1746 has a unique design, with a wheeled buttress which enables the mill to be rotated.

There are two thriving theaters on Nantucket, the Actors Theater, which performs in the Folger Hotel, and the Theatre Workshop of Nantucket, which performs in Bennett Hall, 62 Centre St.

Nantucket Slide Show depicts the history of the island; Performance Center, Methodist Church, Centre St., mid-June–Sept.

SIGHTSEEING TOURS   Island Tours, Straight Wharf Boat Basin (228-0334); Barrett's Tours (Gray Line), 20 Federal St. (288-0174). Both tours run frequently, meeting the ferries, and give a very good overall view of the island.

There are cruises aboard the 31-foot Friendship sloop *Endeavor,* leaving from Straight Wharf, captained by Capt. James Genthner (228-5585).

PARKS, BEACHES   **Parks:** Much of the island is owned by the Con-
AND CAMPING   servancy. Melville called Nantucket "all beach without a background," and it is easy to forget the town, when traversing the dunes and sand of the island's glorious beaches. **Beaches:** Codfish Park, below the bluff at Siasconset is the town's public beach with a lifeguard. Tom Nevers Head, near Siasconset, suffers badly from erosion. Other accessible beaches include Pocomo and Wauwinet in the interior harbor (where, a century ago, visitors used to "bathe"). On the North Shore, there are Jetties (lifeguards, bath house), Dionis (lifeguard), and a children's beach. Brant Point, however, has very strong currents and is dangerous for swimmers (but go there to watch the ferries and other boats arriving on Nantucket.) On the South Shore are Surfside (lifeguard), Cisco (lifeguard), and Madaket (lifeguard). Eel Point, on the northern side of Madaket Harbor, is owned by the Conservation Foundation; currents make swimming dangerous. Bicycling is very popular and is an excellent way to see the island; there are many miles of bike trails. **Camping:** Absolutely no camping is allowed on the island and no sleeping in vehicles is permitted; there is a heavy fine for breaking these rules.

MARINAS   The Nantucket Yacht Club and Nantucket Moorings do not have transient moorings. Nantucket Boat Basin (228-1333), 110 transient slips; maximum length 150 ft.; approach depth 14 ft.; dockside depth 10 ft.; electric power – yes; restaurant within walking distance – yes. Reservations required for slips; send credit card no. or check to George H. Bassett, Jr., Dockmaster, Nantucket Island, MA 02554. The Nantucket Dink Dock has dinghies only. Anchorage in the middle of the harbor is impeded by a grassy bottom.

RESTAURANTS   Chanticleer, New St., Siasconset, Nantucket, MA 02564 (257-6231) is much in demand; it specializes in seafood and wild game.**$$$**

Le Languedoc, 24 Broad St. (228-2552) is on a very historic street near the Whaling Museum, in a building dating from the early 1800s; specializes in continental menu with veal, lamb, and fish.**$$$**

Obadiah's, 2 India St. (228-4430) is in a former whaling captain's house, furnished with antiques. It specializes in fresh seafood.**$$$**

Club Car, 1 Main St. (228-1101) is in a former railroad car with railroad memorabilia and turn-of-the-century decor.**$$$**

Company of the Cauldron, 7 India St. (228-4016) is a Northern Italian restaurant for which reservations are required; harp accompaniment; dinner only.**$$$**

India House, 37 India St. (228-9043) is considered one of the island's best restaurants. It is in an inn and serves both dinner and breakfast. It is especially popular for Sunday brunch.**$$$**

Jared's at the Jared Coffin House (228-2400; see Lodging). The dining room has period furnishings and traditional food.$$$ The Taproom, downstairs, is pine-panelled with a very pleasant formal atmosphere, and good service.$$

LODGING   The Jared Coffin House, 29 Broad St. (228-2400) is a sturdy building, built in 1845, which survived the fire of 1846. Jared Coffin's wife did not like Nantucket; he built the house as an attempt to keep her on the island. The building became an inn in 1847. It is furnished with antiques.$$$

The Chestnut House, 3 Chestnut St. (228-0049) is run by Jeannette and Jerry Carl, artists who came to Nantucket from New York. This guest house is very centrally located, just around the corner from the Whaling Museum. It is beautifully maintained and decorated with Jerry's handmade rugs as well as Jeannette's animal sculptures. Upstairs there is a cozy library. The Carls are enthusiastic converts to life on Nantucket, and are knowledgeable about theatrical events, nearby eating places, and the island as a whole. There are rooms and suites; no breakfast but many nearby restaurants.$$

The Woodbox, 29 Fair St. (228-0587), built in 1709, is Nantucket's oldest inn. It has hand-hewn beams, fireplaces with ovens, and low ceilings.$$$

The Ships Inn, Fair St. (228-0040) was built in 1812 by Captain Obed Starbuck and is furnished with antiques.$$

The White Elephant, Box 359, Nantucket, MA 02554 (228-5500), a sprawling hotel on the harborfront, well landscaped. The Breakers is another building in the complex, containing the most expensive and elegant of the accommodations, with sitting/bedrooms, suites, and patios.$$$

The Harbor House, South Beach St. (228-1500) is a courtyard complex with cottages and houses as well as a main building.$$$

The Wauwinet House, Wauwinet (228-0145) is a turn-of-the-century hotel in a small summer colony 6 miles from the town of Nantucket. It offers ocean walks, tennis, and sailing and is very good for children.$$$

The Summer House, Siasconset (257-9976) is located on a bluff overlooking the sea. It has a swimming pool on the beach, and is known for its Sunday brunches.$$$

(For complete listing of accommodations, write the Chamber of Commerce.)

RENTALS   There are many forms of rentals on Nantucket, including apartments, cottages, and interval ownership. Three agencies specializing in such accommodations are Nantucket Vacation Rentals, Box 426, Nantucket, MA 02554 (228-3131); Nantucket Accommodations, 6 Ash Lane, Nantucket, MA 02554 (228-9559); and the Maury People, 35 Main St., Nantucket, MA 02554 (228-1881).

CONTACT   Nantucket Island Chamber of Commerce, Pacific Club Building, Main St., Nantucket, MA 02554 (228-1700); also the Nantucket Information Bureau, 25 Federal St. (228-0925).

PLUM ISLAND

Area Code 508
LOCATION   3 miles east of Newburyport.

ACCESS   ***Car:*** Over a causeway, which stretches across
                                the salt marsh, from Newburyport. Exit off I-95 to
                                Rt. 113 East (Newburyport/West Newbury). Con-
tinue on Rt. 113 East to Newbury, then follow signs to Plum Island/Parker River
National Wildlife Refuge. ***Private boat.***

HISTORY AND   Plum Island is a natural barrier beach, a long
DESCRIPTION   narrow spit of land. The northern part is residen-
                                tial, cluttered with hundreds of small beach
homes; here there is a public beach. The southern two-thirds of the island is
administered by the Parker River National Wildlife Refuge, which totals 4,662
acres of beaches, dunes, upland forests, and salt marsh. The Refuge was
established in 1942 as a resting and feeding area for migratory black ducks. It is
the home of many species of birds, mammals, reptiles, amphibians, and plants;
saltwater and freshwater marshes provide a good resting and feeding place for
birds on the Atlantic Flyway. The Refuge beaches are open to the public for
swimming and fishing.

The island was discovered by Champlain in 1601 and first mapped by Captain
John Smith in 1616. Large heaps of shells called middens give evidence of the
past use of the island by coastal Massachusetts Indians, but they established no
permanent settlements (it is thought that lack of fresh water played a part in their
decision to go elsewhere). The area became known as Plum Island in the 1630s,
as early settlers noticed the wild beach plums which abound in late summer. An

White-Tail Deer in Winter, Plum Island

early conservation measure became necessary in 1739—the residents of Ipswich, Rowley, and Newbury had been grazing their livestock on the island, depleting the island's vegetation. Grazing had to be prohibited. Salt marsh haying was an industry during the mid-1800s; circular "straddles," used to keep mown hay above tidal waters, can still be seen in the marshes.

In 1806, a road and bridge were built to the mainland. A horsecar line reached the island from downtown Newburyport about 1890. The summer colony grew, and further depleted the vegetation. The bird sanctuary was established in the early 1930s, when the Massachusetts Audubon Society acquired 1,600 acres. The Parker River National Wildlife Refuge was established in 1942, when the U.S. Fish and Wildlife Service acquired the area from the Audubon Society, plus an additional 3,050 acres from private landowners. In 1985, 12 more acres were added and set aside for a future headquarters facility.

POINTS OF INTEREST   Refuge Headquarters are in the old Coast Guard lighthouse at the northern end of the island. Here there is a small fishing dock and a store, Captain's Fishing Party, which sells and rents fishing equipment and charters boats, including the 76-foot *Captain's Lady*. There are self-guided trails through dunes and marshes offering excellent birdwatching. A leaflet is obtainable from the Refuge which lists the species most likely to be seen at various times of the year. In January and February, the snowy owl and northern harrier may be visible (though at times snow blocks the Refuge road). March and April bring waterfowl migrating north and courtship activity; in May and June, geese hatch and broods feed in roadside fields. Warbler migration peaks in May. In July and August, ducks hatch and feed; there are also snowy egrets, shorebirds, and swallows (especially in late August). September and October bring southerly migration; November and December are noted for the migrating Canada and snow geese as well as the American black ducks, horned larks, and Lapland longspurs. People are allowed to pick plums and cranberries (one quart per person) from the Tuesday after Labor Day to October 31.

The Hellcat Swamp Wildlife Trail Guide, a 2-mile nature trail divided into loops, leads off from Parking Lot No. 4. There is no access to the ocean from this trail, because of the fragile dunes. The trail has an observation tower; a pamphlet is available describing the vegetation and wildlife along the way. Over 300 species of birds regularly visit the Refuge; most of them feed and rest in the Freshwater Swamp which is circled by the trail (and is seemingly misplaced, among the sand dunes).

The town of Newburyport is gracious and appealing, with grand Federal-style homes built by ship captains. The novelist John P. Marquand, who lived here, once said, the town "is not a museum piece although it sometimes looks it." Of special interest in Newburyport are the Coffin House (c. 1654), which has the furnishings of 8 generations; the Cushing House Museum, which has furniture, a carriage house, portraits, and other memorabilia; and the Custom House Maritime Museum, depicting the area's maritime heritage spanning 300 years. Towle Silversmiths was one of the town's earliest businesses and is still in operation.

SIGHTSEEING TOURS   None within the Refuge. There are flying tours offered by Air Plum Island from May through Labor Day; they leave from the Plum Island Airport, located on Water Street. Call 462-2114.

PARKS, BEACHES
AND CAMPING

Parks: Visitor hours at the Refuge are from one half hour before sunrise to one half hour after sunset. The only legal entrance to the Refuge is through an automatic gate. In summer, the parking lots are sometimes filled by 9:00 a.m. (they hold about 350 cars); in such cases, the gate remains closed until 3:00 p.m. This measure prevents overcrowding. You can rent bikes on the causeway and enter, even if the parking lot is full. A small day use fee is charged as part of the Emergency Wetlands Resources Act; the revenue helps defray the cost of management. There are nature trails (the Hellcat Swamp Wildlife Trail is of special interest) and surf fishing is allowed. (You need a permit for night fishing). The season for striped bass is mid-May through October. Feeding wildlife is prohibited. **Beaches:** The public beach is 2 miles long; from Memorial Day to Labor Day there are lifeguards. In the Refuge there are 7 miles of beach; some of the dunes are as high as 50 feet. Access is over boardwalks at each parking lot except #4 (reserved for visitors using the Hellcat Swamp Wildlife Trail). All visitors should remain on the boardwalks to avoid damaging the dune vegetation. Swimming is at your own risk; there are no lifeguards, and undertows and tides are very strong. Also, there is a "greenhead season" during part of the summer, when beachgoers are plagued by greenhead flies. Call the Refuge headquarters to find out whether they are present. Alcoholic beverages are not permitted. **Camping:** Camping is not permitted.

MARINAS

There are no marinas on the island itself. Plum Island Sound and Plum Island River connect Ipswich and Newburyport (a 10-mile stretch), but the water is too shallow for anything but dinghies. There are marinas in Newburyport, including the Newburyport Town Dock, Dawn Marina, Bridge Marina, Inc., and Yankee Marine.

RESTAURANTS

The Captain's Fishing Party, a store near the Refuge headquarters at the northern tip of the island, sells refreshments. The Lighthouse Grill, 3 Reservation Terrace, (462-0324) is at the edge of Plum Island on the point, across from a working lighthouse. They serve fishermen's platters, lobster tails, fish and chips, a full turkey dinner, and do their own baking of homemade desserts and pizza dough. The restaurant is open year round.$

LODGING

Walton's Ocean Front, Fordham Way, Plum Island, Newbury, MA 01950 (465-7171), owned by Ann Lee and John Syrene, is an attractive structure, with floor-length windows and wooden steps to the beach. They offer overnight rooms with private baths which do not face the ocean but are 10 steps up a flight of stairs to the sandy beach. There are also studio apartments (see Rentals).$

RENTALS

Walton's Ocean Front (see Lodging) has ocean front studio apartments with kitchenettes, just 20 steps away from the beach. There are also more elaborate ocean front apartments with private decks. Apartments rent from Saturday to Saturday and are furnished with dishes, pans, pillows, and blankets.

CONTACT

Parker River National Wildlife Refuge, Northern Boulevard, Plum Island, Newburyport, MA 01950 (465-5753). Also the Essex North Chamber of Commerce, 29 State St., Newburyport, MA 01953 (462-6680).

THACHER ISLAND

Area Code 508
LOCATION   ³/₄ mile off the coast near Rockport.

SIZE   Approximately ¹/₂ mile long by ¹/₄ mile wide; about 80 acres.

ACCESS   *Boat:* A special boat, the *Landing Barge,* is run by the Thacher Island Association. It was constructed from a wooden boat model made by the Association chairman Ned Cameron; it leaves from T Wharf in Rockport and runs June through September, Saturday and Sunday at 9:00 a.m. and 1:00 p.m. For details, contact Ned Cameron (508/546-2367) or John Bennett (508/546-2849). The boat trip is open to all, not just Association members. *Air:* There is commercial service to Boston. *Private boat.*

HISTORY AND   To those who know it, Thacher Island is a very
DESCRIPTION   special place. Samuel de Champlain sighted it in 1605, as did Captain John Smith in 1614. The island was named for Anthony Thacher; he and his wife were the only survivors of the shipwreck of the *Watch and Wait,* a small boat bound from Ipswich to Marblehead in 1635. Twenty-three others perished. Eleanor C. Parsons, in her excellent history of the island (*Thachers: Island of the Twin Lights;* see Sources for Further Reading), summarizes the tragic history and beauty of Thacher Island:

> Today this island of the *Watch and Wait* ... island of Anthony Thacher and his tragedy; island of all those who have come after him and call his island "home"; island of fishermen, farmers, artists; island of grief, of trouble, of discord; island of the strident, hoarse voice of seagull and fog horn; island of storms both physical and political; island of shipwrecks; island of life-saving light ... watches and waits for its future to unfold.

In 1636–37, the General Court voted to grant Thacher the island "at the head of Cape Ann, as his inheritance." An heir of Thacher, John Appleton, sold the island to the Rev. John White in 1717 for £ 100. In 1771, the year the twin lighthouses were erected and lighted for the first time, the Colonial Government bought the island back for £ 500. In the early twentieth century, five familes lived on the island and ran the lighthouses and fog whistles. Descendants of these families live in Rockport today. In 1919, the fog signal saved the *S.S. America,* which was carrying President Woodrow Wilson back from the European Peace Conference and nearly foundered on the island's rocky ledges. Only light keepers have occupied the island during its long history.

The North Tower light was abandoned by the government in 1932, as an economy measure, but, in 1979, was placed on the Massachusetts list of historic places to be restored. In 1967, the Cosa Nostra gangster Joseph Barboza Baron, his wife, and two-year-old son were held on the island in protective custody (it was said that he did not appreciate the wildlife or stark beauty of the island; a hiding place was later found for him at Eastern Point, Gloucester). The Federal Government threatened to dispose of the island and its twin lighthouses in 1970; for ten years, citizens of Rockport and Cape Ann fought to save the island. Ned Cameron was the principal leader of the movement. In 1980, the town of Rockport leased the south half of the island from the U.S. Coast Guard. That year the U. S. Coast Guard, which had manned the island, removed its last crew, and the south light and fog whistle became automated. Lightkeepers (the first was Russell Grubb) were appointed, not so much to man the remaining lighthouse, which was computerized, as to perform general maintenance, prevent vandalism, and to take care of the island (with no pay). Sheep and goats were brought to the island; they help mow the grass (and regard poison ivy as a delicacy).

The Thacher Island Association was founded in 1981 and has since grown. In July 1982, the dream of the Association was realized when the *Landing Barge* was launched, enabling residents of Rockport and Cape Ann, along with visitors, to savor the unique qualities of Thacher Island.

POINTS OF INTEREST   The Twin Lights are the principal sights on the island; they are two light towers, the North Tower and the South Tower, built in 1771 and replaced by the present 124-foot granite towers in 1861. The North Tower light was re-lit in April 1988. Thacher Island is now unique, the only island in the world with twin lights operating.

The stone Keeper's House, which replaced an earlier dwelling house, was erected in 1816 for Aaron Wheeler, keeper at that time.

SIGHTSEEING TOURS   There are no sightseeing tours.

PARKS, BEACHES AND CAMPING   **Parks:** There are scenic trails on the island, and there are many picnic areas. **Beaches:** There are no beaches but there are scenic vistas visible from the rocky coast. **Camping:** Camping is allowed only by permission and a small donation to the Association.

MARINAS   There are no marinas, but there is a boat house; for landing conditions call 546-2367.

RESTAURANTS   There are no restaurants.

LODGING   There is lodging in guest quarters by permission; a donation is expected.

RENTALS   There are no rentals.

CONTACT   For information about the island and boat schedule, contact the Thacher Island Association, Box 73, Rockport, MA 01966.

NEW HAMPSHIRE

Cornelius Weygandt, writing on New Hampshire for the *W.P.A. Guide* in 1937, holds that New Hampshire people were the "merriest of the Puritans," bringing English country traditions of wit and clowning to country auctions, town meetings, and fairs. There are still festive country auctions and the wit and charm of New Hampshire natives is still evident.

The New Hampshire landscape varies, with a somewhat commercialized coast, scenic inland lakes, and mountains. The state is extremely proud of the White Mountains; Mount Monadnock has been called "the most literary mountain in America." Kipling referred to it as a "wise old giant. . . . Monadnock came to mean everything that was helpful, healing and full of quiet." Emerson, Thoreau, and Mark Twain also wrote of Monadnock. Marian MacDowell, widow of Edward MacDowell, founded the MacDowell Colony at Peterborough, where Thornton Wilder, Aaron Copland, and other creative artists worked. Artists who have celebrated New Hampshire include Albert Bierstadt, Asher Brown Durand, and Frederic Church; the state figures in the literary work of James Russell Lowell, Henry Wadsworth Longfellow, John Greenleaf Whittier, and Oliver Wendell Holmes, among others.

Portsmouth, embarkation point for Star Island, was the site of one of the earliest permanent settlements in the state. In 1623, members of the Laconia Company founded a plantation and fishery. In 1630 travelers on the ship *Pied Cow* disembarked on the banks of the Piscataqua River and, finding fields of wild strawberries, named their settlement "Strawbery Banke." The islands off Portsmouth were not noted on maritime records until Captain John Smith explored the New England coast and mentioned "ye Islandes of Shoales," though it is thought they had been sighted by Verrazano, Gosnold, and other early navigators. The rocky islands were, even then, barren of trees, yet majestic in their rocky desolation.

The New Hampshire lakes and their islands have long been known for their beauty and tranquillity. Squam Lake was featured in the film *On Golden Pond*, and Lake Winnipesaukee has for many years attracted vacationers. Chocorua Island in Squam Lake takes its name from the mountain peak Chocorua, of the Sandwich Range south of the Presidential Peaks; Longfellow once wrote a poem, "Jeckoyva," about an Algonquin chief, Chocorua. Thomas Cole of the Hudson River School painted the scene of his death; he is shown on a high rock with the traitorous white man who had shot him standing below.

During the nineteenth century, steamboats came into service on the lakes to transport freight and passengers. The *Lady of the Lake* began traversing Lake Winnipesaukee in 1849, threading around the hundreds of islands, and in 1872 the sidewheeler *Mount Washington* was launched; she sailed until she was destroyed by fire in 1939. The current *Mount Washington* came from Lake Champlain; she churns across the lake daily in summer, offering a narrated tour of the islands. Even today, the old cry "Here comes the Mount!" summons people to cease their activities until she steams past, a poignant reminder of the heyday of the lake steamers.

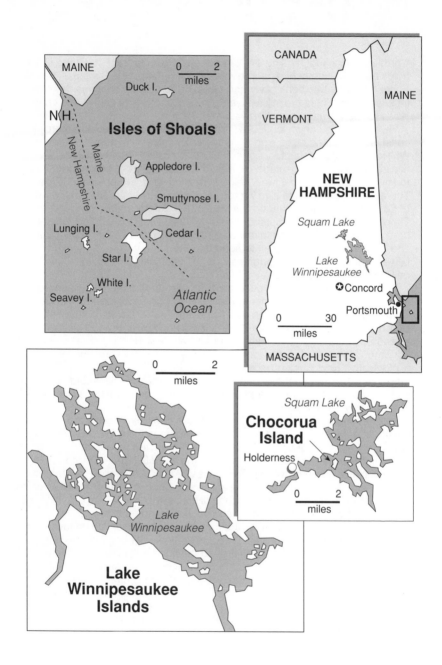

Isles of Shoals

MAINE

Duck I.

0   2
miles

N.H.

New Hampshire

Maine

Appledore I.

Smuttynose I.

Lunging I.

Cedar I.

Star I.

White I.

Seavey I.

Atlantic Ocean

CANADA

MAINE

VERMONT

NEW HAMPSHIRE

Squam Lake

Lake Winnipesaukee

✪Concord

Portsmouth

0   30
miles

MASSACHUSETTS

0   2
miles

Lake Winnipesaukee

Lake Winnipesaukee Islands

Squam Lake

Chocorua Island

Holderness

0   2
miles

NEW HAMPSHIRE

CHOCORUA

Area Code 603

LOCATION — In Squam Lake, near Holderness.

SIZE — A few acres.

ACCESS — Only on Sundays, for church services. Access is by boat only (usually canoes and small motor boats).

HISTORY AND DESCRIPTION — Chocorua Island is a religious sanctuary in Squam Lake (the second largest in the state), which was actually the lake featured in the film *On Golden Pond,* starring Henry Fonda and Katharine Hepburn.

Chocorua Island was the site of America's first residential boy's summer camp, established in 1881 by Ernest Balch; it operated until 1889. Religious services played a vital part in the camp's activity, and in 1903 some of Mr. Balch's relatives and former campers organized the Chocorua Chapel Association for the purpose of "carrying on religious services according to the form of the Protestant Episcopal Church." Clinton Crane, owner of the island, donated it to the Association in 1928. Clifford G. Twombly, one of the Association's founders, led services for 38 years. Since 1940, they have been led by clergy of various denominations; many are summer residents of the Squam area. Nearby is Rockywold-Deephaven Camps, Inc., a long-established and notable family camp which has been in operation since 1897. Some campers take part in the Chocorua Island Chapel services, which are held at 10:30 a.m. on Sundays. The Chapel has a granite altar and a birch cross; the congregation faces the lake, with hills in the background.

Visitors are drawn to Squam Lake by the natural beauty of its shoreline and mountains. James Greenleaf Whittier described it: "Before me stretched for glistening miles, / Lay mountain-girdled Squam; / Like green-winged birds the leafy isles / Upon its bosom swam."

The church services held on Chocorua Island, amid the beauty of the lake and surrounding hills, are a source of special inspiration for those who attend.

POINTS OF INTEREST — The principal place of interest on Chocorua Island is the natural sanctuary where services are held.

The Science Center of New Hampshire is at Holderness; this complex has more than a dozen exhibit buildings and 2 miles of nature trails. Various animals, such as bears, deer, bobcats, and raccoons are kept in settings resembling their natural habitats.

SIGHTSEEING TOURS   None on the island.

PARKS, BEACHES   There are no parks, beaches, or camping on
AND CAMPING   Chocorua Island. No group visits are permitted.
Quiet, limited use of the island by visitors willing
to respect it as a religious sanctuary is permitted.

MARINAS   There are boat rentals at Squam Boats
(968-7721), Riveredge Marina (968-4411), and
Kimbell Marine (968-7182). No boats with motors
of more than 25 HP are allowed. The island has a landing and there are docks in
the inlet behind the main landing.

RESTAURANTS   There are no restaurants on Chocorua, but there
are restaurants near Holderness and many oth-
ers on Lake Winnipesaukee.
The Manor on Golden Pond (see Lodging) has fresh seafood and does its own
baking. In summer there is terrace dining.**$$$**
Squam Lakes Steak House, intersection Rts. 3 and 25, Holderness
(968-7236) has home baking and a fish fry on Friday night; lobster specials are
served on Saturday night.**$$**

LODGING   None on the island. The Manor on Golden Pond,
Box T, Shepard Hill, Holderness 03245, $^1/_2$ mi. SE
on U.S. 3, NH 25 (968-3348), overlooks Squam
lake, and offers a private beach, boats, boat tours, snowmobiles, lawn games, a
swimming pool, and box lunches.**$$-$$$**

RENTALS   None on the island.

CONTACT   Chocorua Chapel Association, c/o Richard V.
Fabian, Treas., Box 223, Holderness, NH 03245.
In case of uncertain weather, call 968-3313.

ISLES OF SHOALS

Area Code 603
LOCATION   6 miles off the Maine and New Hampshire coasts.

SIZE   Appledore, the largest, is less than a mile in
length and width (95 acres).

ACCESS   **Ferry:** From Portsmouth (Capt. Whittaker's Isles
of Shoals Steamship Co., Box 311, Portsmouth,
New Hampshire, 03801; 603/431-5500. **Air:**
There is commercial service to Manchester, NH and Boston, MA.

Gosport Church and Star Island Conference Center
Star Island, Isles of Shoals

HISTORY AND DESCRIPTION "Isles of Shoals" means a place where fish are schooling or shoaling, literally the "Isles of Schooling Fish." The nine Isles were once owned by two Englishmen, who drew an imaginary boundary in 1635, dividing them up. Today, five belong to Maine (Duck, Appledore, Malaga, Smuttynose, and Cedar) and four to New Hampshire (Star, Lunging, White and Seavey). Captain John Smith described them as "many barren rocks, the most overgrowne with such shrubs and sharpe whins you can hardly passe through them; without either grasse or wood, but three or foure shrubby old Cedars." It is surprising that he went on to declare, in his journal in 1616, " . . . of all foure parts of the world that I have seene not inhabited, could I have but the means to transport a Colonie, I would rather live here than any where . . ."

In the early 1600s, the Isles of Shoals became the center of colonial fishing industries and the economic hub of New England many years before that position was held by Boston. As many as 600 British Isles fishermen and their families lived on the Shoals in the 1600s and 1700s and it was considered the wealthiest settlement per capita at the time in the colonies. At the time of the Revolution, however, many islanders retreated to the mainland, and those who remained on the island led a decadent life, alarming members of mainland churches. They sent out ministers bent on rescue. Reforms were accomplished, ministers managed to marry those who had been living together without benefit of wedlock, and churches were built. In 1848, Thomas Laighton of Portsmouth, who had moved his family to the islands, opened the grand Appledore House on Appledore Island, accommodating more than 500 people. This was one of the nation's first summer resorts, and attracted artists, philosophers, and writers. Laighton's daughter, Celia Thaxter, became a famous poet and considered

Hawthorne, Whittier, Richard Henry Dana, James Russell Lowell, Sarah Orne Jewett, Longfellow, and Harriet Beecher Stowe among her literary friends; they all frequented the island. Hawthorne, in his *American Notebooks,* praised the hotel's "long piazza or promenade . . . so situated that the breeze draws across it from the sea on one side of the island to the sea on the other, and it is the breeziest and comfortablest place in the whole world on a hot day." The National Museum of American Art in Washington has a superb painting by Childe Hassam (1859-1935), called "The South Ledges of Appledore," which evokes the striking rocky coastal terrain of the island.

The island has many reefs and coves. Sunsets here now are not very different from the way Celia Thaxter recorded them: "The whole heaven was in a blaze of scarlet, across which sprang a rainbow unbroken by the topmost clouds, with its seven perfect colors chorded in a triumph against the flaming background; the sea answered the sky's rich blue, and the gray rocks lay drowned in melancholy purple. I hid my face from the glory — it was too much to bear." It is fitting that her cutting garden has been restored today as it was planted in 1893, providing a colorful element contrasting with the island's dark-hued rocks.

Although the Isles developed during the early colonial era as the major trading center for English merchants and colonists, by the 1850s they had become known as one of the most sought-after health resorts along the East Coast. It is said that, before telegraph communication was established with the Isles of Shoals, boats would carry carrier pigeons as well as passengers. Once the boat had left Portsmouth, passengers would state whether they expected to dine at one of the Isles of Shoals restaurants, and a pigeon would be dispatched with a note clipped to its leg to make the reservation.

Today, none of the islands have public landings. Appledore and Star are accessible during the summer months; the others are all either privately owned or uninhabitable. Appledore is the home of the Shoals Marine Laboratory, jointly operated by Cornell University and the University of New Hampshire. Marine Science courses are offered from June through August. Both credit and non-credit courses are offered in a variety of subjects, including terrestrial and underwater archaeology, marine biology, marine microbial ecology, and nature photography.

Occasional visitors to Appledore are permitted. If you contact the Ithaca office in advance (see Contact), they will let you know if you or your group can be accommodated. If you have made prior arrangements, and your name is on the list, you will be shuttled by Boston whaler from Star Island to Appledore. If you plan to go, eat lunch on the ferry from Portsmouth to Star Island. This service is *only available by prior arrangement.*

The Star Island conferences first took root in 1896, when Thomas Eliot, who had been affiliated with a summer conference center at Lake Sunapee, N.H., went in search of a health retreat for his wife, who suffered from respiratory ailments. They spent the summer of 1896 at the Oceanic Hotel at Star Island, and Mrs. Eliot felt greatly improved. Eliot asked Thomas Laighton, proprietor of the Appledore House, whether he would consider hosting the religious and educational conferences which had been held at Lake Sunapee. He agreed, and in the summer of 1897, several hundred people came to the retreats at the Oceanic Hotel on Star Island. By 1903, the conferences were so popular the Appledore House was enlisted for the overflow guests. By 1914, the conferences were extremely popular and a benefactor purchased the island that year to secure it for the group until they were able to establish the Star Island Corporation, now headquartered in Boston, which was made up of a group of Congregationalists and Unitarians. Ever since, week-long conferences have been held, for families, religious educators, and anyone interested in cultural, historical, and religious topics. Each evening there is a silent trek up to the chapel, with everyone carrying a lighted lantern. At the end of each conference, staff members say good-bye to "shoalers" (or conference attendants), chanting, "You *will* come back, you *will* come back."

The Oceanic Hotel on Star Island was built in 1873, burned to the ground two years later, and was rebuilt. It stands today as a unique family center virtually unchanged in more than 100 years. You may only stay at the hotel if you are a member of a Unitarian conference group. Meals are served conference guests in the dining room by college-age "Pelicans," who have often attended conferences themselves as children; they compete for the positions. The chapel and several other buildings are constructed of native stone.

The Isles of Shoals Steamship Company runs a 90-foot ship, the *Thomas Laighton,* to Star Island. It is built along the lines of a turn-of-the-century coastal steamship, and carries 350 passengers. The public may disembark on the island by taking the Star Island Stopover trip from Portsmouth; it allows about 3 hours on the island. Only 100 people are allowed to land; make reservations well ahead. If stopover tickets are sold out, you may ride over and return immediately, without disembarking. There is also an evening trip, which does not permit passengers to disembark (see Sightseeing Tours section).

POINTS OF INTEREST   The library and gift shop on Star Island welcome visitors. Betty Moody's Cave, several slender rock crevices, and Haley's Breakwater are also of interest; legend has it that the latter was built in 1820 with pirate treasure dug up on Smuttynose by Captain Samuel Haley.

SIGHTSEEING TOURS   Optional walking tours of Star Island are offered day visitors.

Visits to Appledore are *only available by prior arrangement* (see History and Description section.)

The Isles of Shoals Steamship Co. offers whale watch excursions aboard the *M/V Oceanic* from Portsmouth (431-5500). The company also has a Star Island Sunset and Supply Run (no disembarking on the island) and a Fall Foliage trip to Great Bay and Tributaries.

PARKS, BEACHES AND CAMPING   **Parks:** None as such. **Beaches:** There are no recreational beaches. **Camping:** None.

MARINAS   None.

RESTAURANTS   None; Star Island day visitors may take a picnic, buy a box lunch from the Steamship company, or eat at the island snack bar.

LODGING   Only for those taking courses at Appledore or attending religious conferences at Star Island.

RENTALS   None.

CONTACT   For information on Star Island conferences, write the Star Island Corporation, 110 Arlington St., Boston, MA 02116 (617/426-7988).

For information about the Shoals Marine Laboratory programs, contact the Shoals Marine Laboratory, GH-14, Stimson Hall, Cornell University, Ithaca, NY 14853 (607/255-3717).

ISLANDS OF LAKE WINNIPESAUKEE

Area Code 603

LOCATION   274 islands, within New Hampshire's largest lake (72 square miles).

SIZE   Island size varies a great deal.

ACCESS   May not be visited, but the steamer *Mount Washington* tours the islands from late May to early September (Winnipesaukee Flagship, Box 367, Weirs Beach, NH 03246; 366-5531).

HISTORY AND DESCRIPTION   The Lake Winnipesaukee area is rich in history and, says Robert J. Cole, Fleet Captain of the Winnipesaukee Flagship, it was very important to New Hampshire during the steamboat era (mid-1800s to early 1900s). The most commonly accepted interpretation of the Indian name "Winnipesaukee," according to historian Bruce Heald, is "beautiful water in a high place," though others abound — "The Smile of the Great Spirit," and "Smiling Water Between Hills." All of the above epithets seem to fit Lake Winnipesaukee, with its 274 varied and habitable islands, deep blue water, and panoramic views of mountains in the background. Heald (also the purser of the *Mount Washington*), has carried out research about the region and written *Follow the Mount,* a thorough history of the Indian legends, the lake communities and the steamers which have threaded their way through the islands. Much of the book is based on oral history given by residents of the area. It was published by the Winnipesaukee Flagship Corp., and is available to passengers who take the steamer excursion around the lake and past the islands. There are many Indian camping and hunting grounds, concentrated especially on the west shore at the Weirs and Meredith. The first steamboat, the *Belknap,* was launched in 1833; she was followed by the *Lady of the Lake,* the *Governor Endicott,* the *Maid of the Isles,* and many others. The present vessel dates, in part, from 1888 (portions of the sidewheel steamer *Chateaugay* are incorporated in it).

The *Mount Washington,* with a capacity of 1,250, crisscrosses the lake daily from late May to early September, linking four ports on two triangular, alternating itineraries. Each circuit takes about three hours. About 50 weddings a year are held aboard, along with anniversary parties, reunions, and other special events. The wheelhouse has a rear wall with windows opening onto the observation deck; passengers can view the captains in their native habitat.

POINTS OF INTEREST   The islands of the lake abound in different legends and histories. Among the more interesting are the Dolly Islands, named for Dolly Nichols, who operated a hand-propelled ferry from Meredith Neck to Bear Island. Three Mile Island is one of the summer homes of the Appalachian Mountain Club. Birch Island is the site of the wreck of the steamer *Belknap.* Guernsey Island was

Island in Lake Winnipesaukee

settled by Paul Pillsbury, said to be founder of the Pillsbury flour firm. Rattlesnake Island is one of the largest in the lake, with elevations of almost 400 feet. Governor's Island is one of the most famous in the lake; it was, early on, owned by a succession of New Hampshire governors. It was later the resort of celebrities and housed the staff of the German Embassy during World War I. It now has an exclusive summer colony. Near Wolfeboro, the steamer passes Kimball's Castle, a replica of one on the Rhine River in Germany.

Among the mountains visible from the boat are the Belknaps, the Ossipee Range, and the Sandwich range. On clear days, Mount Washington (6,288 feet, the highest peak east of the Rocky Mountains and north of the Carolinas) can be seen. Besides the huge steamer (230 feet long), there are about 15,000 pleasure craft on the Lake during the summer, including sailboats, power boats, rowboats, and canoes. The steamer, "Queen" of the lake, must make sure to avoid her "subjects."

The port towns include Center Harbor, which is a summer resort at the northern tip of the lake and the home of the New Hampshire Music Festival. The Meredith-Laconia Arts and Crafts Shop shows the work of New Hampshire craftsmen. Weirs Beach has a broad promenade before lakefront Victorian homes, painted in various colors. Wolfeboro, the largest town on the lake, has been an established resort community for two centuries. A major lake port, it still maintains a sedate air. The Clark House, a one-room school, houses the Wolfeboro Historical Society. Alton is a quaint residential community and an old shipping port.

SIGHTSEEING TOURS   During the summer season, the *Mount Washington* departs Weirs Beach and Wolfeboro daily; it also leaves on Monday, Wednesday, and Friday from Center Harbor and on Tuesday, Thursday, Saturday, and Sunday from Alton Bay. In addition, there are special theme cruises, such as a country/western trip and a Hawaiian luau. For full details, contact the Winnipesaukee Flagship (see Access).

PARKS, BEACHES AND CAMPING   There are no parks or beaches accessible to the public on any of the islands, and camping is not allowed.

MARINAS   There are a number of marinas which rent and sell boats. Two are Thurston's Marina at Weirs Beach (366-4811), which has been in business since 1972; and Wolfeboro Marina (569-3200) at Wolfeboro. There are also boat rentals at Goodhue and Hawkins Navy Yard, Wolfeboro (569-2371).

RESTAURANTS   One of the most pleasant meals in the vicinity can be found aboard the *Mount Washington* itself, especially the Sunday champagne brunch. There is a buffet on all cruises, along with a cafeteria and light entrees served in the Flagship Lounge.**$**

The Lakeview Inn Restaurant (see Lodging) in Wolfeboro offers international cuisine.**$$**

The Weirs Beach Lobster Pound and Barbecue Pit at Weirs Beach (366-5713) is a popular family restaurant.**$$**

The Wolfeboro Inn (see Lodging) is in an historic 1812 building; it offers outdoor dining and does its own baking and desserts.**$$**

LODGING   There are many establishments around the lake offering accommodations; the following list of a few near departure points for the *Mount Washington* is necessarily brief.

The Grand View Motel, Box 5051, Weirs Beach 03246 (366-4973) is well landscaped with a good view of the lake.**$$**

The Lakeview Inn and Motor Lodge, 120 N. Main St., Wolfeboro 03894 (569-1335) offers motel units and country inn rooms.**$$**

The Wolfeboro Inn, 44 N. Main St., Wolfeboro 03894 (569-3016) has a private beach on the lake.**$$**

RENTALS   Clearwater Lodges, N. Main St., Wolfeboro 03894 (569-2370) has a cottage colony with 15 1- and 2-bedroom cottages, with a private waterfront, porches, and fireplaces.

Pick Point Lodge and Cottages, Box 220, Mirror Lake 03853, 1¹/₂ mi. West of N.H. 109 on Lake Winnipesaukee (569-1338) also has cottages with kitchens; the complex is on 70 wooded acres with lake frontage.

CONTACT   The Winnipesaukee Flagship, Box 367, Weirs Beach, NH 03246; 366-5531. Also the Chamber of Commerce, Box 547, Wolfeboro, NH 03894 (569-2200).

NEW YORK

"Submit to no models but your own, O city!" wrote Walt Whitman of Manhattan — a dictum surely followed by the nation's metropolis. Today it is the leading commercial and cultural city in the country, with a rich architectural and historic heritage; Christopher Morley once called it the "nation's thyroid gland," which regulates the country's metabolism.

Giovanni de Verrazano entered New York Harbor in 1524; he was followed by Samuel de Champlain in 1609, who explored the Lake Champlain valley, and Henry Hudson, who sailed the river now named for him. When Verrazano arrived, Indian wars were in progress, but by 1570 they formed the Iroquois Confederacy under Dekanawidah and Hiawatha and began a peaceful existence. Manhattan was settled by the Dutch in 1625; in *The Great Gatsby*, F. Scott Fitzgerald evokes the Long Island the Dutch sailors first saw, "a fresh, green breast of the new world. . . . for a transitory enchanted moment man must have held his breath in the presence of this continent."

Today one must leave the environs of the city and venture into the rural upstate area, where dairying and truck farming are still a major source of livelihood, to find a sense of spaciousness and emptiness. There has of late been a shift from emphasis on manufacturing to service industries; business and health services are the state's leading employers. Manufacturing is still important, however; for New York leads in the industries of apparel, printing and publishing, and leather and leather products, among others. The state's terrain is varied, ranging from the Catskill and Adirondack mountain ranges to the piedmont and the coastal plain. The St. Lawrence, the Hudson, and the Mohawk are the principal rivers.

Since the nineteenth century, the islands of New York have been polarized on the economic scale: Fishers, Shelter, and portions of the Thousand Islands have to a large extent been the preserve of the very wealthy, while Ellis and Liberty have been associated with the influx of immigrants. Liberty, of course, stands alone as the emblem of freedom. City Island, in the Bronx, is a curious oasis, with its shipbuilding traditions, within sight of Manhattan. Much of Fire Island is part of the Fire Island National Seashore. Visitors are welcome on the beaches and in the towns, which antedated the establishment of the Seashore, but overnight accommodation is limited; the majority of visitors rent houses or come for the day.

Virtually no state has islands which are less alike than those of New York. Liberty is a national treasure; Fire Island has wide beaches and wind-swept dunes punctuated with architect-designed modern homes; some of the Thousand Islands are large and others so miniscule they are barely able to support a hut and a tree, while still others are graced with mansions and castles. Fishers resists the public, while Fire Island and the Thousand Islands are major recreation areas; City Island and Shelter Island welcome visitors, though City has no lodging.

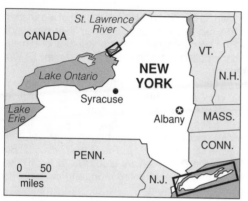
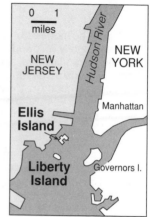
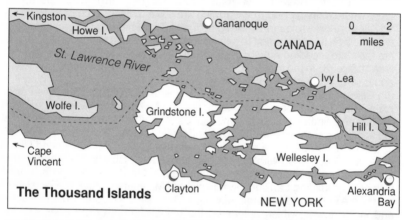

NEW YORK

CITY ISLAND

Area Code 212

LOCATION In Long Island Sound, where the waters of the East River and Sound mix, just across the bridge from Pelham Bay Park in the Bronx.

SIZE 1¹/₂ miles by ¹/₈ mile (230 acres).

ACCESS *Car:* Across the City Island Bridge from the northeast Bronx. *Air:* There is commercial service to New York. *Subway and bus:* Several subway lines from the East and West sides of Manhattan connect with the Bx 12 bus to City Island. Take the Lexington Ave. IRT #6 local marked Pelham Bay Park to the end of the line and follow signs to the end, or take the IND D train marked 205 Street to Fordham Road, take the eastbound Bx 12 bus. If it is marked Pelham Bay Park, ask for transfer to the continuation of the route to City Island. You can also take the IND A train to 207th St., Washington Heights, or the IRT #1 Broadway local to 207th St., to connect with the Bx 12 bus. There is also express bus service to Pelham Bay Station from Madison Ave. (for times and stops, call New York Bus Service, 994-5500); take Bx 12 bus from there. *Private boat.*

HISTORY AND DESCRIPTION Writer Barney Cohen has called it a "proletarian Nantucket." Others view it as a center of boatbuilding (several America's Cup winners were built here). In any case, the visitor to New York who wants to absorb the city's maritime heritage in a festival atmosphere would do well to make his way to City Island, a small bit of land shaped a bit like a seahorse in Long Island Sound.

"The quaint old streets, with their ancient and picturesque dwellings, will repay a desultory ramble," says a 1916 New York guidebook by Fremont Rider. "A bit of New England tucked away in a corner of the Bronx," says the current *I Love New York Bronx Travel Guide*. Both descriptions are a bit off the mark. There are Victorian buildings, but also a touch of honky-tonk on City Island; sailmakers, ships' chandlers, nautical flea markets, and many seafood restaurants crowd its tiny area. Some marine businesses have been replaced by condominiums of late, but the nautical village character of the island remains (residents claim that boats outnumber the population).

The original inhabitants are thought to have been the Siwanoy Indians, part of the Algonquin tribe. They farmed the land and lived in small fishing villages along the shores. Artifacts and arrowheads are still found today, and boaters still paddle the waters in canoes and kayaks, both for pleasure and in competition.

Benjamin Palmer owned the island in the mid-1700s, and was the first person to call it City Island. He hoped to develop it is a major seaport, but the American Revolution put an end to his plans. During the Revolution, the island was a British stronghold. In 1862, the first shipyard opened, located on Pilot St. (It is now known as Consolidated Yachts, an excellent boatyard). As the shipbuilding industry grew, craftsmen from Norway, Denmark, and Sweden immigrated and built luxury yachts; they donated their labor to build the white-steepled Grace Church, next to Consolidated. Scandinavian customs are incorporated in the church; hanging on either side of the altar are two square rigger models, one incoming and one outgoing. City Island was a stopping point for ships waiting for the tide to change, and men from the island often acted as pilots for ships bound for the port of New York.

Today, City Island is a true community in the sense that it is self-sufficient; there are churches, a synagogue, post office, public library, school, newspaper, funeral parlor, launderette, and even an exterminator. The names of businesses reinforce the nautical ambiance: Hair Ahoy Haircutters, Outward Bound Cafe, Lobster Box. "Minneford Boat Yard," proclaims one sign, "The yard that built the cup defenders." This is not an idle boast, for many America's Cup winners were built at Minneford: *The Constellation* (1964), *Intrepid* (1967), *Intrepid* (1970), *Courageous* (1977), *Freedom* (1980).

Most of the side streets on the island stop at the water. They are graced with lovely homes, many Victorian or turn-of-the-century. They face the water, but the passerby can see lawns, gardens, and patios.

Noisy, colorful, and good-natured crowds throng the main street and restaurants. One is as likely to hear Spanish as English here. A blind man's sign says "Por favor, ayude a los ciegos" as well as "Help the blind." There are other, more subdued and often more imposing restaurants, too. Most have parking lots, and a Sunday drive to City Island for dinner seems to be a favorite pastime of Bronxites.

A good time for a visit would be on a weekday in autumn, when many of the yachts are already stowed for the winter, the children are back in school, and there are no crowds at the restaurants.

POINTS OF INTEREST   North Wind Undersea Institute, Inc., 610 City Island Ave. (885-0701), is housed in a renovated and restored Victorian sea captain's mansion. This is a nonprofit educational/environmental organization. It opened in 1981 and is dedicated to educating the public about the need to protect and preserve all marine life as well as to saving beached, injured, or entrapped marine mammals such as whales and dolphins. The museum's director, Captain Michael Sandlofer, is said to have been instrumental in saving the life of a sperm whale that beached itself off Long Island in 1981. A "Rescuarium" was begun in 1985 to house injured or stranded marine animals; three seal pups were the first inhabitants. It offers horse and buggy rides, seal and diver demonstrations, a snack bar, and gift shop. There are also educational programs, including a Pollution Workshop, Equine Heritage Conservancy Program, and a Marine Mammal Workshop. Approximately 25,000 visitors come to North Wind each year.

The City Island Museum, in the old red schoolhouse at 190 Fordham St., houses nautical artifacts and exhibits, including those of the America's Cup winners; the library has many paintings. It is only open on Sundays from 2 p.m. to 5 p.m.

Grace Episcopal Church, on Pilot St., was built in 1862 (see History and Description for part played by Scandinavian craftsmen). The wooden church is in the Gothic Revival style; the rectory is reminiscent of an Italian villa.

There is a ferry, the *Michael Cosgrove,* from City Island to Hart Island, but it is definitely not for tourists. It takes the unclaimed bodies of people who die in New York (presently 1 out of every 29) to Potter's Field, high on a windy hill, for burial, in small New England pine coffins. The public is not admitted, though tours are given for officials, students, professors, and others about once a month. The ferry runs four days a week. New York has had potter's fields for over two centuries, at several locations, including Washington Square and the site of the New York Public Library. Hart Island was purchased for the purpose in 1869.

Two lighthouses off the island, Execution and Steppingstones, are of interest. Execution Lighthouse, east of the island, is infamous as the site of the execution of British prisoners during the Revolution. Steppingstones, at the southern tip, supposedly received its name from a legend that the devil threw stones across the Sound as he escaped to Long Island from Indians in Westchester.

SIGHTSEEING TOURS   The North Wind Undersea Institute has horse and buggy rides (see Points of Interest).

PARKS, BEACHES AND CAMPING   *Parks:* Pelham Bay Park, just across the causeway, has bridle paths, picnic grounds, and golf courses. It is the largest in the city, with over 2,700 acres of settled parkland and wilderness. There are facilities for bicycling, fishing, picnicking, tennis, ball playing, and horseback riding. The Hunter Island Marine Zoology and Geology Sanctuary is here, as well as the marshes of the Thomas Pell Wildlife Refuge. *Beaches:* Orchard Beach is a one-mile crescent-shaped beach near Pelham Bay Park; it is about a 20-minute walk from City Island, and is wide and sandy. There are several eateries here. It is crowded in summer but, off-season, very pleasant. *Camping:* There is no camping allowed.

MARINAS   City Island has one of the major concentrations of boats on Long Island Sound. There are boating services, yacht clubs, shipyards, and marine supply houses. Sagman's Marine (885-1000); 6 transient slips; maximum length 85 feet; approach depth 7 feet; dockside depth 6 feet; electric power—yes; restaurant within walking distance—yes.

RESTAURANTS   Anna's Harbor Restaurant, 565 City Island Ave. (885-1373) has Italian seafood specialties. **$$-$$$**

The Crab Shanty, 361 City Island Ave. (885-1810) specializes in fish dishes; it is a popular restaurant with a pleasant decor.**$$**

Johnny's Reef Restaurant, 2 City Island Ave. (885-9732) is a popular cafeteria-style family restaurant open daily 11 a.m.–9 p.m.; it is just beyond Rochelle St., the terminus for the Bx 12 bus.**$**

The Lobster Box, 34 City Island Ave. Belden Point (885-1952) has been in business over 40 years (it opened in 1945) and has an excellent view of the Long Island Sound. They offer 20 preparations of lobster and many of shrimp, and do their own baking. Closed Mondays.**$$-$$$**

The Sea Shore Restaurant and Marina, 591 City Island Ave. (885-0300) has valet parking and a patio open in summer; reservations are advised.**$$-$$$**

Ellis Island

Thwaite's Inn, 536 City Island Ave. (885-1023) is an old eatery, dating from the Gilded Age (it opened in 1870). It is very popular. One specialty is lobster.$$

LODGING	There are no overnight accommodations on the island.
RENTALS	Mary J. McDonnell, 528 City Island Ave., City Island, NY 10464-0206 (885-1234) handles residential and commercial property.
CONTACT	New York Convention & Visitors Bureau, 2 Columbus Circle, New York, NY 10019 (397-8222) or the Bronx Chamber of Commerce, 367-7200.

ELLIS ISLAND

Area Code 212

LOCATION	In New York Harbor, 1/2 mile from the Statue of Liberty.
SIZE	27 acres.
ACCESS	Ellis Island is closed at present, but, when it reopens, will be accessible by ferry from the Battery in lower Manhattan and from Liberty State Park in New Jersey.

HISTORY AND DESCRIPTION

"It was not Ellis Island that I saw but the magic portal to the new, free, unbelievable world," Leo Rosten wrote of his arrival in America. For over a century, Ellis Island, near the Statue of Liberty, was the gateway to this country. The oral history of countless U.S. families would keep the dream of Ellis Island alive even if it were not being preserved at the site and had not been movingly chronicled by various authors. The island had numerous earlier names (it was called Gull Island, by the Indians, Oyster Island by the Dutch, and Gibbet Island after some pirates were hanged there in the colonial period). Finally, it was called Ellis Island after Samuel Ellis, a New York merchant and owner of a small tavern on the island that catered to fishermen. In 1808, the State of New York bought the island, and later that year it was purchased by the Federal Government. A battery was placed on the island shortly before the War of 1812.

Until 1892, immigration was handled at Castle Garden on the Battery, but it was too small to handle the influx of immigrants and Ellis Island was actually an improvement. In 1890, the government began to prepare it for the role it would assume two years later as an immigration station. On January 1, 1892, Annie Moore, from County Cork, Ireland, was the first person processed at Ellis Island. More than 12 million immigrants, mostly European, were handled here during the time Ellis Island served as an immigration facility, from 1892–1954 (though during and immediately after World War II, it served as a Coast Guard station and was used as a detention center for suspected enemy aliens and as a hospital for returning wounded servicemen). The transatlantic ships actually went first to berths further up the Hudson, where first- and second-class passengers disembarked. Those in third class, or steerage, were loaded onto ferries and brought back to the Ellis Island harbor. The ferries were lined up, immigrants were jammed aboard, and then had to stand for hours until individual ships were called. Those who passed the rigorous examinations (for physical condition, moral character, financial stability, and literacy) were herded back on the ferries and taken to Battery Park or to the railroad terminal in New Jersey. Only 2 percent, from 1892 through 1924, were denied permission to enter — but this was nearly a quarter of a million people. Famous people who passed through Ellis Island included Justice Felix Frankfurter, Rudolph Valentino, Irving Berlin, and Isaac Asimov.

The island, a National Parks Service facility, has undergone extensive restoration and has been closed for several years. It is expected to reopen to the public for museum purposes during the summer of 1990. When the reconstruction is completed, the state-of-the art facilities will be designed to revive the whole immigration experience, including arrival, medical check, mental testing, appearance before a "Board of Special Inquiry," and the joyous moment when one was free to land. There will be four major themes worked out in the displays and exhibits: "The Peopling of America," a graphic look at the history of immigration to America; the "Ellis Island Processing Area," a step-by-step view of the reception process, "Peak Immigration Years, 1892–1924," covering the immigrants' journey to America, and "Ellis Island Galleries," exploring the history of the island and its restoration as well as immigrant artifacts. The entire restoration and museum will cost approximately $140 million.

CONTACT

New York Convention & Visitors Bureau, 2 Columbus Circle, New York, NY 10019 (397-8222).

FIRE ISLAND

Area Code 516

LOCATION About 3 or 4 miles off the south coast of Long Island (some points on the island are closer; others are more distant).

SIZE 32 miles long by $1/2$ mile wide at its widest point.

ACCESS *Car:* There are causeways at the eastern end (the William Floyd Parkway to the Smith Point West Visitor Center) and the western end (the Robert Moses Causeway to the Robert Moses State Park), but no road links these two access points. *Ferry:* There are several ferry companies operating from Long Island to the island. (In New York, call the Long Island Railroad (718/454-5477) for information about getting to the appropriate towns from Manhattan; there are usually vans or taxis at the train station to take people to the boats.) From Sayville to Barrett Beach, Cherry Grove, Fire Island Pines, and Sailors Haven: Sayville Ferry Service, Inc., River Road, Box 626, Sayville, L.I., N.Y., 11782; 589-0810. From Patchogue to Davis Park, Leja Beach, Ocean Ridge, and Watch Hill: Davis Park Ferry Co.; Box 814; Patchogue, L.I., 11772; 475-1665. From Bay Shore to Dunewood, Fair Harbor, Kismet, Ocean Bay Park, Ocean Beach, and Saltaire: Fire Island Ferries, Inc., Maple Ave., Bay Shore, L.I., NY 11706; 665-3600. (Fire Island Ferries also runs a Lateral Ferry in July and August which runs between Kismet and Ocean Beach; 665-3600 or 666-3600). Another ferry from Bay Shore goes to the exclusive community of Point O'Woods; call Captain Artie Weis, Point O'Woods Ferry, Maple Ave., Bay Shore, NY 11706 (665-1568). There are also water taxis serving the island from Watch Hill to Kismet and all the National Seashore parks (Island Water Taxi, 363-2121). Service is also offered by South Bay Water Taxi (583-8885). *Air:* There is commercial service to New York. Waterfront Airways (212/777-3323 or 516/549-1664) offers seaplane service from the 23rd St. Seaplane Base in Manhattan to several Fire Island points, including The Pines and Kismet. *Private boat.*

HISTORY AND DESCRIPTION Fire Island is an island off an island—a straight 32-mile sandbar stretching along the south shore of New York's Long Island from Democrat Point on the west to Moriches Inlet on the east between the Atlantic Ocean and Great South and Moriches bays. It lies parallel to the central one-third of Long Island's south (Atlantic) shore. The width of the island ranges from a few hundred feet to just under a half-mile, making it a fragile ribbon of sand, a barrier island protecting the Great South Bay. The Bay is a shallow sand-bottomed salt water bay flushed by the two inlets at either end of Fire Island, Fire Island Inlet on the west and Moriches Inlet on the east. The depth of water ranges from little more than a foot in many areas to depths of 6 to 10 ft. The normal tide range is 12 to 16 inches. Fire Island is connected to Long Island by bridges at its western end and near its eastern end. But once one has crossed those bridges, or taken the ferries to the island from Bay Shore, Sayville, or Patchogue, there is no place to go except on foot or by bike, for Fire Island has no roads, only boardwalks, paths, and some paved walks. There are 17 separate communities on Fire Island, ranging from the fenced-off private community of Point O'Woods to Ocean Beach, the island's "capital" and only year-round community. Here there is a school, cinema, boutiques, restaurants, and numerous restaurants. There is a predominantly gay community (Cherry Grove, noted for its arts and restaurants) and family settlements such as Saltaire. Some towns appeal to singles and others are a mixture. Technically, Fire Island is part of the National Seashore, but these communities, built primarily for summer recreation, were there long before the designation. The 7-mile stretch from Smith Point West to Watch Hill was designated a wilderness area in 1980, and the Fire Island National Seashore was created in 1964. There are strict regulations governing litter, eating on beaches, and other matters, all aimed at preserving the island's beauty and atmosphere.

Parts of Fire Island are much as they were when Isaac Stratford of Babylon, L.I., set up a whaling station at Whalehouse Point in 1653. The island is rich in marine life, waterfowl, and other wildlife. Walt Whitman, a native of Long Island, once suggested, only half in jest, that Long Island secede from the state of New York and become a small principality called Paumanok (a word used in the aboriginal deeds for the island). Whitman wrote of the "long stretching beaches and sand-islands" on the south side of Long Island; he would surely be grateful for the preservation efforts which have ensured that at least portions of Fire Island have remained intact. Shipwrecks were once frequent here, and survivors would struggle to the shores of the island only to starve. Long Island townships then put up small huts to offer food and shelter to those lucky enough to reach shore.

If there were a single icon applicable to the inhabited portions of the island, it would be the red wagon. Dozens of them are penned up at the ferry landings as though waiting for a bevy of earnest bread-winning children to step off the ferry. When the ferry pulls in, some of those disembarking are met by spouses, friends, lovers, and housemates with wagons, ready to help load them with luggage, flowers, briefcases, wine, and mail. Others disentangle their wagons from the pen and set off, often accompanied by self-important setters and poodles who relish the carefree island summers as much as their owners.

Summer renters, whether young married couples, singles, gays, or families, tend to entertain a great deal. Long Island liquor stores, seafood supermarkets, bakeries, florists, and gourmet shops offer ferry delivery; it is not unusual to see fruit baskets, cheese and nut trays, clam bakes, seafood party platters, and hams traveling across the bay on the daily freight boat for consumption at the Gatsby-like festivities laid on by summer islanders. (Groceries are not allowed on the regular ferries, and there are no big supermarkets on Fire Island, though there are some very adequate smaller stores). Sam's Pet Food and Supplies in Sayville even offers ferry delivery of Nutra Max, Science Diet, and other nourishment for cats, dogs, rabbits, hamsters, gerbils, and wild and exotic birds. Daytrippers had better not plan to picnic, however; food consumption is banned on the beaches.

Barrett Beach is a Town of Islip beach, with many private houses. It has beautiful views, a snack bar, and a marina, but is not a popular gathering spot for people coming to Fire Island for a short time in search of a variety of restaurants, bars, shops, and a more convivial scene.

Cherry Grove is a predominantly gay community. It is famed for its summer theatrical productions, art shows, and the notorious Miss Fire Island Contest (female impersonation). It has very interesting architecture, and a variety of restaurants, bars, and clubs. About 1946, the poet W. H. Auden, who had a genius for discovering unique habitations, purchased (with friends James and Tania Stern) a cottage covered with tarpaper at Cherry Grove, reached then, as now, by the ferry crossing from Sayville. The shack was in a sparsely settled area of the beach, with an unimpeded view of the sea, owing to the 1938 hurricane,

Cherry Grove, Fire Island

which washed away many houses. In "Pleasure Island" he described the island as "a huddle of huts related / By planks, a dock, a state / Of undress and improvised abandon . . . this outpost where nothing is wicked / But to be sorry or sick." He and Chester Kallman were visited at "Bective Poplars" (a takeoff on Stern's family home in Ireland) by Stephen Spender, Christopher Isherwood, and other *literati*. Today, "the Grove" is a lively community, especially in summer, with a large gay population and a relaxed, friendly, free-spirited ambiance. Many of the cottages have names. "Y.M.C.A. – No Vacancy," says one sign. The beach is spacious and inviting.

Davis Park is a small community of about 300 people. It is the most easterly village on the island, and comprises two other small communities, Ocean Ridge and Leja Beach. With electricity installed only a few years ago, Davis Park remains relatively remote; nevertheless, a thriving singles scene exists, centered on the Casino with its restaurant and bar.

Dunewood is a small residential community adjacent to Fair Harbor; there are no commercial facilities.

Fair Harbor, founded in 1923, is an attractive beach community with a restaurant, the Dock, a liquor store, and a food market. If you go to Dunewood or Saltaire, you will need to walk to Fair Harbor for facilities. It has moved away from its traditional role as a family community and now attracts more of a singles crowd. It is popular with advertising and publishing professionals.

Fire Island Pines has made a quantum leap from the pup tents and shacks which once characterized it. The area, once known as Lone Hill, was purchased in 1924 by Dr. Warren Smadbeck, and the metamorphosis slowly began. In 1953, the Home Guardian Company of New York began to subdivide the Pines, advertising them as a remedy for the "atomic age" with "mad rushing about" which "leaves our nerves and body exhausted and often undermines our health to such an extent that we are permanently affected by it." It is now considered by many people to be Fire Island's most glamorous community, with a Botel, hotel, and yachts moored along the Botel dock – as one writer put it, "like gleaming limos parked in front of a posh East Side nightspot." Some of the world's top designers, models, performing artists, and professional people come to Fire Island. Many of the present homes, built to blend with and enhance the natural surroundings, have an understated elegance. At the same time, residents claim to live unpretentiously. "If you normally drive a Rolls-Royce, no one knows it here," architect Gary W. Stluka informed *The New York Times* (he owns a home on Tarpon Walk with his wife and three children). The community, like its sister community to the west, Cherry Grove, counts among its residents and visitors a large gay population. There are parties almost nonstop from Memorial Day through Labor Day, with some guests barefoot in evening clothes. If you survive the festivities, you might wander, the next day, along the famous roller coaster walks between the groves of wild cherry, holly, and pines which form leafy tunnels connecting the bay and ocean. Poison ivy is rampant, however, so it is best not to stray off the boardwalk.

Kismet is where most of the townspeople across the Bay go after working hours. It was devastated by the hurricane of 1938 and is essentially a post-war development. There has been an influx of singles here. It has two restaurants and a large marina.

Ocean Bay Park and **Seaview** are two of the smaller communities on Fire Island. Seaview has a grocery store and a ball field, and Ocean Bay Park has a restaurant with bar which is very popular with both tourists and townspeople. Ocean Bay Park has a reputation as a singles center, and is popular with group renters, while Seaview is more family oriented.

Ocean Beach is the hub of island activity; it is an incorporated village and is the largest and one of the most popular communities on Fire Island. It has a wide array of restaurants, bars, a nightclub, and a cinema. It is also one of the most strictly controlled, with a vigilant police department (in fact, it has been called "The Land of NO."). There are about 600 homes. It is family oriented; there is a nursery program for children up to 5, a day camp with a full schedule of activities for children 4–12, and Youth Group activities for teenagers. Amenities include a playground. Group rentals are restricted and daytripping is not encouraged. No eating or drinking is allowed on beaches or public rocks; there are no public restrooms or locker facilities; use of radios is regulated; and violators are subject to fines up to $250. Residents of Ocean Beach are extremely concerned about fire, so visitors are asked to take every precaution. The beach itself is wide and appealing.

Point O'Woods is an exclusive private residential community.

Sailors Haven, a mile west of Cherry Grove, offers a marina, a visitor center, a guarded beach in the high tourist season, naturalist activities, picnicking, a snack bar, grocery store, and a dog walk. It is a U.S. National Seashore run by the Dept. of the Interior, and the gateway to the Sunken Forest, which has a thick canopy of gnarled holly, sassafras, tupelo, and other vines climbing from the forest floor toward the sun. The trees are unable to grow above the level of the dunes, because the high salt concentration kills thrusting twigs; the smooth canopy protects them from wind damage. The trail, which begins at the Sailor's Haven Visitor Center, is 1½ miles and takes at least an hour for leisurely exploration. The National Park Service cautions visitors against going barefoot, straying from the boardwalk and touching poison ivy.

Saltaire is an incorporated village; it has been a family community since its founding in 1910. There was once a grand hotel here, which guests would reach by taking a horse and carriage out on Long Island, then a boat. Once there, they would often stay for the summer. Saltaire has the only natural harbor on the island, but has no restaurants, bars, or hotels.

Watch Hill is one of the main National Park Service facilities, with a marina, interpretive activities, summer lifeguards, visitor center, picnic tables, a snack bar, grocery store, nature trail with a guide leaflet, a dog walk area, and family and group campgrounds.

The rhythm of summer life on Fire Island is closely linked to the network of ferries crossing from Long Island to Fire Island. Summers on the island marked by intense festivity and, perhaps, by the nostalgia Nick Carraway feels, at the end of F. Scott Fitzgerald's novel *The Great Gatsby,* as he gazes at the "shadowy, moving glow of a ferryboat across the Sound." The ferry may, in fact, have been one of those operated by the Sayville Ferry Service, begun in 1898 by German immigrant Charles Stein. The company is now operated by his great-grandson, Ken Stein, who represents the fourth generation of the Stein family to continue the tradition of one of America's famous ferry dynasties.

POINTS OF INTEREST The Fire Island Lighthouse, 167 feet high, is in the Robert Moses State Park at the western end of the island (it was once on the tip, but shifting sands added 4 miles to the island's length). The present building is an 1858 successor to the first lighthouse, built in 1825; it was relit in 1987 after 13 years disuse. The lightkeeper's quarters of the mid-nineteenth century is a visitor center with exhibits on the history of the site.

The Community House, 577 Coast Guard Walk, Fire Island Pines, has a variety of summer theatrical productions, and also contains the post office, a book swap, and the community manager's office.

The William Floyd Estate is in Mastic Beach, on Long Island, near the Smith Point West Visitor Center; you can drive to it. It is the former home of William Floyd, a Signer of the Declaration of Independence, and is administered by the Fire Island National Seashore.

SIGHTSEEING TOURS There are no sightseeing tours as such, but there are interpretive activities, including walks, at the Smith Point West Visitor Center.

Party boats are popular, especially for bluefishing in late summer. One is the *Frances Ann II,* based in Ocean Bay Park, which offers pickup at Kismet, Saltaire, and Ocean Beach (795-3090). The *Evening Star,* Bay Shore (666-3601) can be chartered for various feasts and lighthouse excursions.

PARKS, BEACHES AND CAMPING **Parks:** Most of the undeveloped lands between Robert Moses State Park and Smith Point County Park are part of the Fire Island National Seashore. There are visitor centers at Sailors Haven, Watch Hill, and Smith Point West, along with interpretive activities and lifeguards, nature trails. The Robert Moses State Park is at the western end of the island (see Points of Interest for description of the Fire Island Lighthouse). The Smith Point County Park is at the eastern end of the island. ***Beaches:*** The beach at Fire Island extends its entire length, with lifeguarded sections at Watch Hill and Sailors Haven. There are access steps to the beach at many points along its length. Note, however, that the interior boardwalk does not extend all the way between towns; if you take a long beach walk in the sun and want to walk back on a shaded boardwalk, it is usually not possible. (see Access for the Lateral Ferry service). ***Camping:*** Watch Hill has family and group campgrounds, the only ones on the island. They have a 4-night maximum (reservations required; 597-6644).

MARINAS   At the western end of the island, Robert Moses State Park has a boat basin for daylight use only. Saltaire and Point O'Woods have private yacht clubs; Watch Hill has a National Seashore marina; 152 transient slips; maximum length 50 feet; approach depth 6 feet; dockside depth 4 feet; electric power — yes; restaurant within walking distance — yes. Sailors Haven also has a National Seashore marina; 43 transient slips; maximum length 50 feet; approach depth 6 feet; dockside depth 4 feet; electric power — yes; restaurant within walking distance — no. Davis Park has a town marina for residents only. Flynn's Marina at Ocean Bay Park (583-5000) is adjacent to Flynn's Casino (see Restaurants); 20 transient slips; maximum length 40 feet; approach depth 6 feet; dockside depth 4 feet; electric power — yes; restaurant within walking distance — yes.

RESTAURANTS   ***Cherry Grove:*** The Compass Rose, south end of Ocean Walk (597-9801) is under new management and offers gourmet dinner specials.**$$-$$$**
Michaels (597-6555) offers casual dining inside or outside.**$$** The Monster, Ocean Walk (597-6888) is a popular disco and bar, also serving dinner, which has been flourishing since 1971.**$$** Top of the Bay (597-6699) has a deck overlooking Great South Bay and a diversified menu.**$$-$$$**

Davis Park: The Leja Beach Casino (see Lodging) has a popular Sunday brunch and specializes in steaks and seafood; it has an ocean view.

Fire Island Pines: The Pines and Dunes Yacht Club, part of John Whyte's Fire Island Pines Botel (597-6500), overlooking the harbor, is a lovely spot to eat and gather.**$$** Other interesting places are the Cultured Elephant (**$$**) and the Restaurant at the Pavilion**$$**. The Pines Pantry is an excellent gourmet food market. The Pavilion is a disco. A new Pines tradition is "High Tea" at the Pavilion, the community's most popular gay nightspot; this is an opportunity to socialize, dance, and network. The Botel has "Low Tea"; this is a competing nightspot attracting many heterosexual people. The Crew's Quarters, at the corner of Fire Island Boulevard and Picketty Ruffwalk, one block west of the Pines Harbor (597-6873) is a popular bar.

Kismet: The Kismet Inn (583-5592) has docking and serves steaks, chops, and seafood.**$$-$$$**
The Kismet Out, Bay Walk (583-7400) is a well-known restaurant serving lobster, clambakes, shrimp fixed in imaginative ways, and other dishes.**$$-$$$**

Ocean Bay Park: Flynn's Casino, on the Bay side of the island (583-5000), formerly Flynn's Hotel, has been a landmark here for over 40 years; it is open for lunch and dinner and, on Sunday afternoons, has an "It's not over yet" party. **$$** Skimmers, Box 334, Ocean Beach, Fire Island, NY 11770 (583-8438), is a local favorite.**$$**

Ocean Beach: The Sand Castle (583-7000) is at Robbins Rest, just west of Ocean Beach. It is an Italian restaurant. It cannot be reached by ferry, but there is docking space for private boats and water taxis.**$$-$$$**

LODGING There is no accommodation for transients in most of the communities, except (weekend prices given):

Cherry Grove: The Belvedere Guest House, Cherry Grove, NY 11782 (597-6448) is a Venetian-style palatial structure with terraces, towers, domes, statuary, fountains, reflecting pools, and ceiling frescoes, almost a scaled-down version of a Newport summer "cottage." The rooms have antiques, and many have private terraces, though not private baths.**$$$**

The Cherry Grove Beach Hotel (597-6600) has deluxe rooms with VCR's and wet bars. Entertainment includes a piano bar and drag shows; the Ice Palace discotheque is popular.**$$$**

Davis Park: The Leja Beach Casino (597-6150) has rooms.**$$**

Fire Island Pines: The Pines and Dunes Yacht Club, part of John Whyte's Fire Island Pines Botel (Yacht Club 597-6500; Botel 597-6131), overlooking the harbor, has accommodations.**$$$** Dune Point (597-6261)**$$$** and the Carousel Guest House (597-6612) also have accommodations.**$$$**

Kismet: Camelot (583-8565) has rooms.**$$**

Ocean Bay Park: The Fire Island Resort Hotel, Box 334, Ocean Beach P.O., Fire Island, NY 11770 (583-8000), has over 50 rooms; it was formerly Flynn's Hotel and is on the ocean side of the island.**$$** The Seashore Motel (583-5860).**$$**

Ocean Beach: Cleaa's (583-5399, **$$**); Houser Hotel (583-5387, **$$**); Bayberry Inn (583-5558, **$$**); High Point (583-9701, **$$**); High Dune Inn (588-9701, **$$$**).

RENTALS Caryl Phillips, Fire Island Land Company, on the dock at Cherry Grove, NY 11782 (597-1182) is very knowledgeable about the island as a whole; she handles rentals and sales (and is very helpful and gracious to floundering visitors). Bob Howard, Fire Island Pines (597-9400) handles rentals, sales, and housemate referrals. Hanlan's, at the Harbor, Fire Island Pines (597-6969) also handles sales and rentals. For Ocean Beach, contact the Village Clerk (583-5940) for a list of realtors.

CONTACT For information about the Fire Island National Seashore, the Superintendent, 120 Laurel St., Patchogue, NY 11772. The Visitor Center at Sailors Haven is 597-6183; the one at Watch Hill is 597-6455; the one at Smith Point West is 281-3010. For information about the island communities, contact the realtors or innkeepers. For information about Ocean Beach, contact the Village Clerk (583-5940).

FISHERS ISLAND

Area Code 516

LOCATION 11 miles off the northeastern tip of Long Island, and about 7 miles southeast of New London.

SIZE 9 miles long by 1½ mile wide.

ACCESS **Ferry:** Ferries have been serving Fishers Island for about 100 years. The Fishers Island Ferry District has been providing the service since

1949, but the ferries are not publicized. Ferries leave year-round, with two to ten sailings a day, depending on the season. Fishers Island Ferry District, Fishers Island, N.Y., 06390; CT: (203) 443-6851; NY: (516) 788-7463. *Air:* There is commercial service to New London. Charter service to the island is provided by Coastal Air Services from Groton, CT (203/449-0166) and Nantucket, MA (506/228-3350). *Private boat.*

HISTORY AND
DESCRIPTION

Fishers Island, a small realm of tranquillity just off the coast of Connecticut, is an enclave of summer homes of the wealthy. Most of the island is privately owned. There are virtually no tourist facilities and islanders are proud of the lack of amenities; neither homeowners nor locals want to be disturbed. Fishers Island Village, with a few stores and a small hotel, the Pequot Inn, is about a 20-minute walk from the ferry. It is appealing, with green lawns, white colonial-style houses, and a war memorial. The island population is about 250, climbing to 2,000 in mid-summer. The island has no taxis, pay telephones, souvenir shops, bike rentals, or camping.

The landscape consists of rolling hills, mostly covered with trees, briars, and bittersweet. There are swans, ducks, ospreys nesting on the telephone poles, and other birds. The architecture ranges from colonial and Victorian mansion style (including the gabled, turreted house where part of *The World According to Garp* was filmed) to modernistic. The road to the eastern two-thirds of the island is closed to the public in summer, but even off-season, if you walk down it, you won't see much of the estates, hidden as they are by the brush and foliage.

Indian tribes, explorers such as Adriaen Block and one of his officers, named Visscher, and the Winthrops of New England all contributed to the island's history. John Winthrop, Jr., was reputedly the first white settler on the island, in 1646; he raised sheep, goats, and horses. He later became governor of Connecticut. Some people suggest the island got its name from Visscher; others think the name stemmed from the fishing the Indians did. In the late nineteenth century, there was a tourist era, with steamers bringing daytrippers, and vacationers staying at hotels and boarding houses (they have vanished now). During World War II, Fort H. G. Wright was headquarters of harbor defenses for Long Island.

The island lies near the east end of Long Island Sound between Fishers Island Sound, which separates it from Connecticut, and Block Island Sound, which is virtually open sea. Despite the Connecticut connection, Fishers Island is actually part of the town of Southold, in Suffolk County, Long Island, N.Y. The quirks of history and politics landed it there (an 1879 agreement between the two state legislatures settled the problem of domain which had vexed it since colonial days).

It has been said that "strangers generally arrive at Fishers by yacht or by marriage." The Friday ferries are a meeting ground for the weekend. As described in *Town and Country,* everyone "clambering aboard in green espadrilles and worn Shetlands knows each other, each other's children and each other's Labrador retrievers and Jack Russell terriers, by name. Strangers become acutely aware of being strangers. Unless, of course, they are houseguests, in which case they are well-introduced houseguests by the time the ferry docks and the Fishers-folk are whisked off in station wagons down tiny lanes to grandmother's house." If you are a resilient and determined, but unbefriended person, and arrive at Fishers Island unheralded, you can walk around the small end of the island, visit the small beach, if you can find it, make your way to the

Statue of Liberty, Liberty Island

Pequot Inn for lunch, and take the ferry back before nightfall. (Bikes can be transported, but they cost $5.) You may fare a little better off-season. If you stray by, appreciative of the scenery and with no island development gleam in your eye, no sense of wanting to improve the beaches or set up restaurants and fast-food outlets, and if you should meet islanders, you may be surprised at the warmth of the welcome. They may offer to drive you around, give you plants from their gardens, acquaint you with local history, make you feel one of the island family, and even urge you to come again. All they ask is that you don't try to change their world.

POINTS OF INTEREST   The older buildings to the right of the ferry land-ing once belonged to the Coast Guard; they have been slated for restoration.

SIGHTSEEING TOURS   There are no sightseeing tours.

PARKS, BEACHES
AND CAMPING

No camping is allowed.

Parks: There are no parks as such. **Beaches:** There are little sand beaches, and long stretches of stony beach on the "seaward" side. **Camping:**

MARINAS

Yachtsmen will find a better reception at Fishers Island than pedestrians, though they are only welcome if they respect the privacy and quiet of the island. The shoreline has several small harbors; West Harbor is best for cruising boats. Silver Eel Pond, where the ferry docks, is not hospitable to visiting boats because of space needed for the ferry. Fishers Island Mobil Dock (788-7311); 6 transient slips; maximum length 120 feet; approach depth 15 feet; dockside depth 15 feet; electric power — yes; restaurant within walking distance — no. Fishers Island Yacht Club (788-7245); 5 transient slips; maximum length 100 feet; approach depth 8 feet; dockside depth 8 feet; electric power — no; restaurant within walking distance — yes.

RESTAURANTS

It is possible to have lunch or dinner at the Pequot Inn (see Lodging), but day visitors must be careful not to miss the ferry back. **$$-$$$**

LODGING

The Pequot Inn, Box 246, Fishers Island 06390 (788-7246) has six rooms, which are often rented to overflow guests of residents. It has no room telephones, central heat, or television and does not serve breakfast. It is open from April until the end of October. The bar and dining room are the center of island news and activity for islanders and summer folk alike (there is a disco on summer weekends). The person sitting next to you at the bar may be the person who caught the lobster you'll eat in the dining room, and the person sitting next to him may be a summer resident whose family name is known nationwide — a Du Pont, for instance. **$$-$$$**

RENTALS

Only if privately arranged.

CONTACT

The Pequot Inn (788-7246) or the Greenport-Southold Chamber of Commerce, Southold, L.I. 11971 (516/477-1383).

LIBERTY ISLAND

Area Code 212
LOCATION

In New York Harbor, about 3 thousand yards southwest of the tip of Manhattan and $1/2$ mile from Ellis Island.

SIZE

12 acres.

ACCESS

Ferry: Circle Line Statue of Liberty Ferry; Battery Park, South Ferry New York, N.Y. 10004; they depart daily, year round, on the hour 9 a.m. to

4 p.m.; 212/269-5755. The vessels on this service are the *Miss Circle Line* and the *Miss Liberty*. From April–Oct., ferries also run from Liberty State Park, Jersey City, NJ; they depart hourly on the hour 9 a.m. to 4 p.m.; 201/915-3400.

**HISTORY AND
DESCRIPTION**
"People were lifting their children, even their infants, to give them a view of the Statue of Liberty," a 1913 Yugoslav immigrant reported. In the heyday of immigration to the United States, when millions of men, women and children made the journey up New York Harbor, the Statue of Liberty greeted them, symbol of all they had come for. Today, many immigrants arrive at other ports and fly to various cities, so that their first glimpse of the Statue of Liberty is on a trip to New York; they take the ferry out from the Battery and see it on departure from Manhattan, as it were, rather than on arrival. Present-day visitors may not be able to empathize completely with those earlier voyagers. Still, the first close view of the massive statue, now brought to her full splendor, her countenance patient and protective, yet indomitable, is usually a startling experience for the visitor. One can understand her first title, "Liberty Enlightening the World." She has been compared with Minerva, goddess of learning, and with Juno, protector of women.

Until 1956, Liberty Island was called Bedloe's Island, after a Walloon named Isaac Bedloe, who owned it in the seventeenth century. There was once a fort on the island. The centennial celebrations in 1986 reminded everyone of the statue's history. Professor Edouard-Rene Lefebvre de Laboulaye, an historian, conceived the idea for a monument to French-American friendship; Frederic Auguste Bartholdi designed it; and Alexandre Gustave Eiffel solved the engineering problems by designing the framework. The Statue was presented to the United States by France in 1886 in commemoration of the American-French alliance during the American Revolution. She is the largest metal statue ever constructed, with a height of 151 feet and weight of 450,000 pounds. She stands on a granite pedestal of 156 feet. The pedestal was lacking at first; the French had subscribed funds for the goddess herself, but not for the base. Joseph Pulitzer, publisher of *The World*, used his paper to chastise the prosperous Irish, who had forgotten the potato famines and now frequented fine hotels, and they, along with other immigrants from all over the country, raised funds for the pedestal. Richard Morris Hunt designed it, and the Statue was dedicated with high ceremony in October 1886, with the famous words by President Grover Cleveland: "We will not forget that Liberty has here made her home; nor shall her chosen altar be neglected."

Over the past century, Liberty's copper patina had been corroded and discolored and some of the framework rusted; the entire Statue badly needed restoration. Over $230 million was raised by a Centennial Committee for her renovation and that of Ellis Island, nearby. The work on the Statue and part of Ellis was completed in 1986. The Statue was unveiled during a spectacular 4-day gala (July 3–6, 1986), celebrated with Operation Sail, a parade of Tall Ships from Verrazano Bridge up the Hudson River, a music festival, fireworks, and other ceremonies. When you visit the Statue, you may go by elevator up 10 floors to the balcony whch runs around the top of the pedestal. In order to reach the crown, you must climb 12 more stories (but there are rest platforms).

The ferry trip to the State has been called "America's Favorite Boat Ride." It attracts riders from all over the world, and has been for decades one of the top tourist activities in New York.

POINTS OF INTEREST   There are two exhibits in the base of the statue, the American Museum of Immigration, which opened in 1972, and the Statue of Liberty Exhibit, which opened after the 1986 restoration. The Museum of Immigration has photographs, mannequins, dioramas, and other artifacts documenting the immigrant struggle.

SIGHTSEEING TOURS   None.

PARKS, BEACHES AND CAMPING   **Parks:** Liberty Island is part of the Statue of Liberty National Monument, administered by the National Park Service.
There are no beaches or camping.

MARINAS   There are no marinas.

RESTAURANTS   There are snack bars on the ships and there is a gift shop and restaurant on Liberty Island, run by the Evelyn Hill Group, the concessionaire for
Liberty Island.

LODGING   There is no lodging.

RENTALS   There are no rentals.

CONTACT   New York Convention & Visitors Bureau, 2 Columbus Circle, New York, NY 10019 (397-8222). (see Access for boat tour contact.)
Also, Superintendent, Statue of Liberty, National Park Service, Liberty Island, New York, NY 10004 (363-3200).

SHELTER ISLAND

Area Code 516
LOCATION   In Peconic Bay, between the two "claws" of land which form the eastern end of Long Island.

SIZE   Approximately 3 miles by 4 miles.

ACCESS   **Ferry:** From Greenport: North Ferry Co., Inc., Shelter Island Heights, NY 11965 (749-0139). From North Haven: Cliff Clark, Box 614, Shelter Island, NY 11964 (749-0007). **Bus:** (From Greenport): The Sunrise Express van/bus connects Greenport, Queens, and Manhattan (516/477-1200; 516/734-5353; 718/767-2775). **Air:** There is commercial service to New York, but no service at present into Shelter Island. **Private boat.**

HISTORY AND DESCRIPTION   Shelter Island, settled in 1638, is one of the most charming parts of Long Island, rich with literary associations. While not ostentatious, it suggests that kindly philanthropists have retreated here for long, cool summers. Carson McCullers, for instance, came out to Shelter Island in 1961 to meet with Edward Albee and discuss the stage adaptation of *The Ballad of the Sad Cafe.*

Shelter Island has a rural atmosphere with woodlands, flowering meadows, sandy beaches, and abundant wildlife. It is peaceful and charming, with a number of well-preserved Victorian houses, covered with gingerbread trim and graced with turrets, with arched windows. People fly the flag here, and groom their lawns, and sit on their porches of a Sunday afternoon — those who are not out sailing, that is, for this is a very sailing-oriented island. At the Chequit Inn, an inexpensive, casual place in Shelter Island Heights, people will sit outdoors having brunch or lunch on a summer Sunday. One gets the impression that it is, perhaps, quite a conservative spot, and certainly full of self-respect and a feeling for the past.

Shelter Island was purchased from the New Haven Colony in the mid-seventeenth century by four sugar merchants from Barbados. The New Haven Colony, an offshoot of the Massachusetts Bay Colony, was involved in the West Indies trade. One of the four purchasers was a member of the Society of Friends and another was very sympathetic to their point of view, if not a Quaker himself. Shelter Island became a place where Friends could live without being persecuted. The name may derive from its having served as a refuge for Quakers or because, geographically, it was an "island protected by islands." There was farming on the island, and the settlers had slaves. The Shelter Islanders, by and large, were sympathetic to the rebel cause during the American Revolution. The British occupied the island and many families fled, to return later. Much of the island history is recounted by Helen Zunser Wortis in *A Woman Named Matilda and Other True Accounts of Old Shelter Island.*

Many of the roads are winding, shaded, and hilly. They invite leisurely driving, walking, and biking. One large area of the island is a nature conservancy. With its jagged coastline, the island has beaches galore, some private and some public. There are hotels and inns, boarding houses and inviting places to eat, but no campgrounds. There is no public transportation, but there is "Go-Fors," a taxi and errand service (749-1168; 749-0925).

House on Shelter Island

Things are not altogether bucolic on the island; the weekly *Shelter Island Reporter* shows that there are problems (pollution, asbestos, minor crime, rising housing costs, etc.) Young people, unable to afford homes, move away, leaving no one to care for the elderly (almost 30 percent of the population in 1980). "Budget" homes begin at $200,000; waterfront homes are over $500,000. Even a waterfront lot can be $300,000 or over. For the visitor, however, Shelter Island is a shelter indeed, from dirt, noise, bad air, hustle and bustle, and tension.

POINTS OF INTEREST   The Sylvester Manor Windmill, built at Southold in 1705 and moved to its present site on Shelter Island, stands as a monument to Nathaniel Sylvester, the first patentee of the island.

The Shelter Island Historical Society's Havens House Museum and Manhanset Chapel Museum are open Memorial Day through Labor Day; they have exhibits of Shelter Island's history and a tour of period rooms.

The Quaker Cemetery recalls the early influence of the Society of Friends. There is a slave burying ground also.

In Greenport, very close, there are several attractions of interest: the Museum of Childhood, with antique dolls and a Swiss village, the Blacksmith Shop (built in the 1800s and still in use) and the 1899 Greenport Railroad Station. The Stirling Historical Society has displays on local history. In Southold, a few miles from Greenport, the Indian Museum, the Southold Marine Museum, the Southold Historical Society and Museum, and the Horton's Point Lighthouse are well worth seeing.

In Sag Harbor, near North Haven, the Sag Harbor Whaling and Historical Museum, Garden and Main Sts., has relics of whaling days and local artifacts in the former home of Benjamin Hunting, a local ship owner. The Custom House on Garden St. is also open; this building served as a late eighteenth-century post office and customhouse.

SIGHTSEEING TOURS   There are guided tours of the Mashomack Preserve (see Parks, Beaches, and Camping).

PARKS, BEACHES AND CAMPING   ***Parks:*** The Mashomack Preserve, South Ferry Road, is open every day except Tuesday for observation and hiking on trails. Guided tours are offered on selected Sundays, May through October; reservations are necessary (check local paper for schedule or call 749-1001). Fishing is a popular pastime; there is no closed season and no license is needed. ***Beaches:*** There are many beaches, owing to the island's jagged coastline. Some are private and some are public. Upper Beach, Lower Beach, Silver Beach, Crescent Beach, and West Neck are all popular. ***Camping:*** There are no campgrounds.

MARINAS   With its irregular coastline, Shelter Island has protected moorings safe for small craft and waters deep enough for seagoing yachts; the island is a boating mecca, and the marinas welcome transients. The Island Boatyard (749-3333); 20 transient slips; maximum length 50 feet; approach depth 6 feet; dockside depth 6 feet; electric power—yes; restaurant within walking distance—no, but the Club Calypso has beach music, tropical drink specials, burgers, salads, and a clam bar. The Coecles Harbor Marina and Boatyard (749-0799) is one of the most complete, with scheduled transportation to stores and restaurants and a gift shop and snack bar; 30 transient slips; maximum length 75 feet; approach depth 6 feet; dockside depth 6 feet; electric power—yes; restaurant within walking distance—no, but the marina operators provide transportation to restaurants. Piccozzi's Dering Harbor Marina (749-0045); 18 transient slips; maximum length 100 feet; approach depth 10 feet; dockside depth 10 feet; electric power — yes; restaurant within walking distance — yes. The Pridwin Hotel has dockside space for vessels up to 40 feet, if you are dining there.

RESTAURANTS The Chequit Inn (see Lodging) serves breakfast and dinner; there is a lobster buffet at 4 on Sundays.**$$**

Clam Diggers, 15 Grand Ave., Shelter Island Heights (749-2005) has a full dinner menu in the dining room and a lighter menu on the patio; it is closed Tuesday. It offers American regional and Northern Italian specialties; there is also a bakery which has a take-out menu.**$$**

Cogan's Country Restaurant, Rt. 114 and Duvall Road (749-2129) is in a country home and offers American regional cuisine; it is open for lunch and dinner; reservations are requested.**$$**

The Dering Harbor Inn (see Lodging) has a French chef who has a number of specialties.**$$-$$$**

The Pridwin Hotel (see Lodging) is open daily for breakfast, lunch, and dinner; reservations requested.**$$-$$$$**

The Ram's Head Inn (see Lodging) offers terrace dining.**$$-$$$$**

The Soundview Summer Theater, in the Soundview Restaurant, Greenport (477-0666) gives dinner theater productions.**$$-$$$**

LODGING The Chamber of Commerce will send a complete list of accommodations. The following is a necessarily brief list. The Belle Crest House Bed and Breakfast Country Inn, 153 N. Ferry Rd., Shelter Island Heights 11965 (749-2041), owned by Yvonne Loinig, is a spacious Dutch Colonial mansion in a

Chimera Guarding Casa Blanca,
The Thousand Islands

garden setting; guest rooms are furnished in early American collectibles and antiques. Rates include breakfast. **$$**

The Chequit Inn, Shelter Island Heights, 11965 (749-0018) is an historic inn, established in 1870. It is a landmark on the east end. It serves old-fashioned country breakfasts and homestyle meals in the dining room (luncheon and supper can be served outside on the terrace).**$$**

The Dering Harbor Inn, Box AD, Shelter Island Heights 11965 (749-0900) overlooks Dering Harbor and has 1- and 2-bedroom suites and a salt-water pool.**$$$**

The Pridwin, Crescent Beach, Shelter Island, 11964 (749-0476) is a delightful resort hotel which offers Edwardian pursuits such as croquet.**$$$**

The Ram's Head Inn, Box 638, 108 Ram Island Dr., Shelter Island 11965 (749-0811) is a country inn overlooking Coecles Harbor; it has a private beach and tennis court.**$$$**

The Shelter Island Resort, 35 Shore Road, Shelter Island Heights 11965 (749-2001 or 0180), on a bluff overlooking the sound, is also pleasant. It has a well-known Sunday buffet.**$$$**

RENTALS There are a number of realtors handling seasonal and year-round rentals. Three are Rheta Conner, Inc., 10 Margaret's Drive (749-2300), Ferry Hills Associates, Inc., 17 Grand Ave., Shelter Island Heights (749-3050), and Foxfire Realty, Jean Brechter, Broker, Box 830, Shelter Island Heights 11965 (749-8830).

CONTACT Shelter Island Chamber of Commerce, 17 Grand Ave., Shelter Island, NY 11964 (749-0399).

THE THOUSAND ISLANDS

Area Code U.S. 315; Canada 613

LOCATION In the St. Lawrence River, where it meets the waters of Lake Ontario.

SIZE Varies from a rock barely large enough to support a tree to several which are more than 5 miles wide and 20 miles long.

ACCESS ***Car:*** Alexandria Bay and Clayton, departure points for the U.S. boat cruises to the Thousand Islands, are accessible from I-81. On the Canadian side, the Thousand Islands Parkway links Gananoque and Brockville; Rt. 401 parallels it, going on to Kingston. ***Ferry:*** Between Kingston, Ontario, and Wolfe Island, Ontario, and on to Cape Vincent, NY via Horne's Ferry (618/385-2291 or 385-2402). ***Air:*** There is commercial service to Watertown and to Syracuse. Alexandria Bay has an air strip. ***Private boat.***

HISTORY AND DESCRIPTION "The Thousand Islands is man perching where he's not supposed to be and making the most of it," says E. T. Jones, a water resource specialist in Fineview, on Wellesley Island, just across the bridge from Alexandria Bay. At Fineview, as on many of the Thousand Islands (actually, there are about 1,870), small houses are tucked against cliffs that have up to 4 or 5 water-view levels. On other islands there are baronial castles.

The Thousand Islands are located on the St. Lawrence Seaway, site of the Seaway Trail, a beautiful recreational trail stretching 454 miles from the New York-Pennsylvania border at Ripley to the Seaway International bridge at Roose-veltown in St. Lawrence County. The Seaway region extends from Oswego north along the shores of Lake Ontario to Tibbets Point Lighthouse, where the lake flows into the St. Lawrence River, which washes the shores of the Thousand Islands; here a 65-mile stretch of the St. Lawrence is broken up by over 1800 large and small islands.

The St. Lawrence Seaway offers a remarkable changing panorama, a con-tinuum of traffic. The lights on the bridge look at night like a mammoth plump Christmas tree, and imposing tankers and lakers glide by, extraordinarily silently for their size. Barges move along swiftly, carrying a variety of cargo—even, one day, a Canadian Air Force plane. Always there are the colorful paddlewheelers, such as the Uncle Sam Boat Tours' pride, the triple decker *Alexandria Belle* from Alexandria Bay, the largest in the area, and the majestic *Canadian Empress* from Kingston. Other cruise ships from Alexandria Bay, Clayton, Gananoque, Brockville, and Kingston mingle, their statuesque white outlines, graced with gingerbread carving, accenting the dark trees and gray rocks. Private boats dart in and out, carrying fishermen, island housewives bound for the city dock at Alexandria Bay to pick up a few groceries, and pleasure boaters. There are still some houseboats on the St. Lawrence, though perhaps not on the scale of the one advertised in the *Thousand Islands Sun* of 1917: "For Sale at a great sacrifice the handsomely furnished and well built houseboat *Idler* with powerful tug G.A.M. Has 7 master bedrooms and accommodations for 6 stewards. Hot and cold water in all rooms and 2 bathrooms."

"There is nothing—absolutely nothing—half so much worth doing as simply messing about in boats," says Water Rat in Kenneth Grahame's *The Wind in the Willows,* and nowhere is this statement more evident than in the Thousand Islands. Boats pervade every aspect of the area. If asked what disadvantages there are to living on an island, people are likely to reply, "None, unless we get too old to drive a boat." When the millionaires began coming to the Thousand Islands in the late nineteenth century and building European-style castles on the islands, they housed their boats as opulently as themselves. The Boldt Yacht House, on Wellesley Island, has reception rooms with stone fireplaces and carved stair balusters; it is listed in the National Register of Historic Places.

"If your family has an island or even a nice place, every child grows up around boats. My parents let me drive a boat alone by the time I was five," says Sheila Norman-Culp, who has known the mass of islands all her life. She grew up on the United States side of the river, and her husband, Paul Culp, grew up on the Canadian side. "Each child has his or her own boat," she continues, "not anything new, but some wooden wreck that we dragged off someone else's shore for free and fixed up. There is always some small daysailer for the kids . . . the family would have one larger boat, to ferry people over, to keep grandmother dry and cozy, a boat to waterski behind, smaller boats for fishing, one or two sailboats, and perhaps a larger one (25–35 feet) if the parents were sailors, a canoe and a rowboat."

The average family may not have a wardrobe of boats, but it is clear, approach-ing the Thousand Islands by car, that boats are ubiquitous. The interstate from Syracuse is filled with cars towing boats. Boats speed through the waters in and around the islands from dawn to midnight, bearing fishermen or recreational boaters; larger yachts and sailboats abound in the marinas tucked in every cove.

In the past, there has been a rather stratified population divided among those year-round inhabitants whose jobs are seasonal and depend on tourists; those involved in agriculture, principally dairying; and a well-to-do summer colony. As a result, many young people leave the region and work elsewhere. The mix is now changing; there are more middle-income tourists, represented by a substantial increase in bus tours, coming from all over the country, including Arkansas and Oklahoma. Increasingly, there are blue-collar, middle-income visitors, especially in July and August, who are campers and cottagers. Tourism is now running a close second to agriculture.

The border region is neither wholly Canadian nor wholly American. There have been many intermarriages, to the extent that it is almost another country, with familial networks and ties extending into the regions on each side of the river. "This is not always visible to strangers," says Michael Quencer, a native of the region. "But it exists, and is one of the most powerful intangible hallmarks of the area; we sometimes feel we live neither in Canada nor the States, but in a third country." Vandalism is, surprisingly, not much of a worry to owners of island homes. Strange boats visiting docks are conspicuous, and the Coast Guard checks on anything out of the ordinary. They even rescued Peggy, a small poodle belonging to the Amsterdam family of Casa Blanca, who fell from a motor launch into the rapid dark waters of the St. Lawrence. She was presented to the astonished family, very damp and thoroughly chastened. Fire is more of a threat; by the time one is spotted and reported, it is often too late; the fire boats reflect what is too often the hopelessness of their mission (Cape Vincent has the *Long Gone;* Clayton the *Last Chance;* Alexandria Bay the *No Hope*). Many hotels and private homes have been lost to fire over the past century, including the gracious Round Hotel and the Frontenac, as well as the Riveredge and Pine Tree Point in Alexandria Bay (both the latter two were rebuilt).

Alexandria Bay has only about 1,200 people but it supports, in season, a number of good restaurants and fine resorts, as well as many boat tours of the islands (see Sightseeing Tours).

Clayton, with about 1,800 people, is the center of the Thousand Islands, which extend for over 10 miles in either direction.

Canadian towns of particular interest, all of which have tours of the St. Lawrence and Thousand Islands (see Sightseeing Tours) are Brockville, Gananoque, Kingston, and Wolfe Island.

Brockville, with a population of about 20,000, was founded in 1765; it is a tourist center and the home of Ontario's oldest newspaper, the *Recorder* (1821).

Gananoque (pronounced Gana-NOCK-kway) is also delightful, a lively small resort of about 5,000. The Thousand Islands Playhouse draws audiences all summer long, and there are good restaurants and interesting shops.

Kingston, at the head of the Thousand Islands, is an old town, founded in 1673 by Count Frontenac, Governor of New France, as a fur-trading post. Today it has a population of about 52,000, and offers an inviting waterfront, old fortifications, and interesting museums.

Wolfe Island is the largest in the Thousand Islands; it was named in 1792 for the British general James Wolfe. It is a farming community. After the Revolution, the island's fine stands of white oak were cleared for ship building.

Note: In the interest of consistency, the style has been standardized as "Thousand Islands" rather than "1000 Islands," even though some businesses and organizations retain digits in their names.

POINTS OF INTEREST   ***United States: Alexandria Bay:*** Boldt Castle, on Heart Island, seen from Alexandria Bay, comes to life in the early morning like a European vista, something which would have been at home in *Ivanhoe*, a revival of the

Boldt Castle, Heart Island, The Thousand Islands

medieval, a Gothic stronghold where a hundred heroines might have been imprisoned. With its stone turrets and towers, it could be a castle on the Rhine River. At night it is lighted, an enduring testament to the vision of the past which guided Boldt in its construction. The interior of the castle is, at present, disappointing, as it had been neglected for many decades and is unfurnished. However, it is in the process of restoration; progress is made each year, but it is an extremely expensive undertaking. The story of the Boldts is a romantic one. The castle was built by George C. Boldt, owner of the Waldorf-Astoria and Bellevue-Stratford Hotels. He purchased the island, had it reshaped as a heart, and began building a castle for his wife, Louise. When she died unexpectedly in 1904, all construction was halted and was never resumed. Boldt never returned to the island, though he had spent $2 million on the project. It is of the same architectural vintage as Biltmore House in Asheville, N.C., which may one day serve as a model for at least partial furnishing.

The Boldt Yacht House on Wellesley Island was completed in 1904, built to reflect the castle design with towers, spires, and gables; it cost over $50,000 and became the center of the yacht-oriented life that Boldt and his wealthy friends enjoyed. The Yacht House even has reception rooms with oak ceilings, moldings and wainscoting, as well as stone fireplaces. The Yacht House and Castle are now the property of the Thousand Islands Bridge Authority and are on the National Register of Historic Places. The Castle also has a playhouse, an Italian garden, a power house, and an underground passage.

Legend has it that Boldt was cruising on his yacht one day and his steward served him an excellent salad dressing. He decided to serve it at all his hotels, calling it Thousand Islands dressing in honor of the beautiful area where it was first prepared (the steward rose to fame as Oscar of the Waldorf).

The A. Graham Thomson Memorial Museum, James and Market Streets, features paintings, a skiff livery, a photographer's studio, and other depictions of Alexandria Bay history. The Thomson family has played a vital role in the history and development of the town; they owned Pine Tree Point as early as 1915. Captain C. S. Thomson and his son, A. Graham Thomson, founded the resort in 1954. Captain Thomson's Resort and Uncle Sam Boat Tours are now part of the conglomerate, which is still run as a family enterprise.

The Cornwall Brothers Store on the waterfront is a pictorial museum of the past, with photographic displays of the hotels, boats, and river life.

Casa Blanca, on Cherry Island, is a 26-room Victorian home built in 1892 by Louis Marx, a sugar and tobacco grower from Havana, Cuba. It is now owned by Edith and Albert J. Amsterdam, who generously open it each afternoon during the season to boat tours. The Amsterdams purchased the home in 1962, saving it from destruction (the prospective purchaser planned to build an A-frame modern house in its place). The house, with many turrets and verandas, has remarkable features: There is a butler's call box; pressed tin walls, eliminating the need for decorative plaster; a railroad desk from Clayton, reflecting the day when island owners traveled in private railroad cars to Clayton and then by steam yachts to their homes; and a gazebo with gargoyles and griffins guarding the house. There is a 4-slip boat house with dressing rooms, a laundry house with a 1915 working Maytag, and a tower room. If Boldt Castle represents thwarted dreams, Casa Blanca is reality; a trip here is a venture back into the nineteenth century, providing a rare look at how affluent families actually lived.

Wellesley Island has long been an important part of the Alexandria Bay area. In 1875, the Thousand Island Park Camp Meeting Association was founded at Fineview by the Rev. John Ferdinand Dayan, who dreamed of a Methodist summer community offering spiritual and physical renewal. The village had 600 cottages by 1894, as well as hotels; speakers such as Carrie Nation talked eloquently of reform. Fire took its toll, however, and by the 1950s only 350 cottages remained. The Thousand Island Park Historic District, with its gingerbread-trimmed cottages, is now recognized as a unique assemblage of late nineteenth- and early twentieth-century architecture; in 1983 it was placed on the National Register of Historic Places.

The Thousand Islands International Bridge has five island-hopping spans connecting the United States and Canadian mainlands. It was dedicated in 1938; at this time, William Lyon Mackenzie King, Canadian Prime Minister, interpreted the bridge as a "vast undertaking," and a bond of Canadian-American good will: "There is indeed no more striking symbol of unity and friendship than a bridge," he said. The bridge was built over the protests of many skeptics. Heated sand is used to remove ice and snow, and the bridge floor has not yet had to be resurfaced. The bridge is within a day's drive of over 100 million people and is now a vital link between the two countries. Its Skydeck Tower on Hill Island, Ontario, one of the area's dominant landmarks; looms 400 feet in the air and has a 25-mile view of the islands in good weather.

Jorstadt Castle, near Chippewa Bay, is a an island estate on 10 acres just 300 feet north of the St. Lawrence Seaway. It has 28 rooms and 5 stories, and is on the scale of some of the Newport, Rhode Island, mansions. It is owned by Dr. and Mrs. Harold Martin; he is the President of the Harold Martin Evangelistic Association. The castle is accessible by boat, but only on Sunday mornings, when the public may attend a non-denominational church service (picnics are permitted). People from both the United States and Canada come to the services from many miles away. The castle is also open to groups by special arrangement. A number of weddings and other events have been held here. Beautifully furnished with knights in armor, oriental rugs, carved furniture, and medieval-style light fixtures, the stone castle was built between 1897 and 1904 by Frederick C. Borne, of the Singer company, who hired Italian immigrant labor. There are secret passages and peepholes for the servants, enabling them to carry out their duties unobtrusively.

Cape Vincent: The Community House Historical Museum, Market St., has records and artifacts of historical interest.

The Cape Vincent Aquarium on Broadway St. features displays of live fish native to the area.

The Tibbets Point Lighthouse is 3 miles west of Cape Vincent; it stands at the outlet of Lake Ontario and at the head of the St. Lawrence River. It has been a beacon since 1827.

Clayton: The Thousand Islands Shipyard Museum, 750 Mary St., features displays of fine crafts, wooden boats, motors, and nautical history. Courses and workshops in folk arts and crafts are offered at the Thousand Islands Craft School here; the school also has a Textile Museum. In August, an antique boat show draws visitors to Clayton from all over the country.

Zavikon Islands (two islands), between the U.S. and Canada, have the shortest international footbridge in the world.

Among the other islands of interest, visible from the tour boats, are Casino, now part of Alexandria Bay Park; Devil's Oven, with 2 trees tilting; Comfort, with a house featuring a widow's walk; St. Elmo's, with a white anchor on the lawn, homage to the patron saint of sailors; and Tom Thumb, with 1 tree, said to be the smallest in the Thousand Islands. About 85 percent of the islands are privately owned; the remainder are public lands.

Canada:

Brockville: Approximately 35 miles east of Brockville is Upper Canada Village, a restoration of a Canadian village of 150 years ago. Brockville has a museum depicting the early history of the area.

Gananoque: The Gananoque Historic Museum is housed in the 1863 Victoria Hotel; it features a collection of military artifacts.

Half-Moon Bay: Here there is a large crescent-shaped inlet where church services are held on the water under open skies in July and August (Sunday afternoons). The worshippers are seated in boats of every sort, from skiffs and rowboats to luxury cruisers. They face the natural stone pulpit, and prayer books and hymnals are passed to the floating congregation by "ushers" paddling about in canoes.

Kingston: The Agnes Etherington Art Centre, Queen's University at University Ave. and Queen's Crescent, has an important collection spanning 6 centuries, emphasizing Canadian art but containing West African and European works as well.

Fort Frederick and the Royal Military College Museum in Kingston have period furniture, historic weapons, and exhibits on the history of Kingston.

Old Fort Henry (exit 623 off Hwy. 401) is well worth seeing; it was built during the War of 1812 and rebuilt between 1832 and 1836. It is a museum of British and Canadian military history.

The Marine Museum of the Great Lakes, 55 Ontario St., is in the historic waterfront district, with interesting changing exhibits and displays on famous shipwrecks and shipbuilding along with the *Alexander Henry,* an icebreaker.

SIGHTSEEING TOURS   The Thousand Islands region abounds in excellent boat tours; there are also tours of other kinds.
United States: Alexandria Bay: Uncle Sam Boat Tours offers tours on several well-maintained vessels, including

Mississippi-style paddlewheelers and original wooden tour boats dating back to the early 1900s. The tour company also provides 5-minute ferry rides to Boldt Castle throughout the day and luncheon and dinner cruises. (Alexandria Bay, NY 13607; 482-2611; NY only 800/253-9229).

Empire Boat Tours, 4 Church St., Alexandria Bay, NY 13607 (800/542-2628) has triple-deck excursion boats offering cruises of various lengths.

There is a helicopter tour leaving from Rt. 12, just off I-81 between the Thousand Islands Bridge and Alexandria Bay (782-6642).

Clayton: The Thousand Islands Seaway Cruises, 604 Riverside Dr., Clayton, NY 13624 (686-3511) has single and double-deck tour vessels and offers dinner cruises.

Canada:

Brockville: There are cruises aboard the *M.V. Brockville II,* a replica of a St. Lawrence River steamboat (Upper Canada Steamboats, Box 692, Brockville, ON, Canada K6V 5V8; 345-6454).

Gananoque: Gananoque Boat Lines offers trips aboard a 3-decker (Water St., Gananoque; 382-2146). There are also horse-drawn trolley tours in season (Thousand Islands Carriage Co., 780 King St. West, Gananoque, ON, Canada K7G 2H5; 800/297-9497 or 382-3226).

Ivy Lea: A few miles east of Gananoque, in Ivy Village, 1 mile from the Thousand Islands Bridge, the Mount Airy Resort offers cruises on small vessels which navigate slender channels (RR1, Lansdowne, ON, Canada KOE 1L0; 659-2293).

Kingston: The *Island Queen,* a showboat paddlewheeler, and the *Island Princess,* a sidewheeler, offer 3-hour island cruises (The Islands Boat Lines, 6A Princess St., Kingston, ON, Canada K7L 1A2; 549-5544).

The *Canadian Empress,* 253 Ontario St., Kingston K7L 2Z4 (549-8091), is an imposing well-appointed ship which stops at Boldt Castle.

Also there are tours on a catamaran, the *Sea Fox II* (Sea Fox Thousand Island Tours Inc., Box 368, Station A, Kingston, ON, Canada K7M 6R3; 384-7899).

Tours leave from *Pecks Marina,* just west of the Thousand Islands International Bridge, aboard the *Wentworth Lady,* one of the original 1950s-vintage Thousand Islands tour boats, go into small coves and narrow channels (Thousand Islands Tours & Travel, Inc.; Wentworth Lady Thousand Islands Cruise, 780 King St. West, Gananoque, ON, Canada K7G 2H5; 800/267-9497).

Rockport: There is a double-decker cruise from here (Rockport Boat Lines, Thousand Islands Parkway, Rockport, ON, Canada KOE 1VO; 659-3402, summer, and 382-4129, winter).

PARKS, BEACHES AND CAMPING

Parks: United States: There are 24 state parks in the region. Grindstone, Mary, and Cedar islands have parks which are accessible by boat only. Wellesley Island has a large state park containing the Minna Anthony Common Nature Center, which has a museum with live collections as well as mounted exhibits. In addition, the Center has 600 acres of varied wildlife habitats. *Canada:* The St. Lawrence Islands National Park has 21 units of the Thousand Islands; the entrance is at Mallorytown Landing on the mainland. *Beaches:* There are few sandy beaches, but many rocky ledges. Grindstone has two natural sandy beaches, and there is a third at Chippewa Bay. Boating is more popular than swimming. On the Canadian side, Mallorytown Landing, headquarters of the St. Lawrence Islands National Park, has a beach with lifeguards; after July 1, the weather is more likely to be warm enough for swimming. *Camping: United States:* There are too many campgrounds to present a complete list, but camping is available at most of the 24 state parks in the region, including

Wellesley Island, Cedar Point, Keewaydin, and DeWolf Point. There are numerous private campgrounds and RV parks also. Booklets listing public and private sites are available from the Thousand Islands State Park Commission (see Contact). The region has over 17,000 acres of park land and caters to campers from all over the world.

Canada: The St. Lawrence Islands National Park has sites on many islands, including Cedar, Aubrey, Georgina, and Gordon islands. For information, contact Supervisor of Parks Operations, Box 470, Morrisburg, ON KOC 1XO (543-2911). There are also numerous private campgrounds; see Contact for Ontario information.

MARINAS There are far too many marinas to offer a comprehensive list; write localities listed in Contact section for detailed information.

United States: The very helpful *Small Boat Guide,* with maps of approaches and navigation notes about the region is available from the Thousand Islands International Council (see Contact).

Alexandria Bay: The Bonnie Castle Yacht Basin Marina (482-2526; see Lodging) is one of the largest in the islands region, with a marine store, docking, lift, covered slips, and other facilities.

Hutchinson's Boat Works (482-9931) is a long-established firm offering custom restorations, mail service, paved parking, dock attendants, covered slips, and transient dockage.

The Riveredge Resort (482-9917; see Lodging) has complete transient dockage facilities, modern hotel rooms, and a central location for exploring Alexandria Bay.

The Thousand Islands Club on Wellesley Island (482-2551; see Lodging) is a noted boating center, and has space for transients as well as a restaurant.

Cape Vincent: Merlins Marina (654-2174) has dockage, haul-out, a marine store, and boat rentals.

Clayton: Clayton Marina (686-3741) has complete marine facilities and a ship's store.

French Creek Marina (686-3621) has transient slips and a restaurant, as well as boat rentals.

Houseboat rentals are available at the Shipyard, 510 Theresa St., Clayton (686-3597).

Canada:

Brockville: Gilbert Marine, Ltd. (342-3462) has boat rentals and other facilities.

Gananoque: Gordon Marine, Ltd. (382-4315) has overnight dockage, but no restaurant.

Ivy Lea: Holidays Afloat Marina (659-3207) also has transient space.

Kingston: Collins Bay Marina (389-4455) has dockage, winter storage, and many other facilities.

Houseboat Holidays, Ltd., RR 3, Gananoque, ON K7G 2V5 (382-2842) has houseboats sleeping 6.

RESTAURANTS *United States:*

Alexandria Bay: Cap's Landing at Capt. Thomson's Resort (see Lodging) is a floating barge with a state-of-the-art kitchen below.$$

The Captain's Cabin, on Old Bridge Rd., Wellesley Island (482-2756) has a nautical atmosphere; reservations are advised.$$

The Crystal Room at Bonnie Castle Manor (see Lodging) has a has a very pleasant atmosphere; there are mirrors and subdued reflected lighting give prominence to the river setting.**$$$**

Oscar's Harborside at the Edgewood (see Lodging) overlooks the river and specializes in fresh seafood and steaks.**$$**

St. James Station, 15 James St. (482-3309) serves lunch and dinner year round and is a local favorite. Specialties are American dishes.**$**

The Voyageur Room, Pine Tree Point Resort (see Lodging) has a very pleasant situation overlooking the St. Lawrence, a rustic atmosphere, attentive service, and good food.**$$**

Cape Vincent: The Sunnybank Restaurant, Rt. 12E (654-2124) has soups, salads, and open steak sandwiches.**$**

Clayton: The Koffee Cove Restaurant, James St. (686-2472) has homemade bread and pies.**$**

The Thousand Islands Inn, 335 Riverside Dr. (686-3030), specializes in seafood, steaks, veal, and quail.**$$-$$$**

Canada:

Brockville: The Alternative Dining Lounge, 26-28 Water St. E. (345-3975) has an informal atmosphere and overlooks the St. Lawrence River.**$$**

Gananoque: The Athlone Victorian Dining Room, in the Athlone Inn (see Lodging) has continental cuisine in a congenial atmosphere.**$$**

The Golden Apple Restaurant, 45 King St. W. (382-3300) is in a stone house circa 1830, with several small and pleasant dining rooms; home baking and good soups and desserts.**$$**

Ivy Lea: The Hideaway Dining Room at the Mount Airy Resort (see Lodging) is popular with boaters and local people also.**$$**

Kingston: Chez Piggy, 68 R. Princess St. (549-7673) is in a renovated livery stable reached via a tunnel and an old stable yard; it has international cuisine and is a local favorite.**$$**

Truffles Dining Room at the Kingston Motel (see Lodging) has continental cuisine and is a popular restaurant; reserve ahead.**$$**

Wolfe Island: The General Wolfe Hotel (see Lodging) received the "Merit Award" in Canada's Year of Tourism. It is not far from the Kingston ferry landing. Patrons arriving by boat have free docking at the General Wolfe Marina.**$$**

LODGING   *United States: Alexandria Bay:* The Bonnie Castle Resort, Holland St., Alexandria Bay 13607 (800/521-5514), owned by Don Cole, has a manor house which was once a seminary for the White Fathers of Africa. There is a 700-seat nightclub where many stars perform, and a 100-room hotel, marina, private airstrip, stables, golf course, and a paddlewheel cruise boat, the *Bonnie Bell.***$$-$$$**.

Capt. Thomson's Resort, James St., Alexandria Bay 13067 (482-9961) has an excellent view of Boldt Castle and is adjacent to Uncle Sam Boat Tours, which is owned by the same concern (as is Pine Tree Point; see below). Many rooms give the feeling of almost being out in the St. Lawrence Seaway, with boats flying past. It is centrally located for wandering along the main streets of the town.**$$**

Edgewood Resort, Edgewood Road, Alexandria Bay 13067 (482-9922) has 160 rooms on 75 acres of secluded St. Lawrence River shoreline. Founded in

1886, it has now been operated for nearly 40 years by the Hebert family. "Bud" Hebert is president of the local Historical Society and an authority on the legends and folklore of the area. The resort has boat tours and jet ski rentals; rooms overlook the water.**$$**

Pine Tree Point Resort, Pine Tree Point, Alexandria Bay 13607 (482-9911) is in a rustic setting, on a wooded peninsula; there are 83 rooms, most of which have water views. There is a heated swimming pool and private docking for boats.**$$**

Riveredge, 17 Holland St., Alexandria Bay 13607 (482-9917) is on the waterfront, centrally located; the newest of the resorts, it was destroyed by fire and rebuilt within the last few years.**$$-$$$**

Thousand Islands Club and Conference Center, Wellesley Island, Alexandria Bay 13607 (482-2551; NY 800/338-0331) is across the river from Alexandria Bay. It has 105 rooms and efficiency villas, as well as deep water dockage, a famous golf course, tennis courts, heated swimming pool, and good water views.**$$-$$$**

Cape Vincent: The Buccaneer Motel, Point St., Cape Vincent 13618 (654-2975) has 10 units.**$**

Clayton: Bertrand's Motel and Hotel, Inc., 229 James St., Box 129, Clayton 13624 (686-3641) has 28 rooms.**$**

The Quarterdeck Motel, 100 State St., Clayton 13624 (686-5588) is open all year and has 12 rooms.**$**

Canada: There are many accommodations, only a selection of which can be listed; to obtain accommodations book, see Contact.

Brockville: The Royal Brock Hotel, 100 Stewart Blvd., Brockville K6V 4W3 (345-1400) is a deluxe hotel, but does not overlook the river.**$$-$$$**

The Seaway Motel, RR1, Brockville K6V 5T1 (342-1357) has a quiet scenic location on the river.**$**

Gananoque: The Athlone Inn, 250 King St. W, Gananoque K7G 2G6 (382-2440) is in a gracious older building, set back from the street.**$$**

The Glen House Resort and Motel, Thousand Islands Parkway, Box 10, Gananoque K7G 2T6 (659-2204) has been a deluxe resort since 1896; it overlooks the St. Lawrence. It has a whirlpool, sauna, and 200 acres of cross-country skiing; it also provides boat and motor rentals.**$$$**

Ivy Lea: The Mount Airy Resort, (RR1, Lansdowne, ON, Canada; KOE 1LO (659-2295) is on the St. Lawrence River and has boat tours, a gift shop, and many other amenities; it has 34 rooms and 5 cottages.**$$**

Kingston: Ambassador Motor Hotel, 1550 Princess St., Kingston K7L 4X6 (548-3605), has indoor water slides and 200 rooms.**$$-$$$**

Seven Oakes Motor Inn, 2331 Princess St., Kingston K7M 3G1 (546-3655) has tennis courts, a sauna, a whirlpool, and other amenities; there are 40 rooms.**$$**

Kingston Motel, 2467 Princess St., Kingston K7M 3G1 (542-4961) is a small motel with a very good dining room, Truffles (see Restaurants).**$**

Wolfe Island: General Wolfe Hotel, Hwy. 96, Box 100, Wolfe Island KOH 2YO (385-2611) has 6 rooms.**$$**

Wolfe Island Inn, Box 99, Wolfe Island KOH 2YO (385-2533) is a pleasant small inn with 6 rooms and 2 cottages.**$$-$$$**

RENTALS

United States: Space prohibits a comprehensive list of housekeeping cottages, but a selection follows; for listing, write the chambers of commerce listed under Contact.

Alexandria Bay: Hi-Da-Way Summer Homes, Dingman Pt. Rd., Box 96, Alexandria Bay 13607 (482-4492) has 7 cottages on the St. Lawrence River.

Griffins Guarding Casa Blanca,
The Thousand Islands

Pinehurst on the St. Lawrence, RR 1, Box 57, Alexandria Bay 13607 (482-9452) has 21 cottages with a pool on Swan Bay (St. Lawrence River).

There are cabins in many of the New York State Parks, including Kring Point State Park, DeWolf Point State Park and Wellesley Island State Park; for information, contact Robert Moses, Thousand Islands State Park Commission (see Contact).

Cape Vincent: Angel Rock, RD 1, Box 46A (654-2495) has cottages on the St. Lawrence.

Clayton: Fair Wind Lodge, Rt. 12E, Box 276, Clayton 13624 (686-5251).

Mil's Motel & Cottages, RD 1, Box 74, Clayton 13624 (686-3891) has 14 cottages with boat rentals.

Canada: There are many housekeeping cabins available; for full list, contact Eastern Ontario Travel Association (see Contact).

Brockville: Chalet Cabins, RR1, Brockville KGV 5T1 (342-6010) are on the St. Lawrence River.

Gananoque: Harmer's Cottages, RR 2, Gananoque K7G 2V4 (382-3675) are on the St. Lawrence River.

Kingston (Wolfe Island): McCready's Cottages, RR2, Wolfe Island KOH 2YO (385-2527) are on the south side of Wolfe Island, facing Cape Vincent, overlooking the St. Lawrence River; there are 5 cottages.

CONTACT   *United States:* Alexandria Bay Chamber of Commerce, Box 365, Alexandria Bay, NY 13607 (315/482-9531); Clayton Chamber of Commerce, 403 Riverside Dr., Clayton 13624 (686-3771); Thousand Islands International Council, Box 400, Collins Landing, Alexandria Bay, NY 13607 (NY 800/5ISLAND; Eastern US 800/8ISLAND; or collect 315/482-2520); also the Thousand Islands State Park Commission, Keewaydin State Park, Alexandria Bay 13607 (482-2593).

Canada: Eastern Ontario Travel Association, 209 Ontario St., Kingston, ON Canada K7L 2Z1 (549-3682).

RHODE ISLAND

Rhode Island sometimes seems like an island itself, so pervasive is the nautical flavor, which has persisted ever since Giovanni da Verrazano, a Florentine navigator, sailed into Narragansett Bay in 1524. The Bay cuts into the state 28 miles from sea, its coves and harbors offering a blue maritime backdrop to the towns and villages on either side. Pleasure boaters flock not only to Newport, but to Bristol Harbor, East Greenwich, Wickford, Jamestown, Barrington, Warren, and many other seaside towns, adding an air of affluence and confirming the love of the sea which has marked the state from its beginning.

To some extent Rhode Island has always been in opposition to established authority; the religious nonconformists William Blackstone, Roger Williams, and Anne Hutchinson left Massachusetts to seek freedom of conscience in Rhode Island in the 1630s. The state was the first to proclaim independence from England (May 4, 1776) and did not attend the 1787 Constitutional Convention, holding on to its colonial charter until 1842. It has been said that the state has four principal assets: the Bay, Brown University, the handsome State House (built by Stanford White), and the Providence *Journal-Bulletin*. (In an intensely Democratic state, the paper is conservative). It also has world-renowned events, such as the America's Cup races.

The entire state is only 48 miles long by 37 miles wide, but for many years it was the most densely populated (a status now surpassed by New Jersey). Surprisingly, however, it seems quite rural as one drives through it, and residents insist it has the flavor of a small town, with people knowing each other.

Newport is the crown jewel of Aquidneck Island, with its palatial estates. The millionaires were latecomers, however, for the state had a seagoing history well established by the mid-eighteenth century, when shipping and commerce had made it one of the three largest Atlantic cities. One corner of the infamous triangular trade route was in Newport, where rum was distilled (the others were Africa, exporting slaves, and the Caribbean, exporting sugar). There were specialty shops, theaters, and a literary society thriving in Newport long before it became a wealthy summer colony. Both Middletown and Portsmouth are also of great historic interest with modern attractions.

Block Island is a Rhode Island outpost which could very well belong to the Hebrides except for its white sandy beaches. With its rolling moors and stone fences, old Victorian hotels, and rocky cliffs, it is an appealing destination for visitors, especially early and late in the season (those planning to take a car must reserve ferry space far ahead). John Greenleaf Whittier's poem "The Palatine Light" commemorates the Palatine Graves area where a Dutch ship was wrecked in 1738 and the crew lie buried.

Prudence Island is far less developed than Aquidneck or Block, but has a special primitive beauty along with a winery offering tours. It does not have lodging and is best for day trips or for longer stays (there is rental property).

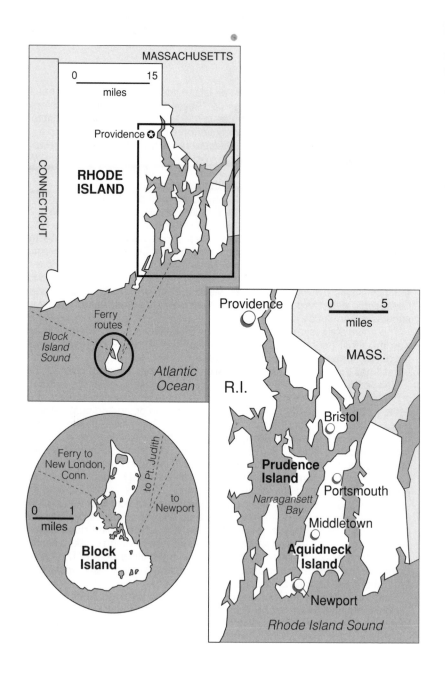

RHODE ISLAND

AQUIDNECK ISLAND
(includes Newport, Middletown, and other towns)

Area Code 401
LOCATION   In Narragansett Bay, SW of Fall River, MA and SE of Providence, RI.

SIZE   Approximately 5 miles by 20 miles.

ACCESS   *Car:* Toll bridge from Jamestown; bridge from Bristol and Tiverton. *Air:* There is commercial service to T. F. Green Airport, Warwick, and a limousine shuttle to Newport. Sakonnet Air Charter provides service to Newport State Airport, Middletown (847-6948). *Private boat.*

HISTORY AND   Aquidneck Island has several towns, including
DESCRIPTION   Newport, at the southern end, Middletown, adjacent to Newport, and Portsmouth at the northern end. The island was originally settled by religious nonconformists. In 1638, Anne Hutchinson, ousted from Massachusetts, founded Portsmouth with her husband and a small group led by William Coddington and John Clarke; in 1639, Coddington moved to the southern end of the island and established Newport. The town prospered with shipbuilding and trade in rum, molasses, and slaves. It was also a haven for refugees from religious persecution, including Baptists, Seventh-Day Adventists, and Jews; the Touro Synagogue is the oldest in the country.

Until 1900, Newport was, with Providence, the joint capital of Rhode Island and it has, since the nineteenth century, been a fashionable resort as well as a prosperous and elegant port. "All that has been said of Newport you may safely set down as an understatement," wrote the turn-of-the-century American critic James Huneker. This is still true of the town today, whether you prefer eighteenth-century colonial simplicity, nineteenth-century Baroque opulence, or contemporary hewn timber/ship's chandlery/yachting ambiance. The "Gilded Age" when the opulent "cottages" were built (1880s, 1890s, and 1900s) is vividly alive today, and a number of the mansions, built by the Vanderbilts and other families, are open to the public. The Cliff Walk affords a good view of some of them. There often seems to be a dichotomy in Newport; the elite and wealthy inhabitants of the mansions are still very much there (the men escape to the yellow frame building, the Reading Room, across Bellevue Ave. from the library, to avoid what has been called their wives' "social wars.") At the same time, the new waterfront area swarms with yuppies in topsiders, who divide their time between touring the mansions, trekking along Cliff Walk, and browsing in the boutiques. There is both a private elegance in the lifestyles of the wealthy inhabitants and a concurrent influx of tourists with an insatiable appetite for a nautical ambiance and for the Gilded Age. "The Great Gatsby" was filmed at Rosecliff. Many visitors are just as eager to see the eighteenth-century homes which are open. The vigilant Preservation Society of Newport has restored a number of these, such as the Hunter House, which has fine Rhode Island furniture.

The Gilded Age was not only one of extravagant spectacle and splendor (one hostess even invited 100 dogs to a dinner party, all chauffeured, naturally), but it also attracted many *literati,* among them Henry James, Julia Ward Howe, Thornton Wilder, and Bret Harte. James deplored the excesses, but referred to Newport in *Daisy Miller* as an "American watering place."

Public admission to the houses began at the end of World War II, when Mrs. George Henry Warren launched an effort to save Hunter House, an eighteenth-century mansion. The Countess Szechenyi offered to open her home for fund raising; her home happened to be the Breakers. The public came in droves, and it became obvious that charging admission would be a way to offset the maintenance of the large houses. Today 7 are open to the public, and 3 others are operated independently. They bring millions of dollars to Newport.

Tournament tennis began at the Newport Casino over a century ago, and today the Casino houses the International Tennis Hall of Fame. Its 13 carefully tended grass courts are the only ones in the country open to the public. The Hall of Fame is host each summer to two international tournaments. The Casino buildings and grounds have been carefully restored, with latticed porches and beautiful landscaping.

Newport is a sophisticated yachting center, and is said to vie with Fort Lauderdale for the title Yachting Capital of the World. Vessels of every size, type, and origin assemble in the harbor during the season, and it is the terminus for the Newport-to-Bermuda race in even years; it has also been the site of the America's Cup trials and races. Today the waterfront has been revitalized and has an international flair, with fashionable boutiques and restaurants ranged along several wharves, among them Bowen's, Bannister's, and Commercial. The complex is frankly for tourists more than for boating people, but the wharves are a lively transformation of the waterfront.

Middletown is the second oldest community in Newport County, with many old residences and farmhouses. St. George's School is here, noted for its English Gothic chapel, along with the Norman Bird Sanctuary and Museum, which has seven miles of walking trails.

POINTS OF INTEREST   **Newport:** The Newport Mansions, seven of which may be seen on a single ticket, are the main attraction here. They are the Breakers, built for Cornelius Vanderbilt (1895); Chateau-sur-Mer, built for William S. Wetmore (1852); Marble House, built for William K. Vanderbilt (1892); the Elms, built for Edward J. Berwind (1901); Hunter House, built by Jonathan Nichols (1748); Kingscote, built for George Noble Jones (1839); and Rosecliff, built for Mrs. Hermann Oelrichs in 1902. (The same ticket covers admission to the Green Animals Topiary Gardens in Portsmouth.) There are other houses open as well,

Newport and Harbor

including the Astors' Beechwood, with historical interpretations by actors, and Hammersmith Farm (1887), summer White House of the Kennedys and former home of the Auchincloss family, where Jacqueline Kennedy made her debut. (The bedrooms all have chaises for naps, so as not to disturb the bed coverings.)

Touro Synagogue, Touro St., is a National Historic Site (1763).

The Newport Historical Society Museum, 82 Touro St., with colonial art and changing exhibits, is well worth visiting.

The International Tennis Hall of Fame and Tennis Museum, Newport Casino, 194 Bellevue Ave., is a special attraction.

The Redwood Library and Athenaeum (1747) is said to be the oldest library building in the country in continuous use.

The Friends Meeting House, Marlborough and Farewell Sts., is one of the oldest meeting houses in the country.

The Naval War College Museum, Coasters Harbor Island (enter Gate 1 of the Naval Education and Training Center), is open to the public.

The Newport Art Museum and Art Association, 76 Bellevue Ave., has changing exhibits in an 1862 building.

Middletown: Prescott Farm and Windmill House, 2009 W. Main Rd., Rt. 114, Middletown (847-6230) consists of an operating windmill, built about 1812, a country store, and British General Prescott's Guard House.

St. George's School Chapel, in the English Gothic style, is of interest.

The Whitehall Museum, Berkeley Ave. (846-3790), built by Bishop George Berkeley and maintained by the Colonial Dames in Rhode Island, is open to the public.

Purgatory Chasm is a scenic overlook on Purgatory Rd. Here a narrow cleft in the rock ledges has been formed by the waves.

Portsmouth: The Green Animals Topiary Gardens, ³/₄ mi. off Rt. 114 on Cory's Lane, is one of the leading attractions here. The gardens contain 80 sculptured trees and shrubs shaped in animal forms (giraffe, elephant, lion, etc.). Thomas E. Brayton, Treasurer of the Union Cotton Manufacturing Co. in Fall River, Mass., had long been fascinated with the topiary gardens created by ancient pharoahs and European kings. Topiary had reached the zenith of its popularity during the seventeenth century in Europe, and Brayton sought to emulate the form on his estate on the shore of Narragansett Bay. He and his Portuguese gardener, Joseph Carreiro, developed this rare garden, and the estate was preserved by his daughter, Alice Brayton. The New York Botanical Garden offered to transport the entire garden to the Bronx, but Miss Brayton refused, saying, "I couldn't bear the idea of seeing my giraffe leaving through the front gate." At her death (1972), the Preservation Society of Newport County took over the estate. There is also a small children's Victorian Toy Museum on the grounds. The Green Animals may be seen separately or on a combined ticket with several of the Newport mansions.

The Friends Meeting House, Middle Rd. and Hedley St., was in use by 1700.

The Portsmouth Historical Society, corner E. Main Rd. and Union St. (683-3858), has a collection of early household and farm artifacts.

Portsmouth Abbey, Cory's Lane, is a Benedictine Monastery and Preparatory School (683-2000); the contemporary church, designed by Pietro Belluschi, has a noted wire sculpture by Richard Lippold. Call in advance.

SIGHTSEEING TOURS   Viking Tours of Newport, 184 Thames St. (847-6921) offers both bus tours and boat trips aboard the *Viking Queen.*

United Tours, 1 America's Cup Ave. (849-8005) offers trolley tours along Ocean Drive (you can stop at attractions and reboard) as well as rail tours to Middletown and Portsmouth aboard the Old Colony and Newport Railway. The firm also has harbor tours aboard the *Amazing Grace,* sailing from Oldport Marine, Sayer's Wharf (849-2111).

If you are not visiting Newport by boat, a harbor tour is excellent for viewing the variety of craft in Narragansett Bay as well as the other islands.

Auto tape tours are available at the Paper Lion, Long Wharf Mall (472-5133).

PARKS, BEACHES   *Parks:* Fort Adams State Park, Ocean Drive, New-
AND CAMPING   port; good water views; ferries go from here to Block Island. Brenton Point State Park, Ocean Drive, Newport also has good sea views. *Beaches:* Aquidneck has many beaches. Easton Beach, Newport, is popular. Sachuset Beach, Middletown, has sand dunes and is guarded. Sandy Point Beach, Portsmouth, also has life-guards. *Camping:* Melville Ponds Campground, 181 Bradford Ave., Portsmouth (849-8212); Middletown Campground, Second Beach, Middletown (846-6273); Meadowlark Recreational Vehicle Park, 132 Prospect Ave., Middletown (846-9455); Paradise Mobile Home Park, 459 Aquidneck Ave., Middletown (847-1500); Sunset Cabins, 1172 West Main Rd., Portsmouth (682-1874).

MARINAS   *Newport* Goat Island Marina, Inc., Goat Island, Newport, RI 02840 (849-5655), 4 transient slips; maximum length 140 ft.; approach depth 16 ft.; dockside depth 18 ft.; electric power — yes; restaurant within walking distance — yes.

Long Wharf Mooring Marina, 142 Long Wharf, Newport, RI 02840 (849-2210), 40 transient slips; maximum length 65 ft.; approach depth 14 ft.; dockside depth

The Chinese Teahouse, Marble House, Newport

30 ft.; electric power — yes; restaurant within walking distance — yes.

Treadway Inn & Marina, 49 America's Cup Ave., Newport, RI 02840 (847-9000), 60 transient slips; maximum length 100 ft.; approach depth 15 ft.; dockside depth 15 ft.; electric power — yes; restaurant within walking distance — yes.

Newport Yachting Center, America's Cup Ave., Box 549, Newport, RI 02840 (847-9047), 75 transient slips; maximum length 150 ft.; approach depth 15 ft.; dockside depth 15 ft.; electric power — yes; restaurant within walking distance — yes.

Ida Lewis Yacht Club, Wellington Ave., Newport, RI 02840 (846-1969), 3 transient slips; maximum length 50 ft.; approach depth 10 ft.; dockside depth 5 ft.; electric power — yes; restaurant within walking distance — no. (The well-known club is named for the daughter of a lighthouse keeper; at his death, she assumed her father's duties and saved many sailors shipwrecked off Castle Hill).

Bannister's Wharf, West Pelham St., Newport, RI 02840 (846-4500), 30 transient slips; maximum length 200 ft.; approach depth 15 ft.; dockside depth 15 ft.; electric power — yes; restaurant within walking distance — yes.

Portsmouth: Pirate Cove Yacht Sales and Marina, 109 Point Rd., Portsmouth, RI 02871 (683-3030), 20 transient slips; maximum length 85 ft.; approach depth 10 ft.; dockside depth 20 ft.; electric power — yes; restaurant within walking distance — no.

East Passage Yachting Center, One Lagoon Rd., Portsmouth, RI 02871 (683-4000), 50 transient slips; maximum length 100 ft.; approach depth 15 ft.; dockside depth 15 ft.; electric power — yes; restaurant within walking distance — yes.

For a full list of marinas in the area, write the City of Newport Harbormaster, Harbor Center, Ann St. Pier, Newport, RI 02840 (847-4370).

RESTAURANTS   **Newport:** The Ark, 348 Thames St. (849-3808) has traditional British and American entrees.**$$**

The Black Pearl on Bannister's Wharf (846-5264) is popular because of its dockside atmosphere and French cuisine.**$$$**

The Clarke Cooke House, Bannister's Wharf (849-2900), specializes in seafood and has water views.**$$$**

Frick's, 673 Thames St. (846-5830) has imaginative meals with an Austrian flair. Reservations are a must. No liquor is served here; only wine.**$$$**

The Inn at Castle Hill (see Lodging) has excellent food and a beautiful view of Narragansett Bay.**$$$**

La Petite Auberge, 19 Charles St. (849-6669) is an intimate country French restaurant; the cuisine and the atmosphere are authentic.**$$$**

Le Bistro, Bowen's Wharf (449-7778) has French specialties and an informal, noisy atmosphere.**$$$**

The Pier, West Howard St. (847-3645) has casual waterfront dining rooms overlooking piers.**$$$**

The White Horse Tavern, Marlborough St. and Farewell St. (849-3600) is a colonial tavern, originally constructed before 1673, with a very pleasant atmosphere. It is reputed to be the oldest operating tavern in the United States.**$$$**

Middletown: The South Sea Restaurant, 268 W. Main Rd. (849-2112).**$**

The Ocean View Restaurant, 28 Aquidneck Ave. (847-9406).**$**

Portsmouth: The Sea Fare Inn, 3352 E. Main Rd. (RI 138; 401/683-0577), is housed in an 1887 historic building with ornate mirrors and chandeliers; it specializes in seafood.**$$$**

LODGING   **Newport:** The Hotel Viking, 1 Bellevue Ave. 02840 (847-3300) is a long-established hotel. The original portion of the building is on the National Historic Register.**$$$**

The Inn at Castle Hill, Ocean Dr. 02840 (849-3800), high above the Bay, was the former summer home of geologist Alexander Agassiz. Thornton Wilder stayed here and wrote of a turret room in *Theophilus North* "from that magical room I could see at night the beacons of six light houses and hear the booming and chiming of as many sea buoys."**$$$**

The Sheraton Islander Inn, Goat Island 02840 (849-2600); this inn, on a small island in the harbor, has a glorious view of the yachts and ongoing marine activity, but book well ahead.**$$$**

The Treadway Newport Resort and Marina, 49 America's Cup Ave. 02840 (847-9000), at the edge of the restored waterfront, is a good choice if the harbor holds any attraction for you (reserve well ahead). From here you have a good view of the continual activity of yachts, tenders, and other traffic. Parking near the harbor is a formidable problem during the summer, and only guests may use the inn parking lot. From here you can wander among the boutiques and restaurants on Bowen's Wharf and Bannister's Wharf, take harbor tours, and do other sightseeing.**$$$**

Middletown: Easton's Inn and Greenhouse Restaurant, 30 Wave Ave., Middletown, RI 02840 (846-0911) is on the beach a mile from the center of Newport.**$$-$$$**

Portsmouth: Ramada Inn, 144 Anthony Rd., Portsmouth, RI 02871 (683-3600).**$$$**

RENTALS   **Newport:** Capital Realty, 30 Bellevue Ave., Newport, RI 02840 (849-4220); Avenue Associates,

Southeast Light, Block Island

208 Bellevue Ave., Newport, RI 02840 (849-8806); Carey, Richmond & Viking, 49 Bellevue Ave., Newport, RI 02840 (849-7000).
   Middletown: Island Homes, Ltd., 539 E. Main Rd., Middletown, RI 02840 (846-8466); Nunes Realty, 575 E. Main Rd., Middletown, RI 02840 (847-4800).
   Portsmouth: Portsmouth Real Estate, 2631 E. Main Rd., Portsmouth, RI 02840 (683-1500).
   Further listings are available from the Chamber of Commerce (see Contact).

CONTACT   Newport County Chamber of Commerce, Ten America's Cup Ave., Newport, RI 02840 (847-1600).

BLOCK ISLAND

Area Code 401
LOCATION   In Block Island Sound, 12 miles from the Rhode Island coast.

SIZE   3 miles by 7 miles.

ACCESS   *Ferry:* From New London, CT (summer) and Galilee, near Point Judith, RI (all year); advance reservations for cars mandatory in summer (Interstate Navigation Co., Galilee State Pier, Point Judith, Rhode Island, 02882; 789-3502). Also from Montauk, Long Island, NY (summer, passengers only); Captain Paul G. Forsberg, Box 730, Montauk, L.I., NY (516/668-5709) and Captain Howard Carroll, Box 461, Montauk, NY 11954 (516/668-2214). Also from Providence and Newport (summer, passengers only); Nelseco Navigation Co., Box 482, New London, CT 06320 (203/442-7891). *Air:* Commuter service from several New England locations is provided by Action Airlines (800/243-8623) and New England Airlines (800/243-2460). *Private boat.*

HISTORY AND DESCRIPTION   "Encapsulated on a stage in the middle of the ocean is this beautiful little island," says Joseph Connolly, who has resided on the island for a number of years and is a columnist for the *Block Island Times.* The island has about 740 registered voters and, at least off-season, is the sort of place where one can put a classified ad in the *Times:* "Lost or strayed: 4 bottles white wine on 5 p.m. boat" and confidently expect full restoration. Residents relish the island's tranquillity but often, in summer, feel its resources are strained by the thousands of visitors who flock over by ferry and plane (some people, in fact, fly over for the day with a picnic hamper, taxiing down to one of its noted beaches). The summer population is about 7,000. The terrain is consistently appealing, with narrow grass-bordered roads winding between stone fences (there are over 300 miles of stone walls on the island). On a misty day, it looks like a compressed segment of Ireland, with gray and green vying with each other in intensity. Almost every hill is crowned by a shingled home (each with an emergency fire number prominently posted in red numbers). In 1876, William P. Sheffield, a descendant of the first settlers and author of an island history, described the topography as resembling "the sea running high before a northeast gale." Everywhere one has the sense of the sea just at hand, swept by winds which have kept the bayberry bushes low. The island was gradually denuded of trees; the lumber was used for homes, barns, and shipbuilding. It is a major flyway, and ornithologists often visit to watch the spring and fall bird migrations. Originally there was no natural harbor; The construction of Old Harbor on the east side of the island was completed in 1878, and Great Pond Harbor (New Harbor) was finished in 1900. The Point Judith, New London, Providence and Newport ferries dock at Old Harbor, which is the home of the fishing fleet and of hotels, boutiques, and restaurants. New Harbor provides protected anchorages and moorings for private boats. During summer weekends there are as many as 1,200–1,500 boats anchored in New Harbor.

Block Island was once inhabited by the Manissean Indians, a branch of the famous and powerful Narragansetts. They settled the island early, calling it "Manisses" (Island of the Little God), but the name did not endure. Nor did "Claudia," which the Italian explorer Giovanni da Verrazzano called the island, after the mother of Francis I of France, who had commissioned his voyage. Ultimately, it was named for the Dutch fur trader and navigator Adriaen Block, who landed on the island in 1614. On his chart, he marked "Adriaen's Eylant." It was not until 1661 that 16 white families, under the leadership of John Alcock, a physician and one of Harvard's first graduates, came ashore with their livestock and settled at Cow Cove. These first settlers bought Block Island for £ 400, more than it was actually worth, taking to the island a vision of religious freedom and democracy which was revolutionary (they believed a voter did not have to own property). Beginning in 1672, their philosophy was put into action at town meetings. The settlers fished and farmed, depleting much of the forest, and penning in their livestock with the stone fences so characteristic of the island landscape today. Block Island was later frequented by pirates and smugglers. More than a thousand ships have foundered on the offshore rocks lurking beneath the surface of the water. Block Islanders were among the earliest colonists to struggle against the British Crown, and passed a resolution of independence in March 1774.

In 1853, steamship excursions to the island began, but the island had no proper harbor until 1878. In 1880 regular boat service was established. During the Victorian period, it was a fashionable watering place; Newport and Narragansett doctors sent patients to the island to recover their health. President Ulysses S. Grant visited the island in 1875. Among the Victorian hotels which survive today are the National and the Surf. One famous hotel, built in the 1870s by the Honorable Nicholas Ball, who had become wealthy in the California Gold Rush, was the Ocean View, which was one of the largest on the Atlantic Coast (it burned in 1966). The 1938 hurricane destroyed most of the fishing fleet and barns, which was devastating to the livelihood of islanders. After World War II, however, the island began attracting a new breed of the "rusticators" who once frequented Maine resorts, and who appreciated the simplicity and even the bareness of the island.

The island has become a posh destination for summer daytrippers and for others staying a longer time. The ferries from Point Judith and Montauk are crowded, as are flights. Bicycles and mopeds are widely available for rental, and are popular with visitors coming from Montauk to New Harbor. Remember, though, that after Labor Day they may not be available at New Harbor, which means you must walk to Old Harbor. The mopeds have been the source of continuing controversy on the island, as many islanders feel that they disturb its tranquillity and cause substantial problems. The state has refused to impose a helmet law for this type of vehicle, and some summer Sundays there are many serious accidents. Local residents must leave their jobs and cope with caring for the victims, who must often be evacuated by air to the hospital at Westerly.

A popular form of entertainment for islanders and boating people is the New England Clambake. Complete clambakes can be ordered from the National Seafood Co. with chowder, clamcakes, lobster, fruit salad, brown bread, steamers, mussels, and other items.

POINTS OF INTEREST   Mohegan Bluffs, 200 feet high, at the end of Mohegan Trail at the southern end of the island, affords a dramatic view of the rocky shoreline and the sea. The name is derived from the Mohegan Indian warriors, who, after invading the island, starved after being driven to the bluffs by the Manissean Indians.

The Southeast Lighthouse, built in 1874, stands on Mohegan Bluffs 163 feet above the beach; its 3-million candlepower beacon is visible 35 miles out to sea and its fog horn carries 11 miles; it is the most powerful electric beacon on the eastern U.S. coast. There are nature programs at the bluffs.

The North Light at Sandy Point, now abandoned, was built in 1867, replacing three earlier ones which were destroyed (those dated from 1829, 1837, and 1857). The North Light Commission is working to restore the lighthouse as a maritime museum.

The Block Island Historical Society, Old Town Road and Ocean Ave. (mid-June through mid-September), has interesting island memorabilia.

Settlers' Rock, Cow Cove, is a monument erected in 1911 by descendants of the original settlers, commemorating their historic 1661 landing site.

Southeast Light and Mohegan Bluffs, Block Island

Palatine Graves, Cooneymus Rd., near Dickens Point, burial ground of a group of shipwrecked Germans from the ship *Palatine,* is famous because of John Greenleaf Whittier's poem "The Palatine." The wreck was said to be caused by false signals and wreckers, and its flaming specter, the "Ghost of Fire," was allegedly visible to later mariners.

SIGHTSEEING TOURS   None.

PARKS, BEACHES AND CAMPING   *Parks:* Veterans Park, near New Harbor, is of interest. The Maze, 11 miles of carefully cut paths meandering through pine forests, near Settlers' Rock, ends in a scenic overlook, with a view of the cliffs, at the northeast end of the island. Rodman's Hollow is one of five wildlife refuges; this is a natural ravine left in a glacier's wake. Many paths wind their way down to a point below sea level. *Beaches:* The east side of the island has excellent sandy beaches, with clear water; they are almost never crowded. Crescent Beach, a wide, sandy strip stretching from Old Harbor to Jerry's Point, has several excellent sandy beaches; the State Beach has expert lifeguard protection and a pavilion. Charleston Beach near Harbor Neck is less accessible. *Camping:* None, by town ordinance.

MARINAS   Champlin's Marina, New Harbor (466-2641); 100 transient slips; maximum length 150 ft.; approach depth 20 ft.; depth alongside 20 ft.; electrical power—yes; restaurant within walking distance—yes.
Block Island Boat Basin, Box 412 (466-2631); 90 transient slips; maximum length 100 ft.; approach depth 16 ft.; depth alongside 10 ft.; electric power—yes; restaurant within walking distance—yes.

Payne's New Harbor Dock, Ferry Landing (466-5572); 50 transient slips; maximum length 100 ft.; approach depth 20 ft.; depth alongside 20 ft.; electric power—yes; restaurant within walking distance—yes.

Smuggler's Cove Marina (466-2828); 16 transient slips; maximum length 64 ft.; approach depth 6 ft.; depth alongside 10 ft.; electric power—yes; fresh water yes; restaurant within walking distance—yes.

Old Harbor Dock (Town Dock) (466-2526); 30 transient slips; maximum length 80 ft.; approach depth 10 ft.; depth alongside 15 ft.; electric power—yes; fresh water yes; restaurant within walking distance—yes.

RESTAURANTS   The Block Island Broiler, Water St. (466-5811), is a favorite with local people.**$$-$$$**

Dead Eye Dick's, New Harbor (466-2654) is within easy walking distance of several marinas and overlooks the water. Specialties include scallops, lobster, and shrimp.**$$**

Samuel Peckham's Tavern, New Harbor (see Lodging) offers food and "spirits" and serves crock pot items Monday through Friday.**$$**

Winfield's, Corn Neck Road (466-5856) is a popular restaurant and a short walk from the ferry landing at Old Harbor. The restaurant, according to owner Arnie Flaig, caters to local people, yachtsmen,and private plane owners "used to fine dining, but who would rather escape from a coat and tie." It adjoins the Yellow Kittens, which offered dancing during the island's Victorian days (part of the building dates back to 1876); after the restaurant closes, Yellow Kittens comes to life as a leading island night spot.**$$-$$$**

The Hotel Manisses (see Lodging) serves dinner in pleasant surroundings.**$$-$$$**

LODGING   Most accommodation is seasonal, only open from spring through early fall. The Atlantic Inn, at the top of High St. 02807 (466-2005) has been newly decorated; it is a large pleasant 3-story structure with a porch.**$$$**

Ballard's Inn, Water St., 02807 (466-2231) has rooms with two double beds and private bath. The owners of Ballards also have a facility in New Harbor adjacent to Champlin's Marina; this hotel, the Overlook, has a good view of New Harbor and the ocean. Reservations for the Overlook are made through Ballard's Inn.**$$**

The Harborside Inn, 44 Water St., 02807 (466-5504), is on the National Register of Historic Places. This is a small pleasant hotel overlooking the ferry landing; there is a patio with umbrellas and good views of the water and ferry operations (across the small town parking lot).**$$-$$$**

The Hotel Manisses and the 1661 Inn, just up from the ferry landing, 02807 (466-2421), under the same management, are a colonial inn and a Victorian hotel a short walk from each other. The Inn was acquired by Joan and Justin Abrams in the 1960s when, sailing their Triton from East Greenwich, RI, to Block Island, they decided to buy land on a hill overlooking the sea and had to take an old dilapidated inn along with it. They have since devoted themselves to the hotel business. The Inn, which overlooks the ocean, has 16 rooms. It was renovated and opened in 1970 and was renamed the 1661 Inn in honor of the first settlers. The Inn is now managed by the Abrams' daughter Rita and her husband, Steven Draper. In 1972, the Abrams family bought the Manisses Hotel, which was about to be bulldozed, and renovated it. The hotel is furnished with Victorian antiques and combines traditional coziness with modern amenities. There are 17 rooms, each one unique; all have private baths, ceiling fans, Victorian furniture, and

Prudence Island

fresh flowers. Each room is named for a famous shipwreck. A lavish breakfast buffet is prepared and served at the Inn for guests in both establishments.**$$$**

The National Hotel, 44 Water St. 02807 (800/225-2449), built in 1888, is a Victorian landmark. It has been renovated, yet the decor retains its original Victorian flavor. The wide shady porch, with striped awnings, offers a perfect vantage point from which to watch the harbor activity.**$$$**

Old Town Inn, Box 351, Block Island 02807 (466-5958) is a delightful bed-and-breakfast inn run by Ralph and Monica Gunther and David Gunther. The inn is in a large and attractive old home which is one of the oldest on Block Island; it was the original residence of Lorenzo Littlefield, who was a prominent citizen of the island in the late 1800s. One section was built about 1832 and is the only surviving building of the old town center, which was moved in 1900 to the Old Harbor area. The East Wing was added in 1981 and features large rooms with private baths. Room rates include a full breakfast served in an old-world dining room furnished with antiques.**$$**

Samuel Peckham's Tavern, New Harbor 02807 (466-2439), is a sprawling 3-story structure, with porches, which offers special winter rates as well as weekly rates with or without meals.**$$$**

The Surf Hotel, Dodge St. 02807 (466-2241), is another Victorian landmark with wide porches, centrally located.**$$**

The White House, Spring St. 02807 (466-2653), is a very pleasant bed-and-breakfast inn run by Joseph and Violette Connolly. A full breakfast is served in the large sunny kitchen, filled with antiques; the Connollys are experts on what to see and do on the island.**$$$**

For other restaurants and accommodations, write the Chamber of Commerce for a list.

RENTALS   Block Island Realty, Dodge St., Box 721, Block Island 02807 (466-5887); Blake Phelan, Water St., Block Island 02807 (466-2816); Sullivan Real Estate, Box 144, Block Island 02807 (466-5521); Shirley Wood, Box 142, Block Island 02807 (466-2575).

CONTACT   Block Island Chamber of Commerce, Drawer D, Block Island, RI 02807 (466-2982).

PRUDENCE ISLAND

Area Code 401

LOCATION   In Narragansett Bay, between Aquidneck Island (site of Newport) and East Greenwich.

SIZE   Approximately 1 mile by 6 miles.

ACCESS   ***Ferry:*** From Bristol, Church St. Wharf (Prudence Ferry, Inc., c/o Blount Marine Corp., Box 368, Warren, RI 02885; 253-9808). ***Air:*** There is commercial service to Providence. ***Private boat.***

HISTORY AND   Prudence Island was originally bought from the
DESCRIPTION   Indians by Roger Williams. He sold half of it to
finance his trip to England to secure the charter for Rhode Island. The Indian name for the island was "Chibachuwese" or "Chibachuweset," meaning "a place of separation of the passage." The first ferry to Prudence ran between Warwick Neck in Warwick to the north end of Prudence in 1724. On February 14, 1777, a British schooner ran aground between Patience Island and Prudence. The authorities in Providence were quickly notified and they ordered the sloop *Providence* to capture her. Before she reached the scene, the British sailors set fire to the schooner and blew her up, rather than have the "rebels" capture her. For a short time in 1672, Prudence Island had its own Governor and was the smallest Republic in America.

Much of the island is still primitive and undeveloped, with oak and pitch pine forest, cranberry bogs, and rocky shores. It has a casual, rural, relaxed atmosphere with uncluttered beaches, dirt roads, and the opportunity for clamming, bird watching, jogging, and bicycling. Homestead and Sandy Point landings are on the eastern shore. Another large section of the island is owned by the Heritage Foundation of Rhode Island and is open for walking.

The Prudence Island ferry runs year round, and there are about 60 families living on the island year round. The summer population ranges from about 3,000–4,000. Cottages may be rented. There is no town or shopping district as such, though there are two small grocery stores, Marcy's and Deano's, carrying everyday items. Dairy and baked goods come daily from the mainland, along with daily newspapers. Freddy's Fresh Fruit and Vegetable Market, offering a good selection of produce, is opposite the lighthouse. The Anchorage Gift Shop, on Governor Paine Road off Wells Lane from Narragansett Ave., sells historic books about Prudence Island and also stocks post cards, gift items, and local crafts. There are two pay telephones on the island, one at the Homestead Ferry Landing and one at the South Prudence State Park. No alcoholic beverages are sold on Prudence, and there is no lodging. If you wish to bring your car over from Bristol, advance reservations are essential (253-9808). Prudence Island makes a good base from which to explore Newport and Providence; it is possible to reach both and return within a day.

The Prudence Island Vineyards, with an underground wine cellar, is a thriving concern; it is located at Sunset Hill Farm, a 400-acre estate located $1/3$ of a mile uphill from the Homestead Ferry Landing. The vineyard is owned by William Bacon. The farmhouse was built in 1783 and has been lived in by eight generations of Mrs. Bacon's family. The principal wines produced are Pinot Noir and Chardonnay (the latter has won a number of awards in wine competitions).

Another project on the island is the Oyster Farm, a private aquaculture industry which has been successful.

POINTS OF INTEREST   Prudence Island Vineyards, Inc. Sunset Hill Farm (683-2452). Visitors are welcomed for informal tours May 30 through Labor Day, daily 10 a.m. to noon and 2 p.m. to 4 p.m. or by appointment; the rest of the year, visitors are encouraged to come on weekends from 10 a.m. to 3:30 p.m.

Pulpit Rock is 200 feet in from the road north of the center of the island. Some people believe it was the throne of Canonicus and Miantomomi of the Narragansett Sachems. Roger Williams preached to the Indians from this site in about 1637.

The Heritage Foundation Nature Walk, a mile long, runs through a thickly forested area; old stone walls and foundations can be found along the trail.

The Sandy Point Lighthouse was originally built in 1823 and was located on Goat Island in Newport. In 1851, it was moved to Prudence. It is the oldest existing lighthouse in Rhode Island. In the Great Hurricane of 1938, five people lost their lives at the Point, including the lighthouse keeper's wife and son. (The same storm destroyed the post office and for a time Postmistress Louise Chase ran the post office from her car.)

The schoolhouse, known as the Prudence Park School, was built in 1896; the addition dates from 1954.

Indian Spring is a spring enclosed in a circular concrete wall, located ³/₄ of a mile from the eastern shore near the center of the island. It was used by the Indians and early settlers.

The R. I. Historical Cemetery has pre-Revolutionary stones.

In Bristol, the departure point for the Prudence Island ferry, there are two major attractions. The Herreshoff Marine Museum, formerly the Herreshoff Manufacturing Co., is at 18 Burnside St. (253-5000), near the harbor. Here many famous yachts were built, including the *Reliance* and the *Yankee*. Lewis Herreshoff originally built the Sandy Point Dock on Prudence Island in 1911. It washed away in the 1938 and 1954 hurricanes, but was quickly rebuilt each time. South of the Herreshoff Marine Museum, on Ferry Road, are the Blithewold Gardens and Arboretum (253-2707), a historic 33-acre estate overlooking Narragansett Bay where many exotic plants are grown.

SIGHTSEEING TOURS   None, but there are naturalist programs in the Bay Islands Park Camping Area.

PARKS, BEACHES   **Parks:** The southern and northern ends of the
AND CAMPING   island are part of the Bay Islands Park System, with over 1,300 acres of park land (the middle portion of the island is privately owned). The two parks are North Prudence Bay Islands Park, at the northern end of the island and South Prudence Bay Islands Park, at the southern end of the island. North Prudence is the largest park site and boasts the most varied landscape; it has sheltered coves, windswept hills, hedgerows, crumbling stone walls, and salt marshes. It has 10 miles of trails and is protected by sanctuary status. South Prudence is the center for the Bay Islands Park, offering camping, fishing, and picnicking. Throughout the summer, naturalist programs are held here. In addition, there is the Heritage Foundation of Rhode Island Park, with 475 acres of natural landscape for hiking, bird watching, and photography. The entrance is on Broadway at the center of the

island. At the north end of the island, the Narragansett Bay Estuarine Sanctuary has been established as an outdoor laboratory for research; there are hiking trails, and fishing and shellfishing are permitted. The parks offer large areas of land for leisure walks, picnics, and the observation of wildlife (there are said to be more deer here per square mile than any other place in New England). *Beaches:* The beaches on the island are uncluttered and pleasant. There is a sandy beach just below Pine Hill Point. No vehicles of any kind are allowed on the island beaches. *Camping:* Camping is allowed only in the South Prudence State Park. The camping area is 3 miles from the Ferry Dock. You must obtain a reservation and permit from Colt State Park in Bristol (253-7482). Note that all trash must be taken away with campers; no open fires are allowed. Water resources are limited on the island.

MARINAS   Potter Cove, on the northern section of the island, offers 3 state transient slips and a good undeveloped anchorage, but has no facilities. It is a natural harbor inside a curving sandspit.

Prudence Bay Islands Park (near the T-Dock) has 5 state transient slips, but this anchorage tends to be crowded. Docking at floats at the north end of the island is permitted for ten minutes only to board and let off passengers. Small boats may be beached on the island except in salt marshes and in areas marked "no landing."

RESTAURANTS   None.

LODGING   None.

RENTALS   Frederick R. Stevenson and Margaret H. Stevenson, Prudence Island Realty, Governor Paine Rd., Prudence Island, RI 02872 (683-9026) handle rentals as well as sales.

CONTACT   Tourism Division, Rhode Island Department of Economic Development, 7 Jackson Walkway, Providence, RI 02903 (277-2601).

VERMONT

It has been said that Vermont is the only place in America for which a person can feel homesick before he has left it. Calvin Coolidge once gave a speech at Bennington delineating the character of the state: "I love Vermont because of her hills and valleys, her scenery and invigorating climate, but most of all, because of her indomitable people. They are a race of pioneers who have almost beggared themselves to serve others. If the spirit of liberty should vanish in other parts of the Union and support of our institutions should languish, it could all be replenished from the generous store held by the people of this brave little state of Vermont." Vermonters still have the reputation of being staunch individuals, as well as being taciturn self-reliant New Englanders, little given to chatter. At the same time, they are neighborly and egalitarian (farm and domestic workers don't "work for" employers but "help them out.") They are prescient about everything rural, especially the weather.

Tourism is one of the state's leading businesses. The ski trails, rolling farms, white church spires, evergreen forests, meeting houses, and dulcet mountains beckon visitors, who feel almost universally compelled to stop at least once at a roadside stand to taste the various grades of maple syrup offered in elfin-sized pleated paper cups. The scholar/writer Noel Perrin writes in *First Person Rural* of seeing a welcoming sign near Lebanon, New Hampshire: "Welcome to Vermont, Last Stand of the Yankees," and reflects that the state "makes a business of last stands . . . the last stand of farmers who plow with oxen and do the chores by lantern light. . . . of covered bridges that really bear traffic. . . . of weathered red barns with shingle roofs . . . a whole ancient and very appealing kind of rural life."

Other writers who have lived in Vermont are Robert Frost, Rudyard Kipling, Bernard Malamud, and Pearl Buck. Frost, though a San Francisco native, was elected Vermont's Official Poet Laureate; he lived in several towns before moving to Ripton, near Middlebury College. It is Frost's poetry, such as "Stopping By the Woods on a Snowy Evening," "After Apple-Picking," "Blueberries," and "The Mountain," which perhaps most shapes our conceptions of Vermont.

Lake Champlain runs like a leitmotif through any account of Vermont; the indexes to books about the state often list references as occurring *passim*. For 112 miles, it serves as the state's western border, and is so large at its northern end as to be an inland sea. The islands in the lake, cast against the background of the Adirondacks, form a scenic resort area which is unique in New England.

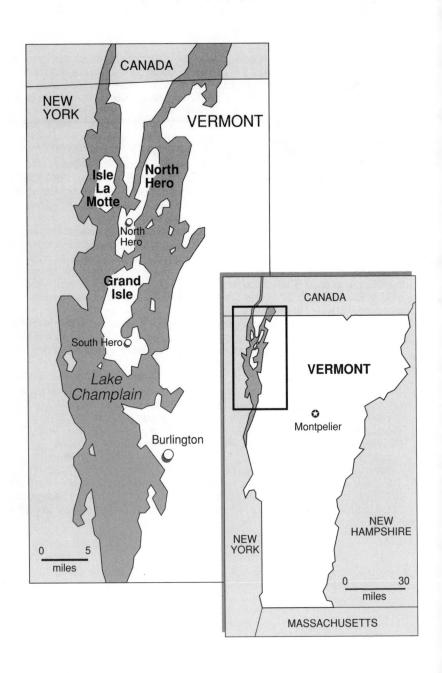

CANADA

NEW YORK

VERMONT

Isle La Motte

North Hero

North Hero

Grand Isle

South Hero

Lake Champlain

Burlington

0   5
miles

CANADA

VERMONT

Montpelier

NEW YORK

NEW HAMPSHIRE

0   30
miles

MASSACHUSETTS

VERMONT

GRAND ISLE / SOUTH HERO

Area Code 802

LOCATION   In Lake Champlain.

SIZE   6¹/₃ mi. long, ranging from ¹/₄ to 4 mi. in width.
                                      (The town includes Two Sisters Islands off the
                                      northwest shore, about 10 acres, and Savage
Island to the east, about 200 acres).

ACCESS   **Ferry:** From Plattsburgh, NY (Lake Champlain
                                     Transportation Co., King Street Dock, Burlington,
                                     VT 05401; 864-9804); Sand Bar Bridge from
Milton, VT. **Air:** There is commercial service to Burlington and Plattsburgh.
Private boat.

HISTORY AND   Grand Isle and South Hero are one island; Grand
DESCRIPTION   Isle is the northern portion and South Hero
                                     makes up the southern end. (Grand Isle was, in
fact, once known as Middle Hero, which clears up the mystery of the names to
some extent). The South Hero section of the island is connected to Vermont by
the unique Sand Bar Bridge, and to New York by ferry to Plattsburgh. There are
orchards, herds of cows, and silos. The French explorers, understandably,
named the region *Vert Mont,* or "Green Mountain."

The first settler here was Ebenezer Allen, said to have been a cousin of Ethan
and Ira Allen; he kept an inn here for many years and also ran a ferry. Ethan Allen
captured Fort Ticonderoga from the British in 1775 and was a member of the
Green Mountain boys, the rag-tag but successful band of rebel irregulars. The
Vermont Legislature grouped Grand Isle/South Hero and North Hero in a charter
to Ethan Allen, Ira Allen, and 362 others, all veterans of the Revolution. The
Allenholm Farm in South Hero, owned and operated by Ray Allen, is the oldest
commercial orchard in Vermont. Another place of interest is the Apple Farm
Market, with cider doughnuts for sale.

Grand Isle has more of a resort flavor, with gardens, lawns, hedges, and tidy
wooden homes. Alexander Gordon was the first settler here, arriving the same
day Ebenezer Allen landed at the southern end and claimed priority on South
Hero. The view from the Grand Isle-Plattsburgh ferry is magnificent, with the
shining lake between the mountain barriers, the Green Mountains to the east
and the Adirondacks to the west.

The Hyde Log Cabin, Grand Isle

POINTS OF INTEREST   The Hyde Cabin, Grand Isle, dating from 1783, is considered the oldest log cabin in the United States that is still standing in its original condition. It is maintained by the Vermont Board of Historic Sites, but in 1956 was turned over to the newly formed Grand Isle County Historical Society. This group now uses the cabin as a meeting place, museum, and local information center. During the Revolution Captain Jedediah Hyde, Jr., enlisted at the age of 14 in the Connecticut Grenadiers; his father fought at the Battle of Bunker Hill in the same unit. In 1783, he and his father surveyed Grand Isle; Captain Hyde, Sr., obtained land grants, and Jedediah, Jr., then built the house of hand-hewn logs on his father's property. He and his wife raised ten children here. One of the first buildings erected on the "Two Heroes," it has been in the Hyde family for nearly 150 years. It is furnished with domestic artifacts and has one room and a sleeping loft.

The Bicentennial Museum, Main St., South Hero, is a converted library featuring farming and household artifacts.

Another landmark on the island is the Round Barn, built around the turn of the century and converted into a residence for the elderly in 1981.

A major museum just 7 miles south of Burlington is the Shelburne Museum at Shelburne, well worth a side trip. This has over 30 buildings filled with Americana, from the 220-ft. steamer *S.S. Ticonderoga,* which once ran on Lake Champlain to folk art, quilts, furniture, and all the artifacts which once figured in the lives of New Englanders. Among the buildings are a schoolhouse, livery stable, church, sawmill, inn, toy house, apothecary shop, and a number of historic houses. It is open from mid-May to mid-October.

SIGHTSEEING TOURS   None from the island, but there are lake excursions from Burlington, VT, on a two-masted schooner, the *Homer W. Dixon* (453-4811). There are also dinner, sunset, and moonlight cruises aboard the paddlewheeler *Ethan Allen* (Green Mountain Boat Lines, Ltd., Box 4306, S. Burlington, VT 05401; 862-9685) and cruises from Plattsburgh, NY, on the *Juniper* (518/561-8970).

PARKS, BEACHES   **Parks:** Grand Isle State Park, on US 2, is a
AND CAMPING   popular focal point for Lake Champlain recreation. It has camping and boat rentals. The Sand

Bar Wildlife Area is just opposite South Hero on the mainland. **Beaches:** There is no swimming at Grand Isle State Park, but there is swimming at Sand Bar State Park, at Colchester, just over the bridge on the mainland. White's Beach at South Hero is the town beach; there are no lifeguards. **Camping:** Make reservations at Grand Isle State Park well in advance; the area is quite popular. Campgrounds include Silent Cedars Campground, 70 campsites in orchard and cedar woods (372-5938); Grand Isle State Park, 256 sites including 31 lean-to shelters; and Cedar Ridge Kampgrounds of America (KOA), 75 sites, store (372-5070). Ice fishing is growing in popularity in Vermont, as in many other northern areas. Smelt, perch, walleye, northern pike, and other fish may be caught. Appletree Bay, South Hero (372-5398) has 100 sites. Others are Camp Skyland, South Hero (372-4200) and White's Lakeshore Campground, Grand Isle (372-4478).

MARINAS   Tudhope Sailing Center, at the Bridge, Grand Isle (372-5545 or 372-5320); almost all slips are for regular customers, but if they have space the approach depth is 6 ft. or better. A restaurant is 2¹/₂ miles away.

Appletree Bay (see Camping) has nightly moorings. There is a public boat launching area, Keller's Bay Access, east side of Rt. 2, north of Rt. 314 (Ferry Rd), South Hero.

The Sandbar Motor Inn and Restaurant (see Lodging) has a private beach and marina.

RESTAURANTS   Commodore's Table, Rt. 2, Keeler's Bay, South Hero (372-4345) is a family restaurant open for three meals per day.$ Donna's Restaurant, Rt. 2, Keeler's Bay, (372-5025) is open year round, serving three meals daily.$

Apple Blossom Time, Grand Isle

The Sandbar Motor Inn and Restaurant, in South Hero (see Lodging) is popular with boaters and has a good view of the mountains and lake; it is famous for good Vermont food. It serves fresh fish, homemade breads, and sinfully good desserts.**$-$$**

LODGING   Sandbar Motor Inn and Restaurant (Route 2, South Hero 05486; 372-6911), open from "May through Foliage," is owned by Jim and Lee Metzger and Cliff and Poe Sheard. The Inn is within a mile of the Sand Bar Wildlife Refuge, where heron, among other species, can be seen. The dining room is filled with plants, pictures, and leftovers from grandmother's attic. The inn is on the lake, and has a private beach with a good view of the mountains; some rooms are equipped for light housekeeping.**$**

RENTALS   Hislop's Landing, U.S. 2, Grand Isle (372-8309 or 372-8229) has housekeeping cottages on the beach with boat launching facilities. Camp Skyland, South Hero (372-4200), on Lake Champlain, also has housekeeping cottages.

Outer Bay Cottages, South Hero (864-0174) has cottage rentals and can arrange for boat rentals.

CONTACT   Lake Champlain Islands Chamber of Commerce, Box 213, North Hero, VT 05474 (372-5683).

ISLE LA MOTTE

Area Code 802
LOCATION   In Lake Champlain, between Alburg and the western shore.

SIZE   Approximately 10 miles by 3 miles.

ACCESS   **Car:** Bridge from S. Alburg. **Air:** There is commercial service to Burlington and Plattsburgh, NY.

HISTORY AND   Isle La Motte is the site of the first European
DESCRIPTION   settlement in Vermont. Many historians believe that it was on Isle La Motte that Samuel de Champlain made camp after he entered the lake on July 4, 1609. In 1665, the French sent a contingent south to prepare a site for a fort; in the summer of 1666, Captain Pierre de St. Paul, Sieur de la Mothe (or la Motte) was sent to construct the fort. It was completed in July 1666 and dedicated to St. Anne. The fort was used for a few years, but was abandoned in 1670. French settlers apparently inhabited Isle La Motte by 1748, but their claims were disputed by the British who also attempted to claim the island. For decades the region remained something of a "no man's land," unsafe for settlement. Benedict Arnold anchored his fleet off the western shore of Isle La Motte before fighting the battle of Valcour Island in 1776. It was not until the American Revolution that settlers began to make their homes in the islands.

The island also has the famous quarries which were the source of the highly prized black marble used in many stately buildings, such as the U.S. Capitol and Radio City Music Hall. The quarries were the first to be worked in Vermont and are still open today, although they are not open to the public.

Isle La Motte village has stone and brick buildings lining Main St. The library is made of the special blue-gray stone for which the island is well known. Fleury's Country Store has a complete line of groceries and gifts. The island has about 400 year-round residents, many of whom commute off-island to jobs. Farming, however, is still important on the island.

POINTS OF INTEREST   St. Anne's Shrine is on the site of Fort St. Anne, the first European settlement in Vermont (1666). Visitors are welcome at services; there is a roofed-over outdoor seating area. It was here that the first mass in Vermont was celebrated; raids against the Iroquois were also launched from this spot. The fort was constructed in 1666 under the direction of Capt. de La Motte for refuge from the Mohawks; French Jesuit missionaries were housed here for protection. There is an enormous granite statue of Samuel de Champlain opposite the shrine, sculpted in Expo 67 in Montreal. Near the shrine is a dock for visitors who arrive by boat, as well as a pleasant beach, picnic tables, and a cafeteria with a store and gift shop.

Coral outcroppings on one of the island farms indicate that the Isle La Motte was once submerged in a sea; many eminent geologists come here to study the coral formations. Visitors might also be interested in a Vermont specialty, the country auction. The Alburg Auction House holds auctions on Saturdays (796-3572 or 796-3441).

SIGHTSEEING TOURS   None from the island, but there are lake excursions from Burlington, VT, on a two-masted schooner, the *Homer W. Dixon* (453-4811). There are also dinner, sunset, and moonlight cruises aboard the paddlewheeler

St. Anne Shrine, Isle La Motte

Ethan Allen (Green Mountain Boat Lines, Ltd., Box 4306, S. Burlington, VT 05401; 862-9685) and cruises from Plattsburgh, NY, on the *Juniper* (518/561-8970).

PARKS, BEACHES AND CAMPING	There are no formal parks or campsites, but there are picnic tables near St. Anne's Shrine and at the southern tip of the island; there is a public fishing

access area on the western shore, and swimming beaches on North Hero. Summer Place Campground and Cabins (928-3300) has a fishing pier, beach, marine facility, full hook-ups, and tent sites.

MARINAS	None, but there is a public boat launching area from Rt. 129 on the west side of the island.
RESTAURANTS	Ruthcliffe Lodge and Motel Resort (see Lodging), on the lake, serves breakfast, lunch, and dinner 7 days a week.$$
LODGING	Ruthcliffe Lodge and Motel Resort, Isle La Motte, Vermont 05463 (928-3200), has boating, swimming, and fishing. It is located on the lake.
RENTALS	Only if arranged privately.
CONTACT	Lake Champlain Islands Chamber of Commerce, Box 213, North Hero, VT 05474 (372-5683).

NORTH HERO

Area Code 802

LOCATION	In Lake Champlain.
SIZE	15 miles long.
ACCESS	*Car:* Bridge from Grand Isle and the Alburg peninsula (Rt. 2). *Air:* There is commercial service to Burlington and Plattsburgh, NY.
HISTORY AND DESCRIPTION	North Hero is the shire town of Grand Isle County. Main Street runs along the shore, facing Lake Champlain, with tall elms and tidy wooden

houses with pretty gardens. There is a population of about 450, greatly augmented in the summer by boaters and other visitors; in winter, ice fishing and cross-country skiing are drawing more and more tourists.

North Hero and Grand Isle/South Hero were grouped together in the 1779 charter to Ethan Allen, Ira Allen, and other Revolutionary War veterans (see description of Grand Isle/South Hero). At its narrowest point there is a place still called the "Carry," where Indians first carried canoes across to avoid a lengthy water trip. This spot was later used by smugglers, who would carry their booty across to avoid federal agents (after the 1807 Embargo Act made trade with Canada illegal). There is a magnificent view from the bridge to Grand Isle/South Hero. On October 10, 1776, the British fleet anchored between these two islands. The next morning the fleet sailed south along the shores of North and

The Adirondack ferry, Lake Champlain

South Hero. Benedict Arnold lay in wait behind Valcour Island on the New York side and fought a rear-guard action which allowed his fleet to reach Fort Ticonderoga safely. The resulting battle, though technically a British victory, delayed the British advance by a year. (Kenneth Roberts, in *Rabble in Arms,* describes the battle).

POINTS OF INTEREST   There are no historic monuments or museums on the island, but the views of the lakes and mountains and the beautiful sunsets and sunrises draw people here.

SIGHTSEEING TOURS   None from the island, but there are lake excursions from Burlington, VT, on a two-masted schooner, the *Homer W. Dixon* (453-4811). There are also dinner, sunset, and moonlight cruises aboard the paddlewheeler *Ethan Allen* (Green Mountain Boat Lines, Ltd., Box 4306, S. Burlington, VT 05401; 862-9685) and cruises from Plattsburgh, NY, on the *Juniper* (518/561-8970).

PARKS, BEACHES AND CAMPING   *Parks:* Knight Point State Park, with picnic area, swimming beach, and rental boats (372-8389), is at the southern end of the island. North Hero State Park (372-8727) has 399 acres. *Beaches:* There is a swimming beach at Knight Point State Park and at Sand Bar State Park, along the Sandbar Bridge leading into South Hero. White's Beach, South Hero, is the town beach; no lifeguards. *Camping:* Make reservations well ahead; the area is quite popular. Carry Bay Marina and Campground, run by Bob and Carol Eldred, has RV sites, boat rentals (372-8233); North Hero State Park has campsites in lowland forest, beach for campers only, boat launch. King's Bay Trailer Park has lakefront lots (372-4407); Isle of Nites Primitive Campground, on Knight Island between North Hero and St. Albans, isolated and uninhabited since 1909, has no facilities (372-4083).

MARINAS   Carry Bay Marina and Campground (see Parks and Camping), launch area. Anchor Island Marina, North Hero 05474 (372-5131) has no transient slips free as a rule, but can take boats up to about 40 feet long. A restaurant is across the street.

RESTAURANTS   North Hero House (see Lodging), overlooking the lake, prides itself on fresh fish and baking; its cheerful flower-filled solarium is popular with boaters; the inn has its own steamship dock, where yachts are often moored. The Sunday evening buffets are popular.**$$**

Shore Acres Inn and Restaurant (see Lodging) has also been long known for good food and has a friendly maple dining room).**$$**

If you are there in mid-August, plan to attend the North Hero Firemen's Roast Beef Dinner, so popular with locals and visitors there are now 4 sittings.

LODGING   Charlie's Northland Lodge, Box 88, North Hero 05474 (372-8822) is small country inn with good views; open year round, it also offers ice fishing.**$**

Holiday Harbor Motel, Rt. 2, North Hero (372-4077) has clean rooms; no restaurant.**$**

North Hero House, Box 106, North Hero 05474 (372-8237), is a a large, square, attractive inn overlooking the lake, long famous for good accommodations. There are rockers on the porch from which there is an excellent view of Mt. Mansfield across the lake. The Apgar and Sherlock families are innkeepers. Many of the rooms have sliding glass doors opening onto balconies overlooking the lake. There are tennis and shuffleboard courts. Open seasonally.**$$**

Shore Acres Inn and Restaurant, Rt. 2, North Hero 05474 (372-8722) has lakeside rooms and a restaurant along with 50 acres of rolling grounds and a peaceful rural setting. Open seasonally.**$$**

RENTALS   Parker Lodge, North Hero (372-8792) has rental cottages with dockage for renters' boats. Charlie's, North Hero (372-4667) has cottages with electric heat and tennis.

Birdland, North Hero (372-4220) has housekeeping cottages, as does Carry Bay Marina and Campground (see Camping).

CONTACT   Lake Champlain Islands Chamber of Commerce, Box 213, North Hero, VT 05474 (372-5683).

EASTERN CANADA

"Not to know an island," says Scottish poet Hugh MacDiarmid, "is like having a blunt sensation in the tips of your fingers. Horrid! But to know a whole lot of islands is like having a portfolio of pictures and an adjustable frame, which enables you to hang up any picture for a day, a week, or a month. . . . an island is an almost startling entire thing, in these days of the subdivision, of the atomization, of life."

The easternmost islands of Canada are an excellent illustration of MacDiarmid's point. They are a portfolio of the various Canadian provinces, in microcosm; also, far more than United States islands, they exhibit the vestiges of their European heritage. One does not go far on Cape Breton before becoming aware of an Celtic overlay, with Scottish highland dancing and Gaelic place names. The sad Acadian saga haunts the western coast of Cape Breton as well as the Fortress of Louisbourg and sections of Prince Edward Island and New Brunswick. The Magdalen Islands, part of Quebec, are French-speaking, as are St. Pierre and Miquelon, which do not actually belong to Canada at all but are two communities making up a territorial collectivity of the French Republic. They cling fiercely to the French way of life (including excellent cuisine).

The prospective island visitor may get ample toll-free information about the various provinces (Nova Scotia even has a toll-free Check-In service to handle reservations). The islands are very welcoming to Americans, with a cleanliness, honesty, and roominess which comes as a welcome relief to urban dwellers or those who have visited more crowded islands in the States such as Nantucket or Fire Island. The scenery on the easternnmost islands, such as Grand Manan, Campobello, and Cape Breton, is somewhat similar to that in Maine, though Grand Manan has more striking cliffs and Cape Breton a high and beautiful scenic drive, the Cabot Trail (the closest equivalent on a Maine Island would be the loop going through Acadia National Park). Further north, Prince Edward Island and the Magdalens have dramatic red rocks, eroded to form arches and other exotic shapes.

Seven islands are discussed, all accessible by car with the exception of St. Pierre/Miquelon, which must be reached by plane from Montreal, Halifax, or Sydney, or by pedestrian ferry from Fortune. Sometimes the distances are surprising; the ferry crossing from Souris on Prince Edward Island to the Magdalens is five hours, longer than from Newhaven to Dieppe, across the English Channel. Reservations for cars should be made in advance on some ferries; details are given in the individual entries. Prices given are in Canadian dollars.

In 1534, when Jacques Cartier discovered Prince Edward Island, he declared it "the fairest land 'tis possible to see." The other islands in the Maritime Provinces are just as "fair" and, in MacDiarmid's words, "startling" and "entire." Individually, they have distinct characters; collectively, they are peopled with friendly, sensible, sympathetic, imaginative, and, above all, hospitable Canadians.

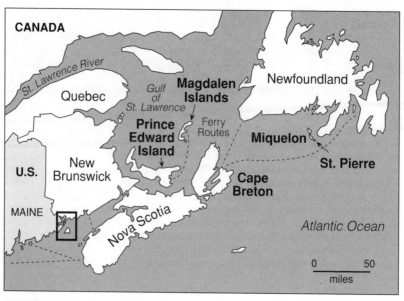

CANADA

St. Lawrence River

Quebec

Gulf of St. Lawrence

Magdalen Islands

Newfoundland

Prince Edward Island

Ferry Routes

Miquelon

U.S.

New Brunswick

St. Pierre

MAINE

Cape Breton

Nova Scotia

Atlantic Ocean

0   50
miles

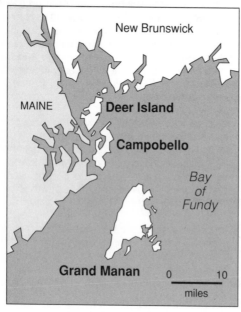

New Brunswick

MAINE

Deer Island

Campobello

Bay of Fundy

Grand Manan

0   10
miles

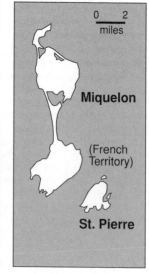

0   2
miles

Miquelon

(French Territory)

St. Pierre

EASTERN CANADA

CAMPOBELLO
New Brunswick

Area Code 506

LOCATION Off the coast of Maine and Canada, east of Eastport, ME and south of Blacks Harbour, N.B.

SIZE 13 miles by 3 miles.

ACCESS *Car:* Accessible year round by the toll-free Frank-
lin D. Roosevelt International Memorial Bridge at
Lubec, ME. *Ferry:* July and August only, from
Deer Island, N.B. (East Coast Ferries Ltd., c/o Stanley Lord, Lord's Cove, Deer
Island, 747-2159). East Coast also runs ferries in summer from Eastport, ME, to
Deer Island; it is easy to transfer to the second ferry to Campobello. *Cruise ship:*
The Clipper Cruise Line, 7711 Bonhomme Ave., St. Louis, MO 63105
(800/325-0010) calls at Campobello on several cruises leaving from Boston in
July and August. *Private boat.*

HISTORY AND Of the Fundy Isles, Campobello seems the most
DESCRIPTION connected with the United States. The year-
round population of 1,300 do their shopping in
Lubec, Maine (in fact, there is no longer even a grocery store on Campobello),
and rely on hospitals in Maine. The ten-minute drive across the International
Bridge is far shorter than the commuting and shopping runs made by most
American families. Still, the flavor of the island is clearly Canadian. It is clean and
spacious. The landscape is adorned by wildflowers, not neon, and traffic is
sparse enough for U-turns and for roadside stops by water vistas. Don't look for
nightclubs or shopping malls. But if you prize simplicity and a quiet pace, if you
relish rocky outcroppings, splashing waves, cobbly beaches, primroses, fireweed, and coves sheltering migratory shorebirds, you will delight in Campobello.

Explorers Samuel de Champlain and the DeMonts visited Campobello in
1604, and it is thought that the island had early French settlers. After the
expulsion of the Acadians from Nova Scotia, large grants of land were made to
attract English settlers. One of the first was Captain William Owen, who named
the island Campo-Bello after Governor William Campbell of Nova Scotia, who
granted him the "Outer Island." Campobello was part of Nova Scotia until 1784,
when the province of New Brunswick was formed. At the end of the American

Revolution, the traitor Benedict Arnold lived at Snug Cove with his wife, the former Peggy Shippen of Philadelphia. She found it dull, so they moved to Saint John, New Brunswick, where they lived from 1789–93.

Campobello Island was once the summer home of the Franklin Delano Roosevelt family. Roosevelt always referred to Campobello as "my beloved island." His passion for the island was founded in his childhood. James and Sara Roosevelt first visited Campobello in 1883, the year after Franklin was born; they bought several acres and began building a house, which was completed in 1886. When Franklin brought Eleanor to the island in 1903, the Roosevelts' next-door neighbor, Mrs. Hartman Kuhn, stipulated that Sara Roosevelt could purchase her home for the young couple. The house, with 34 rooms and no electricity, became a refuge for the Roosevelts, especially after Franklin entered politics. Traveling by boat one day to St. Andrews in New Brunswick, Eleanor wrote: "The sun is out, and the fog is rolling out to sea, and I'm sitting in the bottom of the boat, sniffing salt air and now and then looking over the water to my green islands and gray rocky shores." According to historian Stephen O. Muskie, the Roosevelts were "like an army on the march" each summer when they went to Campobello, with "a nurse for each of the small children, three to five other domestics, mountains of trunks, valises, and hat boxes." The only Roosevelt summer homes were those of James and Sara Roosevelt and Franklin Delano Roosevelt. The James Roosevelt home was torn down after Franklin's death.

The park is now operated jointly by the United States and Canada, the only arrangement of its kind in the world (see Points of Interest).

POINTS OF INTEREST　　　The foremost site of interest is the Roosevelt Campobello International Park, established in 1964, a memorial to Franklin Delano Roosevelt. It is open from late May to mid-October. The centerpiece of the park is the 34-room maroon, gambrel-roofed summer "cottage," built in Dutch colonial style, which Franklin Delano Roosevelt and his wife were given as newlyweds. The house is marked by patrician simplicity, with many bedrooms for the children, staff, and guests, but so understated that everything seems subordinate to the lawns and

Head Harbour Lighthouse, Campobello

The Roosevelt Summer Home, Campobello

water views. It was here that Franklin Delano Roosevelt spent summers from 1883 to 1921, when he was stricken with polio (from 1921-1933, Roosevelt's paralysis kept him from visiting the island). The house contains four water-colors given by Mme. Chiang Kai-shek to Mrs. Roosevelt, and also a megaphone for hailing offshore boats and calling family members in for meals. You may hear a tape of Roosevelt's most famous speeches and his D-Day prayer, via a nostalgic old-time radio containing a tape recorder. There is also a 30-minute film in the Visitor Centre which follows the President's political career.

Friar's Head is so named because of the detached pinnacle called the "Old Friar" off the outer end of Friar's Head in the Roosevelt Campobello International Park. The British reputedly used the "Old Friar" for cannon practice during the occupation of Eastport under Sir Thomas Hardy in 1814 and altered its outline.

The Head Harbour Lighthouse, also known as the East Quoddy Head Lighthouse, at the northern tip of the island, is well worth visiting. It is red and white, as are all Canadian lighthouses, and is very appealing with its red-roofed outbuildings. You can view it from a distance, but should only walk to it at low tide; incoming tides, with swift and dangerous currents, rise 5 feet per hour, and may leave you stranded.

Friar's Bay, north of the Roosevelt home, has large summer homes.

Welshpool is a town where Captain Owen originally settled in 1835; he called it New Warrington, but the name was changed to Welshpool after his home in Wales. The historic Anglican church of St. Anne's, which Roosevelt attended as a young man, is well worth seeing. It was built in 1855 by Admiral William Fitzwilliam Owen, Captain Owen's son. Admiral Owen and his first wife, Martha, are buried in the cemetery behind the church. The block of stone from which the font was carved was brought from the Church of the Knights Templar at Malta; it dates from 1843. The rood screen, representing the Gates of Heaven, was brought from England. Three generations of Roosevelts have worshipped here, as well as former president Lyndon Johnson. The small white Victorian-style church, with its green trim, is a landmark on the island and well worth a visit.

Wilson's Beach was the location of the first English settlement on the island. There is a large pier here, where fresh and salted fish and sardines are sold. Sardines are packed from herring fish in the cannery here.

Harbour de Loutre is reminiscent of the French settlement of the island (the whole island was once called the Outer Island). There are a number of French place names still evident.

The Sugar Loaves are two large rocks off the southern end of Liberty Head that resemble loaves of sugar. The Boring Stones lie just outside the Sugar Loaves and are only visible at low tide. The tide covers them, then uncovers them. In the early days of sail, it was necessary to navigate inside the Boring Stones to get around Liberty Point, a delicate maneuver.

SIGHTSEEING TOURS   Cline Marine offers scenic search tours aboard the *Cathy & Trevor* June through September; whales are sighted on better than 8 out of 10 trips. The boat originates in St. Andrews and calls at Deer Island and Campobello if passengers are waiting. To reserve, call Osprey Travel, St. Andrews (506/529-8844) or Stroh Gift Shop, Lighthouse Road (752-2124) or the Cline Marine Office (747-2287).

A pleasant day trip for those staying in Campobello is to take the ferry to Deer Island, board the adjacent one to Eastport, Maine, and have lunch and shop at the Cannery Wharf Restaurants (the Cannery, the Clam Kibbin, and the Pickling Shed, a bar). All of these are located at the ferry landing.

Scenic Bay Tours leaves from Lubec, Maine, just across the International Bridge, on the *M. V. Seafarer,* offering a chance to view whales and bald eagles. Call Captain Butch Huntley, 207/733-5584.

PARKS, BEACHES   **Parks:** Roosevelt Campobello International Park,
AND CAMPING   is the principal park on the island. It has over 8 miles of walking trails and several vehicular drives. There are picnic areas at Mulholland Point, which has an 1885 lighthouse, and at Friar's Head. The Herring Cove Provincial Park is ideal for picnics and has a good 9-hole golf course, open to the public, the Herring Cove Golf Lodge, as well as a pro shop. Cart rentals are available. The course is both scenic and challenging; it is very popular in summer months because of cool ocean breezes. For information, call or write Afton Green, Herring Cove Provincial Park, Welshpool, N.B. E0G 3H0 (752-2396). **Beaches:** There is a clean 1-mile beach at Herring Cove Provincial Park, but, in general, the water is very cold for swimming. **Camping:** Tent and trailer camping are allowed at Herring Cove Provincial Park, which has all necessary facilities. Afton Green, superintendent for over 16 years, takes a personal interest in all the campers and spends the winter corresponding with an ever-widening circle of previous campers and beneficiaries of his attention. One very elderly couple from Kentucky have come for many years, with increasing difficulty and wrecks on the way; Afton and his wife Terry, ably assisted by Alice Gough, help with grocery shopping and any other necessary errands.

MARINAS   There is docking at several public wharves. One well-known and popular spot is Head Harbour, an established stop-over for yachts coming up or down the eastern coast. It is completely landlocked, so it is a safe harbor at all times. It has ample room for most private boats; no maximum length; approach depth at low tide 25 ft. or more; dockside depth 17 ft.; electric power—yes; restaurant within walking distance—no.

RESTAURANTS   Friars Bay Restaurant and Motorlodge, Welsh-
                         pool, N.B. E0G 3H0 (752-2056) specializes in
                         seafood.**$**

The Campobello Club Lodge (see Lodging), has an inviting dining room with
the ambiance of a presidential retreat, with high-backed comfortable chairs and
water views; specialties include local haddock, lobster, and seafood newburg.
Lodge rates include breakfast and dinner.**$$**

Herring Cove Provincial Park (see Camping) has a pleasant dining room.**$**

LODGING   The Campobello Club Lodge, Box 16, Welshpool,
                         N.B. Canada E0G 3H0 (752-2487) is an example
                         of preservation at its best. These rustic cottages,
built as a summer residence between 1907 and 1915 by the Adams family (Mrs.
Adams was a first cousin of Franklin Delano Roosevelt), were almost torn down.
Instead they were rescued and converted into very comfortable accommoda-
tions by the Campobello Company, based in Little Rock, Arkansas, which leased
them from the Canadian government. Rates include breakfast and dinner.
Among the rooms is the Lobster Trap Suite, with a private cathedral-ceilinged
living room. Reserve well ahead. (The same company is also offering ocean-
front lots and tracts of land for sale).**$$-$$$$**

The Owen House, Welshpool, Campobello, N.B., Canada E0G 3H0
(752-2977) is owned by artist Joyce Morrell. This is a large colonial inn, the 1829
home of Admiral William Fitzwilliam Owen. It is said that for more than a century
the Owen family ran the island of Campobello as a feudal estate. Admiral Owen
loved the sea so much he built a quarterdeck on which to pace. There are water
views from every room. Rooms are furnished with antiques and hand-made
quilts. Guests usually gather around a fire in the evening. Greer Garson stayed
here during the filming of *Sunrise at Campobello.* Painting and photography
workshops are often held here, and breakfasts, for as many as 14, in the large
sunny dining room, are so festive as to preempt almost all other activities for the
day. "When I see the guests around the table, in animated conversation, I know
they'll be there most of the morning," says Joyce Morrell. Some of her paintings
are on display in the inn, as well as in galleries on the mainland. The Deer Island
ferry is nearby for expeditions to Deer Island and Eastport.**$-$$**

The Welshpool Guest House, Welshpool Road, Campobello Island, N.B. E0G
3H0 (752-2040), is run by a warm and attentive couple from Connecticut, Bud
and Kathleen MacFeat. Guests are coddled in spotless rooms with fluffy linens,
and served an excellent full breakfast in a panelled breakfast room adorned with
pewter and flowers.**$**

RENTALS   Quoddy View Cabins, c/o M. Newman, Wilson's
                         Beach, N.B., E0G 3L0 (752-2981).**$**

CONTACT   The Tourist Information Center, Welshpool, N.B.,
                         30G 3H0 (752-2396) or Tourism New Brunswick,
                         Box 12345, Fredericton, New Brunswick, Canada
E3B 5C3 (800/561-0123).

CAPE BRETON ISLAND
Nova Scotia

Area Code 902

LOCATION   Cape Breton Island is the northeastern section of Nova Scotia, joined to mainland Nova Scotia by the Canso Causeway at Port Hastings.

SIZE   Approximately 100 by 70 miles.

ACCESS   *Car:* The island is accessible via the Canso Causeway at Hastings. *Ferry:* From Port-aux-Basques, Newfoundland to North Sydney and from Argentia, Newfoundland to North Sydney (Marine Atlantic, 121 Eden St., Bar Harbor, ME 04609; Continental US 800/341-7981; ME only 800/432-7344; Maritime Provinces 800/565-9470; Newfoundland and Labrador 800/563-7701; Quebec and Ontario 800/565-9411). Note that advance reservations are necessary on both routes. *Air:* There is commercial service to Sydney. *Private boat.*

HISTORY AND DESCRIPTION   "Many men have loved the island of Cape Breton," the eminent Canadian novelist Hugh MacLennan observes in *Each Man's Son.* He writes of the Highlanders who, defeated by the English, left their homeland at the

Scenery on the Cabot Trail, Cape Breton

end of the eighteenth century, "with the pipes playing laments on the decks of their ships . . . the pipes played again when they waded ashore on the rocky coast of Cape Breton Island." Bagpipes may still be heard on Cape Breton, whose Scottish heritage is very much alive today. "Ciad Mile Failte," "One Hundred Thousand Welcomes," say the signs greeting tourists. The Ceilidh Trail, along the Western Shore, rings with Scottish place names: Inverness, Strathlorne, Boisdale, and Loch Lomond. All evoke the Scottish homeland of the settlers, and many older residents, even today, are fluent in the Gaelic language. Many Cape Breton girls, with their green eyes and reddish hair, look as though they could be descendants of Anne of Green Gables, who was a Nova Scotia orphan and had "decidedly red hair" and eyes "that looked green in some lights and moods and gray in others." Cape Breton's Scottish heritage is particularly notable in summer, with Highland dancing, step dancing and fiddling competitions, square dances, ceilidhs, and Highland Village Day, held the first Saturday in August at Hector's Point, Iona. Cape Breton bears out the words spoken in 1758 by Donald "Og" MacNeil, a native of Barra, Scotland, who was serving in the British Army: "Besides fuel in the forests, water in the ground and fish in the sea, you will find there, shelter from the North wind, better ripening harvests and good fishing grounds." The first Scottish pioneers settled on the Northern bank of the strait in 1800, in what is now called Iona. Others followed, most from the islands of Barra and South Uist, bringing their deep religious convictions, industry, honesty, and Celtic language. The only Gaelic College on the North American continent is in Cape Breton at St. Ann's (see Points of Interest). The Centre Bras D'Or at Baddeck has a noted summer festival, established in 1985 by Cape Bretoners to promote its heritage and culture, much of which is Gaelic. In recent years, groups such as the Barra MacNeils have performed music and step dancing; the group Mabou Jig has brought more step dancing and traditional and contemporary Cape Breton music.

Cape Breton, with its deep blue lakes, salmon streams; rugged coast with gray granite promontories and red sandstone cliffs, bears out the statement by Alexander Graham Bell: "I have travelled around the globe. I have seen the Canadian and American Rockies, the Andes and the Alps and the Highlands of Scotland; but for simple beauty, Cape Breton outrivals them all."

The island was probably visited by Europeans long before John Cabot, the English explorer, arrived in 1497; Cape Breton fishermen were here as early as 1504. In 1713, the French founded the Fortress of Louisbourg; the British captured the Fortress twice, in 1745 and 1758 (the second time leaving it in ruins). In 1763, Cape Breton became part of the British Empire. At the time it was mainly inhabited by Micmac Indians, Jersey fishermen, French settlers who escaped the expulsion, and some Irish settlers. During the American Revolution, many Loyalists came to Cape Breton; they were joined by Scottish immigrants. Today you may hear four languages in Cape Breton: Micmac, English, French, and Gaelic. It is the aura of the Gaelic settlers, however, which hovers over the island, distinguishing it from the other Maritime provinces and giving Cape Breton a unique flavor.

POINTS OF INTEREST   ***Baddeck:*** This is a sailing center on the beautiful Bras d'Or Lake, and makes an excellent base from which to tour the Cabot Trail and the remainder of Cape Breton. The town is reminiscent of an elegant turn-of-the-century Maine seacoast resort, perhaps Bar Harbor in its better days, though it is not so large. The backdrop of the lake seems to provide a soothing counterpoint to the slow traffic crawling through town; everywhere there is the *leitmotif* of brightly colored sails and shimmering blue water. The Alexander Graham Bell National Historic House has three large exhibit halls documenting Bell's life and work; the grounds are beautifully landscaped, and there are interesting scientific displays which demonstrate many of his experiments. Historical talks, evening slide presentations, and kite-making workshops are also offered by the museum. The Bell home in Baddeck, where Bell lived, is not open to the public.

Cabot Trail: The 184-mile Cabot Trail is one of the most dramatic highways in North America; it winds around the northern shore of Cape Breton, linking isolated Scottish, English, and Acadian communities. There are many scenic overlooks, giving a kaleidoscopic view of the clear blue water, rocky beaches, and cliffs. At times, it is misty, evoking Longfellow's description in "Evangeline"of the mountains where "sea-fogs pitched their tents." Some people drive around the Cabot Trail in one day; this is possible, but not recommended. Others take two weeks or more. One couple, searching for amethyst veins in the rocky beaches, was spending each day on different sections of the rocky beaches or exploring the nature trails; they were staying in several different inns at various points around the trail. For the traveler who lacks the luxury of so much time, the ideal solution might be to see the trail in two segments, possibly beginning at Baddeck. You might spend the night at the government-run Keltic Lodge (see Lodging), which is itself a point of interest along the trail and well worth a stop (for a meal or a break, if not a night). The Trail from the Keltic Lodge around through Cheticamp and on to Inverness is manageable in one day, and the inland journey from Inverness back to Baddeck is easily accomplished in the brilliant late summer evenings.

Cape Breton Highlands National Park: This park is in the northern section of Cape Breton; part of the Cabot Trail goes through the park (see Parks section).

Cheticamp: This is the heart of Acadian Cape Breton. Acadia was first founded in 1604, destroyed several years later, resettled in 1632, and became prosperous until the Great Expulsion of 1755, which was the subject of Long-fellow's poem "Evangeline." In 1758, after the fall of Louisbourg, the Acadians refused to swear loyalty to the British Crown; they were deported throughout the Atlantic coast to Boston, Georgia, and other places. In 1785, the Acadians returned and settled in Cheticamp. Many French names are evident in the town today, and, in the shops, some of the girls have French names and look as though they might have modeled for the illustrations of the beatific Evangeline.

St. Peter's Church, which dominates the village of Cheticamp, is well worth seeing, with a Baroque-style interior and an impressive stone exterior.

Fortress of Louisbourg, Cape Breton

Les Trois Pignons is an eighteenth-century-style building serving as an historical, cultural, genealogical, and information center. It houses the Dr. Elizabeth LeFort Gallery as well as a museum of Acadian furnishings and artifacts. Elizabeth LeFort's tapestries are known worldwide and can be found in the White House, the Vatican, Buckingham Palace, and the Canadian House of Commons.

Glace Bay: The Miners' Museum (849-4522) is well worth touring; this is an underground tour given by a retired miner. At bed-and-breakfast inns, all over Cape Breton (and other places in the Maritimes as well), the main subject of conversation at breakfast each morning is likely to be the Glace Bay mine, to the astonishment of inn owners. The exhibits relate the past, present, and future of coal mining, and there are miners' houses on display. The most memorable part of the tour, however, is donning a cape and helmet and, stooping painfully, following the miner through the various tunnels of the Ocean Deeps Mine, hearing of his decades in the mines and the small pittance he was paid. There is an underground garden in the mine, still blooming.

The Men of the Deeps is a well-known singing group, consisting of retired and working coal miners from Cape Breton. The choir was formed in 1967. They have gathered music from mining communities around the world; many have Celtic roots. When they perform, they enter the concert hall in total darkness, coveralls, and hard hats, as they entered the mine; at first, only the lamps on their helmets illuminate the audience. They have even toured China and performed at Expo 86 in Vancouver.

Iona: This village, not far from Baddeck, is on Rt. 223. Here the Nova Scotia Highland Village Museum was built by a nonprofit society dedicated to preserving Scottish culture. It is devoted to the life of early Scottish settlers, and has a carding mill, forge, country store, school, and log cabin.

Louisbourg: The Fortress of Louisbourg National Historic Park is a reconstruction of eighteenth-century French Louisbourg; it is the largest historic reconstruction project in Canada. One-fifth of the original town enclosed by the Fortress walls has been reconstructed in absolute detail. Local people in period dress perform the duties they might have performed at the time; there are gardens, animals, living quarters, period rooms, and shops, all faithful to their eighteenth-century origins. Many French-speaking visitors come; *"très beau et enchanteur,"* a New Brunswick visitor has written in the guest book. *"Ça radait le voyage,"* writes a Montreal tourist. *"Une partie de notre histoire,"* says one from Quebec. West Germany is represented, as well as a presumably youthful visitor from nearby Glace Bay who states, "I liked the Bread Boy best." (A young boy demonstrates bread baking in the King's bakery.)

North East Margaree: The Margaree River offers some of Canada's finest salmon fishing. There are two museums of interest here: the Museum of Cape Breton Heritage, which has tartans, exhibits of weaving and spinning equipment, and embroidery displays, and the Margaree Salmon Museum, showing the salmon life cycle.

St. Ann's: The Gaelic College here was established to preserve and foster the Scottish Heritage and offers immersion courses in the Gaelic culture. The Great Hall of Clans commemorates the heritage of the many clan members who settled in Cape Breton. A Gaelic Mod is held here each August, when prizes are awarded to the best performers in various competitions (bagpipe music, Highland dancing, step dancing, fiddling, etc.) It is the only school on the North American continent to teach Gaelic; it was founded in 1939.

SIGHTSEEING TOURS   There are boat tours from Pleasant Bay aboard the 43-ft. *Gail Marie;* call Captain Ariland Fitzgerald, Pleasant Bay, N.S. B0E 2P0 (224-2547). The cruises offer views of mountain scenery, marine mammals, seabirds, and wildlife.

From Baddeck, June 1 through late September, there are trips aboard the 56-ft. *Eastern Star,* a European ship built for King Frederick IX of Denmark. The boat had come into Nova Scotia with hashish aboard and Josie and Allan Gillis purchased her from an interim owner who had acquired her at a crown asset sale. They offer a sail on the Bras d'Or Lake past the Alexander Graham Bell estate (not open to the public); passengers can see bald eagles and other birds in a bird sanctuary. Tours leave from Government Wharf (call 295-2028).

Bannockburn Tours, Ltd., in Baddeck (295-3310) offers daily Cabot Trail tours in a minibus, with pick-up from motels and campgrounds by prior arrangement. There are stops for refreshments, gift shopping, and picture taking.

There are boat tours twice daily, at 10 a.m. and 1:30 p.m., from Big Bras d'Or to the Bird Islands, which are the nesting grounds of Atlantic Puffins, Razor-Billed Auks, Black Guillimots, Blackback and Herring Gulls, Great Cormorants, and Double Crested Cormorants. Contact Mountain View by the Sea, RR # 1, Bras d'Or, Nova Scotia B0C 180 (674-2384).

From Baddeck, a free government ferry takes visitors to Kidston, a 35-acre island with walking trails and life-guarded beach.

PARKS, BEACHES   ***Parks:*** The Cape Breton Highlands National Park
AND CAMPING   (see Points of Interest) is the major park on Cape Breton; it covers 367 square miles of rugged mountains circled by the sea. Recreation, bathing, hiking, golf, tennis, fishing, and camping are offered. There are also numerous provincial parks. In the West, there are parks at Craigmore, Mabou, Margaree, Trout River, and Lake O'Law. The Northern Highlands has, besides Cape Breton Highlands, parks at Cape North (Cabot's Landing Provincial Park), Cape Smokey, North River, and St. Ann's, as well as Plaster Provincial Park on the North Shore. In the Central Lakes, there are parks at Iona and Boularderie. Another, the Barachois Provincial Park, was once an old farm and is now a picnic park with a walking trail leading down to a marshy lagoon. The Southern area of Cape Breton has parks on Isle Madame and at St. Peter's, among others. In the East, the Two Rivers Provincial Wildlife Park is popular; you may see bobcats, lynx, black bears, and deer. The Mira River Provincial Park and the Dominion Beach Provincial Park are also pretty. ***Beaches:*** There are many beaches on Cape Breton. In the West, there is Jockie's Beach, south of Judique off Rt. 19, a sandy beach at Port Hood, two popular beaches at Mabou, one with a lighthouse, and a sand beach at Inverness. Among the Northern Highlands beaches are those at Cheticamp Island, Aspy Bay, Neil's Harbour (which also has an impressive lighthouse), North Ingonish, and Ingonish Beach. The latter two are especially attractive; in fact, Ingonish has been called Cape Breton's most famous beach. In the Central Lakes area, the beach at Kidston, near Baddeck, is pretty; others are at Iona, Groves Point, and Pipers Cove. Popular beaches in the South are at Point Michaud, Pondville, St. Peter's, and Isle Madame. In the East, there are good beaches at Kennington Cove (in Louisbourg National Park) and Dominion. One of the most popular is at the Mira River Provincial Park, which has a crescent-shaped beach with a boat launch and campsites. ***Camping:*** Camping is allowed at many of the provincial parks and in Cape Breton Highlands National Park.

There are numerous private campgrounds, all listed in the free *Nova Scotia* guidebook. A few private ones are these: Ceilidh Cottages and Trailer Park at Mabou (945-2486), which has an attractive setting near West Mabou Beach. The Broad Cove Campground in Ingonish is on the ocean (285-2524). Bras d'Or Lakes Campground, run by Sandy andJanice Hudson, in Baddeck (295-2329) is on the lake. The Meat Cove Campground, run by Kenneth A. McLellan (Meat Cove, Inverness Co. N.S. B0C 1E0; 383-2379) is on a bluff overlooking the ocean on the northernmost part of Cape Breton.

MARINAS   Baddeck is the major sailing center for Cape Breton. Here, the Government Wharf welcomes transient craft; Philip McCrae is the wharfinger. There are ample transient slips and size is not a problem; approach depth 60 feet; dockside depth 60 feet; electric power—yes; restaurant within walking distance—yes.

RESTAURANTS   **Baddeck:** The Inverary Inn Resort (see Lodging) has two dining rooms; the more formal is in the main inn, and the more casual is the Fish House, near the lake. Both have very good food.**$-$$**

The Telegraph House (see Lodging) has a pleasant dining room; this is where a reception was held in honor of his Royal Highness, Prince Michael, brother of the Duke of Kent, on February 23, 1984, on the occasion of the 75th anniversary flight of the *Silver Dart,* the 1909 flight which took place as one of Dr. Alexander Graham Bell's experiments.**$$**

The Bell Buoy (295-2581) is a cozy little seafood restaurant near the Government Wharf.**$-$$**

Cabot Trail: The Keltic Lodge (see Lodging) has several dining rooms, some quite formal. One, away from the main Lodge, is a large informal restaurant overlooking the water, where light meals and snacks can be obtained.**$-$$**

Cheticamp: Laurie's Motel (see Lodging) has a nice cocktail lounge and an attractive dining room, with seafood dishes a specialty. There are homemade soups and breads.**$**

Margaree Valley: The Normaway Inn, Box 121, Margaree Valley, N.S. B0E 2C0 (800/565-9463 or 248-2987) is in a beautiful setting right on the Margaree River. The innkeeper is now David MacDonald. It has been open since 1928.**$-$$**

North Sydney: The Gowrie House (see Lodging) is run by C. J. Matthews and K. W. Tutty. Each night during the summer season, they cook a multi-course gourmet fixed-price meal to which townspeople and visitors not staying in the inn may come. The food is superb, with a choice of entree and dessert.**$$$**

LODGING   Nova Scotia has a unique "Check-In Service," with toll-free telephone calls from anywhere in North America (from U.S. except Maine 800/341-6096; from Maine 800/492-0643; from Nova Scotia, New Brunswick, and Prince Edward Island 800/565-7105; from Central and Southern Ontario 800/565-7140; from Northern Ontario, Manitoba, Saskatchewan, Alberta, British Columbia, and the Northwest Territories and the Yukon: 800/565-7166. The caller can make guaranteed reservations at resorts, hotels, motels, inns, and campgrounds, as well as check ferry schedules, book a car-top camping kit, and get weather forecasts. Cape Breton has dozens of inns, hotels, and motels; the following is a necessarily brief list.

Baddeck: The Inverary Inn Resort, Rt. 205 (295-2674), owned by the

MacAulay family, is a sprawling complex, with two heated pools, a whirlpool, boats and rental canoes, a dock, tennis, rental bicycles, a playground, and paddleboats. The rooms are in different buildings; the main in has a pleasant dining room and gift shop. The resort is on Bras d'Or Lake, but not all rooms have a lake view.**$$**

The Telegraph House Motel, Box 8, Baddeck B0E 1B0 (295-9988), is where Dr. Bell chose to stay. Built in 1861, it has long been a town landmark. In *Baddeck and That Sort of Thing,* published in 1896, Charles Dudley Warner recalls his first sight of the Telegraph House: "We came into a staggling village: that we could see by the starlight. But we stopped at the door of a very unhotel-like appearing hotel. It had in front a flower garden. It was blazing with welcome lights. It opened hospitable doors and we were received by a family who expected us." The Telegraph House still treats guests in the same way, with warmth, open fire-places, and home-cooked meals. It is an attractive large house in the center of town, with a porch and a charming dining room, with a colorful collection of cranberry glass in the windows. No matter what you order, try the Telegraph House Oat Cakes; they are not like those packaged in stores and are delicious. Eggs Benedict, made with a wine French cheese sauce, are a specialty at breakfast. The inn will arrange boat cruises on Bras d'or Lake.**$$**

Cabot Trail: The Keltic Lodge, Box 70, Ingonish Beach, N.S. B0C 1L0 (285-2880) is a splendid Tudor-style country inn owned and run by the Canadian government. The Main Lodge has 32 rooms with private baths; the White Birch Inn has 40 rooms with private baths plus a guest lounge with fireplace. The golf course was designed by Stanley Thompson and one visitor from Edinburgh said the golf course itself was worth making the trip from Scotland to Nova Scotia. There are vistas overlooking land and sea; some of the trails off the winding road up to the main lodge fairly call for canvas and brush or camera. The Lodge is very near the East Gate Cape Breton Highlands National Park. There are tennis courts, a pool, a beach, deep-sea and freshwater fishing, and nature trails.**$$$**

The Glenghorm Resort, Box 39, Ingonish, N.S. B0C 1K0 (285-2049), is a large and appealing complex with 74 units on 22 acres with ocean frontage; there is a pool, licensed dining room, and gift shop.**$$**

Cheticamp: Laurie's Motel, Box 1, Cheticamp, N.S. B0E 1H0 (224-2400), run by the McKeown family, was established in 1938 by Laurie Chiasson, who operated a bed-and-breakfast inn in the old homestead. The inn has expanded

Deer Island Ferry, Deer Island

to include three different buildings; most have a view of the Gulf of St. Lawrence or the Highlands.

Margaree Valley: The Normaway Inn, Box 101, Margaree Valley, N.S. B0E 2C0 (248-2987) is in a beautiful setting right on the Margaree River. It has been in operation since 1928.**$$**

North Sydney: The Gowrie House, a bed-and-breakfast inn owned by C. J. Matthews and K. W. Tutty, 139 Shore Rd., Sydney Mines, N.S. B1V 1A6 (544-1050) is in a handsome home overlooking the water, filled with antiques and an extraordinary art collection. Shore Road is not too far from the dock for the Newfoundland ferries and would make a good stopping place if you intend taking one of the ferries. The immense square rooms are beautifully furnished; they have shared baths. The very large breakfast is served in a sunny dining room overlooking the garden. The inn stays full during the summer, so reserve well ahead. Sometimes archaeologists working at the Fortress of Louisbourg stay here. Conversation at breakfast might range from Chinese export porcelain to pre-Socratic philosophers (with an inevitable tinge of the Glace Bay mine tour).**$**

RENTALS   The Keltic Lodge (see Lodging) has 2- and 4-bedroom cottages. There are many housekeeping cottages in Cape Breton, all described in the *Nova Scotia* guide. One, in Ingonish Beach, is Cape Breton Highlands Bungalows, owned by Pat and Marilyn Donovan, Box 151, Ingonish Beach, N.S. B0C 1L0 (285-2000); they have 25 cottages, a playground, pedal boat, canoe rentals, a laundromat, and offer lake swimming. Another, in Sampsonville, in the vicinity of St. Peters, is Carter's Lakeside Cottages, owned by Charles & Ann Carter, RR2, St. Peters, N.S. B0E 3B0 (535-2453); they have cedar log cabins with ocean swimming, boating, hiking trails, lawn and water games, and a daily boat cruise.

CONTACT   Nova Scotia Tourism, 4th Floor Cornwallis Place, 1601 Water St., Halifax, N.S. B3J 3C6 (424-5000) or Cape Breton Tourist Association, 20 Keltic Dr., Sydney River, N.S. For toll-free numbers to call about lodging and general information, see Lodging.

DEER ISLAND
New Brunswick

Area Code 506
LOCATION   Between the Bay of Fundy and Passamaquoddy Bay, north of Eastport, ME and south of Letete, N.B.

SIZE   9 miles by 4 miles.

ACCESS

Ferry: Year-round from Letete, near St. George, a toll-free government ferry, a 20-min. crossing (453-2600); July and August only from Eastport, ME and Deer Island, N.B. (East Coast Ferries Ltd., c/o Stanley Lord, Lord's Cove, Deer Island, 747-2159). **Air:** There is commercial service to Bangor, ME and Saint John, N.B. **Private boat.**

HISTORY AND DESCRIPTION

Deer Island, which has been called the "Masterpiece of the Picture Province," is a tranquil, appealing island, with narrow roads running over hills and an abundance of coves. The very place names suggest limitless and pleasurable summer days—Fairhaven, Hibernia, Little Meadow, Big Meadow Lake, and Chocolate Cove.

As is often the case with islands, there was a lengthy chronological gap between discovery and European settlement. The Champlain-DeMonts expedition passed through the surrounding waters in 1604, but it was not until the 1760s that the region was settled by former British soldiers who had fought against the French and by Loyalists escaping the American Revolution. The latter earned their livelihoods through farming, fishing, and boatbulding. In 1813, the earliest pink-sterned vessel on record was built by Thomas Pendleton, a Deer Island fisherman. The Quoddy sailing pinks were famous and in use until about 1900, when gasoline engines were introduced. In 1890, George E. Richardson took over his father's boatshop, where many innovations in boatbuilding had taken place. Island boatbuilders were well known and practiced the traditional craft of boatbuilding into the present century. Today, there is an aquaculture project in Lord's Cove, pioneered by native Art McKay. Farming of the Atlantic salmon has become a substantial business. Herring weirs, lobster pounds, salmon pens, the fishing fleet, and processing plants are all prominent features of the island.

At the turn of the century, Deer Island, St. Stephen, St. Andrews, Eastport, Campobello, Back Bay, and L'Etete were linked by the *Viking,* a steamboat of 25/30-ton capacity. Steam ferries have been a feature of the Passamaquoddy Bay area at least since the turn of the century, and probably before. The very earliest steamboat, according to *Steamboat Days on the St. John 1816–1946,* a comprehensive history by MacBeath and Taylor, was the *Woodstock.* She sailed on her first trip down the Bay in September 1836; the route was St. Andrews, the West Isles (Campobello, Indian, and Deer Islands), Eastport, Maine, and Calais, Maine. The service was short-lived; the next year she was sold and put on a route between Saint John and the head of the Bay. It is believed she was returned to Passamaquoddy Bay after 1837. Later, the *Eastport, Lubec,* and *Campobello,* operated by the Passamaquoddy Steam Ferry Co., ran during the summer months. They served Lubec, North Lubec, Eastport and Welshpool, Campobello Island.

One has only to read the Deer Island notes in the *Quoddy Tides* (published in Eastport, ME but printed on Deer Island) to detect the affinities Deer Islanders have for their roots. The summer unites families, bringing back a sizeable quota of far-flung relatives from Connecticut, Ohio, California, Tennessee, Massachusetts, Maine, Prince Edward Island, and other locations in the U.S., Canada, and elsewhere to stay on the island, sometimes for weeks, renewing their spirits and ties of kinship.

"What do people do here?" people sometimes ask Audrey Cline, an island teacher who has a bed-and-breakfast inn in her home. "Well, we're in boats quite a bit," she replies. "Then we have sunsets, stargazing, meteor showers, beaches, sunrises, bird and whale watching, wildflowers . . . Deer Island is a place where nothing is planned; there are no malls, no theaters—but we give visitors a chance to appreciate nature, restore the soul, and renew their perspective; we don't need crowds for that." She suggests going as a foot passenger aboard the government ferries *John E. Rigby* and *D. L. McLaren* and watching for osprey, bald eagles, seals, porpoise, and occasionally even whales. Mrs. Cline is an expert on where to find special flora and fauna, such as Indian Pipes and beach heather, as well as Great Blue Herons and other birds.

Dale Barteau, who owns a mill and is the former owner of the Eastport-Deer Island ferry, and his wife Glenna are both descended from early island families. They have a microfilm reader in their home and are transcribing for posterity early records important in the island's history. "There were eight souls in Chocolate Cove last winter," says Barteau. In conjunction with the West Isles Historical Society, he was active in reenacting the first Fenian incursion on Canadian soil, by embittered Irish emigrants, which occurred at nearby Indian Island in 1866. The Fenians captured the customhouse Union Jack and later burned a wharf and some warehouses. The Fenian action helped sway the vote of the Maritime provinces for Canadian union. Chocolate Cove was also the site of Canada's first summer theater (1959; not presently operating).

High school students commute to St. George by bus and ferry. Until 1930, there was no regular ferry service between Deer Island and the Canadian mainland. In 1935, ferry service was established between Deer Island and Eastport, Maine, and, in the mid-1960s, the Campobello-Deer Island ferry service was begun. Today, Deer Island is an important link on the newly established "Quoddy Loop," a suggested tourist route which encompasses such Maine points as West Quoddy Head State Park, Calais, and Eastport, as well as Campobello, Grand Manan, and St. Andrews, N.B. The route is really shaped more like a mobile than a loop, hung with side trips and excursions by ferry. It takes in the region's rugged coastal byways, lakes, rivers, and islands. A luxurious jumping-off spot for Deer Island, not too far from Letete, is St. Andrews by-the-Sea. Here the Algonquin Hotel is an institution in the Maritimes, a grand Victorian hostelry which celebrated its centennial in 1989. It is a Canadian Pacific hotel. At the turn of the century, the steam yacht *Tourist* was chartered by the hotel to make daily trips about Passamaquoddy Bay and the islands. The hotel has 190 rooms, and looks like a mammoth Norman manor house. At sunset, the kilted bellhops lower the flags to the accompaniment of bagpipes. Refreshments are served on the open-air veranda and there are tennis courts and golf courses. The town has many Victorian and Edwardian homes, appealing boutiques, and pleasant water views. The population is about 850 in winter, and about 950–1000 in summer. The majority of summer visitors have roots on the island.

POINTS OF INTEREST   Northern Harbour has the world's largest lobster pound (at certain times of the year, it holds up to a million pounds of live lobster). It was the first ever built, in the mid-1930s, by Edwin Conley of Leonardville. Conley pioneered the marketing of fresh lobster by air to Europe.

The "Old Sow," on the southern end of the island, between Deer Island and Moose Island, is a giant tidal whirlpool visible and audible from Deer Island Point

Herring Smokehouses, Grand Manan

Park when conditions are right. It is particularly evident when the tides are strong, on the new and full moons. Tides in the Fundy region are the highest on the continent, with a fluctuation of 28 feet at the mouth of the Bay of Fundy, and 40 feet at the head of the Bay.

There is much interesting architecture on Deer Island, such as the Baptist Church at Lambert's Cove and the Church of Christ in Leonardville. Both are much the same as when they were constructed over a century ago, with has detailed interior and exterior carving. Many of the houses have mansard roofs, gingerbread trim, square and rounded bay windows, and hand-carved shingles.

The Boat Shop Gallery at Leonardville features watercolors by Jerome Andrews, an outstanding Deer Island artist.

SIGHTSEEING TOURS   Cline Marine offers scenic search tours aboard the *Cathy & Trevor* June through September; whales (Finback, Minke, and Humpback) are sighted on better than 8 out of 10 trips. The boat originates in St. Andrews and calls at Deer Island and Campobello if passengers are waiting. To reserve, call Osprey Travel, St. Andrews (506/529-8844) or the Tourist Information Centre at Butlers Point Ferry Landing on Deer Island (747-2997) or the Cline Marine Office (747-2287).

A pleasant summer day trip is to take the ferry to Eastport, Maine, and have lunch and shop at the Cannery Wharf Restaurants (the Cannery, the Clam Kibbin, and the Pickling Shed, a bar) at the ferry landing, an interesting waterfront complex, or at Romano's, just up the street and overlooking the marina traffic in Quoddy Roads between Eastport and Campobello.

Guests at West Isles World Bed and Breakfast are offered boat tours to nearby islands and whale watch/bird watch cruises.

PARKS, BEACHES   **Parks:** Deer Island Point Park has picnic sites;
AND CAMPING   one may observe the surging tides of Passama-

quoddy Bay here; they rise and fall as much as 28 feet. If conditions are right, you can also see and hear the Old Sow, the Western Hemisphere's largest tidal whirlpool. *Beaches:* The water is cold, but there is a sandy beach at Cummings Cove, Deer Island Point Park. *Camping:* There is camping at Deer Island Point Park, Deer Island Point.

MARINAS   There is a public wharf at Chocolate Cove.

RESTAURANTS   The 45th Parallel Motel and Restaurant, Fair-
                               haven (see Lodging), is the island's only sit-down
                               restaurant.**$**
The Hillside Bakery in Richardson has daily specials such as clam pie, chili, and fish chowder to go.**$**
Maudie's Ship Ahoy take-out restaurant, North West Harbour, near the Big Meadow Pond also has food to go.**$**
Wendy's take-out restaurant is near Pendleton Fisheries and has very good fresh fish dinners.**$**

LODGING   The 45th Parallel Motel and Restaurant, Fair-
                               haven, Deer Island, N.B. E0G 1R0 (747-2231) is
                               run by William and Diane Bustin. Open in sum-
mer only, it has 10 units and 3 housekeeping units.**$**
West Isles World Bed and Breakfast, Lambert's Cove, Deer Island, N.B. E0G 2E0 (747-2946), is a a very appealing inn run by Audrey J. Cline, a native islander and local teacher and her husband Ralph, a semi-retired fisherman who has spent a lifetime in Fundy waters. There are three rooms, all sunny and pleasant, plus a kitchenette available for guests' use. Boat tours to some of the nearby islands are offered also.**$**
Other bed-and-breakfast inns are Fairhaven, run by Mr. and Mrs. B. Calder, Fairhaven, Deer Island, N.B. E0G 1RO (747-2961); McKenney's Bed & Breakfast, Lord's Cove, Deer Island, N.B. E0G 2J0 (747-2959); Mitchell's Bed and Break-fast, Lord's Cove, Deer Island, N.B. E0G 2J0 (747-2275), and Darby Hill Bed and Breakfast, Lambertville, Deer Island, N.B. E0G 2EO (747-2069). (All are moder-ate.)
The Algonquin Hotel, St. Andrews, N.B. E0G 2X0 (529-8823) is a luxurious resort within easy reach (see History and Description).**$$$**

RENTALS   There are cottage rentals only if privately
                               arranged.

CONTACT   Cline Marine (747-2287) or Tourism New
                               Brunswick, Box 12345, Fredericton, N.B., Can-
                               ada E3B 5C3 (800/561-0123), or Quoddy Bay
and Fundy Isles Tourism Office, Box 9, St. Stephen, N.B., Canada E3L 2X3 or Box 688, Calais, ME 04619 or Tourist Information Centre, Butlers Point Ferry Landing (747-2997).

GRAND MANAN
New Brunswick

Area Code 506

LOCATION   Approximately 9 miles off the coast of Maine in the
Bay of Fundy.

SIZE   6¹/₂ miles by 21 miles.

ACCESS   ***Ferry:*** From Blacks Harbour, N.B. (Coastal Transport, Ltd., Brunswick House, Suite 1501, 44 Chip-
man Hill, Saint John, N.B. E2L 2A9;
506/634-8513.) ***Air:*** The island has a landing strip, recently paved and lighted,
suitable for private aircraft. There is commercial service to Bangor, ME and to
Fredericton, N.B. and Saint John, N.B. ***Private boat.***

HISTORY AND   The largest of the Fundy Isles, Grand Manan, 6¹/₂
DESCRIPTION   miles by 21 miles, has all the elements of an ideal
island — a ferry voyage for access, steep cliffs,
and lighthouses. It is at once both solid and vulnerable, with imposing striated
cliffs rising over 400 feet. As yet, there only scattered homes and beachfront
cottages; it is mercifully lacking in condominiums and shopping centers.

Many visitors are naturalists (birdwatching and offshore whale-watching are
excellent); others, such as the theologian who rents house-keeping cottages on
the island each summer for himself and his researchers, are seeking a quiet
refuge and inspiration from the sea and a tranquil ambiance. The island has
always been a mecca for birdwatchers; James Audubon visited here in 1833, and
later sketched, aboard the sailing ship *Ripley,* the birds he had seen. There are
whalewatching cruises every day from mid-August through mid-October. Laurie
Murison, Manager of the Grand Manan Whale and Seabird Research Station,
says that no matter how prepared visitors think they are, the sound of the whales
blowing is a stunning and unforgettable experience.

Grand Manan is of great interest geologically because its eastern side is
formed of sedimentary rock and the western section of volcanic rock. The
dividing line is visible at Red Point, near Seal Cove.

Access is from Blacks Harbour, a 2-hour crossing. In summer the ferry is
actually the pulse of the island. According to Bill Daggett, a native Grand
Mananer and Tourism Officer of the Anchorage Provincial Park, time can be
measured by the surge of vehicles from the ferry every two hours. The trails take
2–5 hours; backpacking is discouraged.

For the visitor, the only awkward occasion may arise if he is offered a tangy,
salty, dark purple delicacy called dulse, an edible seaweed with iron and
phosphorus. Dark Harbour is the center of the dulse harvesting. It is dried on
nets along the rocky beach, then eaten raw or toasted, or added to soups. True
Grand Mananers munch dulse from paper bags as we would eat potato chips or
popcorn, but, sadly, most visitors find it an acquired taste. It is said that beer
accompaniment helps.

Grand Manan is not an island with neon or night clubs; much social activity
centers on the island's 15 churches. For the visitor, evening entertainment on the
island is likely to take the form of a film on the day's whalewatching (presented
each evening at the Marathon Inn) or a quiet stay on the bench at the Whistle to
watch the sunset. One can also stroll about the harbor and peer at one of its most

memorable features, the heart-shaped weirs (called "wares"), built to trap herring. Herring are a staple of the island economy (for smokehouses, see Points of Interest).

The novelist Willa Cather and her companion of 40 years, Edith Lewis, spent numerous summers on Grand Manan, at Whale Cove, in a small cottage she built. Edith Lewis described Grand Manan as "tranquilizing to the spirit, opening up great spaces for it to roam in." She stated that Willa Cather found the island "a quiet resource, a congenial place to write in that beautiful silence, with the wind blowing in the elder bushes and the songs of hundreds of birds."

The population of the island is about 2,800, year round and as many as 10,000 in summer. Grand Mananers feel a very strong pull to return to their roots; island houses are seldom sold, but retained by families who move away and then return each summer. The headquarters of Anchorage Provincial Park is a stately Victorian home built by the great-grandfather of the present superintendent, Bill Daggett; he and his wife Linda Joan enjoy living in his ancestral home.

"Development can't happen here; we're too inaccessible," Grand Mananers say hopefully, but, alas, the examples of Ocracoke and Nantucket belie their optimism. Islander Laurie Murison realizes the danger. "People are too naive here," she says, "and we don't always appreciate how important it is to preserve what we have." She considers that visitors' questions hint of the almost imperceptible edge of change — "they ask, 'why do you not have street signs? Where are the shopping centers?'" As it is, Grand Manan is replete with all the necessities a sensible person could want. There are water vistas from every part of the island, 16 hiking trails, colorful wildflowers (lupens and fireweed are dominant in the summer season), and an abundance of birds (over 250 species have been sighted). Dolphins and whales are just offshore, as well as seals.

It comes as something of a shock to learn how many homes and parcels of property are actually owned by people from the United States (Vermont, Kentucky, Pennsylvania, and New Jersey, to name only a few). Some American property owners have put up "No Trespassing" signs, which is considered very bad form on Grand Manan: "It is just not our way," say islanders. "Our way of life is to help each other."

In fact, a sense of property often seems absent on Grand Manan and its small sister island, White Head. On White Head, it is not unusual for residents to offer their cars to strangers at the wharf, so that they may tour the island. The same generosity prevails on Campobello, where Afton Green, of the Herring Cove Provincial Park, drives down to the wharf to offer his car to visiting yachtsmen. The evils of stateside litigation may, like killer bees, be working their way north, but they have plainly not reached New Brunswick or its "children of the sea."

POINTS OF INTEREST Swallowtail Lighthouse (1860) is one of the first features of the island visible from the ferry on the voyage to the island. It is a congenial subject if you have a telephoto lens. The Southwest Head Light (1880) is at Southern Head, which has the steep gray cliffs which are one of the more striking topographic features of Grand Manan. A third light, the Long Eddy Point Lighthouse and fog horn, at the Whistle, is at the northern tip of the island.

The Grand Manan Museum in Grand Harbour offers the Moses Memorial Bird Collection (Allen Moses spent a lifetime observing birds and collecting specimens for Canadian and United States museums), the Gannet Rock light lens, and a good geological display.

Shoreline, Grand Manan

One of the few remaining herring smokehouses in the Atlantic Provinces is located in rust-red buildings at Seal Cove; here, passers-by can see the herring hanging in the unshuttered window. It takes a month to smoke the herring. Most of the smoked herring, however, is sent off-island.

The former home of novelist Willa Cather is at Whale Cove. You can park your car and walk in to view the old house, which sits in the center of a field.

SIGHTSEEING TOURS   Ocean Search (662-3804), *weather permitting,* offers daily sailing expeditions to view whales, porpoises, seals, and pelagic birds, mid-July through September.

Sea Watch Tours aboard the *Sea Watcher* (662-8296) are very popular; they leave from Seal Cove and go to Machias Seal Island, where there are nesting Atlantic puffins, razorbills, artic terns, and other birds (mid-June through first week in August). Reservations are essential as the number of people allowed to land is restricted. The same company runs a few whalewatching trips each season from August through September.

An interesting side trip is to take the ferry *Lady White Head* from Ingalls Head to the small offshore island of White Head. Here townspeople often offer their cars to visitors for island exploration. For information, call Coastal Transport, Ltd., 634-8513.

Visitors from the States bound for Grand Manan may well wish to plan a night enroute. A luxurious jumping-off spot for Grand Manan, not too far from Blacks Harbour, is St. Andrews-by-the-Sea; it is well worth spending a night at the Algonquin Hotel, an institution in the Maritimes (see the entry for Deer Island).

PARKS, BEACHES   *Parks:* The Anchorage Provincial Park, 500
AND CAMPING   acres, occupies a beautiful site by the sea; it is a game refuge (no hunting). *Beaches:* Deep Cove Beach, long and curving, is popular, though the water can be cold. Grand Mananers, as a rule, are not avid beach-goers, but a scan of cars on a typical day

reveals tags from New York, Quebec, New Hampshire, Ontario, and Nova Scotia.
Camping: There are 51 sites at the Anchorage Provincial Park, with expansion
expected in the very near future. The Park had a very busy season in 1989.

MARINAS   The North Head Marina (Coastal Transport, Ltd.,
                               634-8513 or Kenny Brown, 662-3350) can
                               accommodate private boats. There is no limit on
length and the number of private boats is usually not a problem. Approach depth
15 feet; dockside depth 9 feet; electric power—yes; restaurant within walking
distance—yes.

RESTAURANTS   The Marathon Inn at North Head (see Lodging)
                               has a large dining room with a potbellied stove.
                               However, the Inn recently acquired a lounge
license, so the dining room may become a lounge or bar, and the present living
room the dining room. In any case, the menu has fresh seafood and the food is
generally plain and nourishing.**$-$$**
   The Compass Rose (see Lodging) is very popular.**$-$$**
   The Griff-Inn restaurant is at North Head (see Lodging).**$**
   The Water's Edge Restaurant is at Sea Cove.**$**

LODGING   An attractive bed-and-breakfast inn, with full
                               breakfast, is the Compass Rose (North Head,
                               Grand Manan, N.B. E0G 2M0; 662-8570). It is
right on the harbor with a fine terrace.**$**
   The Grand Harbour Inn, Grand Harbour, Grand Manan, N.B. E0G 1X0
(662-8681) is a country inn with antiques where Teddy Roosevelt once stayed;
rates include a continental breakfast.**$**
   The Marathon Inn, North Head, Grand Manan, N.B. E0G 2M0 (662-8144), is a
sprawling complex built in 1871 by a Captain James Pettes, and is run by Jim and
Judy Leslie. On a hill set back from the harbor, the inn has plain rooms and
mostly shared baths, but an excellent water view. The lounge has a library
promising enough delights for a summer's stay (such as works by Mrs. Humphry
Ward and other Victorian novelists, along with *Monsters of the Purple Twilight).*
Each night during the summer there are films and narrated presentations about
the whale watching cruises which for visitors are perhaps the island's most
popular activity.**$-$$**
   The Surf-Side Motel, North Head, Grand Manan E0G 2M0 (662-8156) is the
only motel on the island at present; it has 26 units and 1 housekeeping unit.**$**
   There is also a bed and breakfast inn on White Head Island, Sand Dollar
Cottages (662-3437), very clean and appealing, run by Mr. and Mrs. Colby
Cossaboom.**$**

RENTALS   There are many housekeeping cottages on the
                               island, but reserve well ahead for July and
                               August. One popular cottage cluster is Cliff by the
Sea Cottages at Deep Cove (Gerald and Maude Hunter, Seal Cove, Grand
Manan, N.B., Canada E0G 3B0; 662-3131); another is Spray Kist Cottages (Mrs.
M. Laffoley, Seal Cove, Grand Manan, N.B., Canada E0G 3B0; 662-8640).

CONTACT   Grand Manan Tourism Association, Box 193,
                               North Head, Grand Manan, N.B., Canada E0G
                               2M0 (call Anchorage Provincial Park, 662-3215 or
New Brunswick tourist information, 800/561-0123).

THE MAGDALEN ISLANDS
(Îles-de-la-Madeleine)
Quebec

Area Code 418

LOCATION

In the Gulf of St. Lawrence, approximately 133 miles from the Gaspe Peninsula and 80 miles from Prince Edward Island.

SIZE

Approximately 60 miles by 5 miles.

ACCESS

Ferry: From Souris, Prince Edward Island, the *Lucy Maud Montgomery* makes a daily 5-hour crossing from April 1 until the end of January (C.T.M.A. Traversier, C.P. 245, Cap-aux-Meules, Îles-de-la-Madeleine, Quebec, Canada G0B 1B0, 418/986-6600). The ferry leaves Souris at 2 p.m. *except Tuesdays;* on Tuesdays it leaves Cap-aux-Meules at 8 p.m. and Souris Wednesday mornings at 8 a.m. From Montreal, there is a weekly cargo boat, the *CTMA Voyageur,* which can accommodate 15 passengers (Inter-Voyages, Montreal, 514/866-8066 or Cap-aux-Meules, 418/966-6600). *Air:* There is commercial service to the Magdalens from Toronto, Montreal, Charlottetown, Halifax, and many other destinations. The airlines are Canadian International, Inter-Canadian, and Air Alliance. Note that in English the airport is designated as Grindstone, the English name for the Île du Cap au Meules. *Private boat.*

HISTORY AND DESCRIPTION

You can fly to Havre-aux-Maisons, in the Magdalens, but the most enjoyable trip (or, as islanders say, *un voyage inoubliable*), is aboard the *Lucy Maud Montgomery.* This is a paradoxically English name for the ship serving this most French of islands. The 5-hour sea voyage provides a fast

Grosse-Île, The Magdalen Islands

immersion course in the Gallic heritage and orientation of the Magdalens. Slim French women, who have perhaps been on a group trip to Montreal or Quebec, converse animatedly as they apply eye makeup and blush in the ladies' room. Bright-eyed, dark-haired toddlers, chattering eagerly in French, bring life to the shipboard "jardin d'enfants," a colorful, picket-fenced play area with toys and games. It is these cherubic children, awash in books and educational toys, who will grow up to carry on the vibrant cultural life which distinguishes the Magdalens from many other islands. In the Café de la Grave at Havre-Aubert, for instance, a unicorn mobile advertises poetry readings with such well-known poets as Gaston Miron of Quebec. There is a theater at Havre-Aubert with plays, jazz, and folk music. Violinists, writers, and painters are at work on the island. The lower, French-speaking portion of the islands have the more intellectual pursuits, along with some superb restaurants. The smaller English-speaking population inhabiting the northern region of the islands is, as a whole, less inclined to seek the off-island university educations and graduate degrees off-island which many of the French-speaking young people have acquired. Your visit will be richer, naturally, if you speak French, but there is much for the English-speaking visitor to enjoy.

The islands are part of the province of Quebec. The archipelago is made up of about a dozen islands, six of which are connected to one another by very long, thin sand dunes. The four sections representing the inhabited islands are the Île du Havre Aubert and Île d'Entrée to the south; the Île du Cap aux Meules; the Île du Havre aux Maisons and Île aux Loups in the middle; and the Île de la Grande Entrée and Gross-Île to the north. All are linked by dunes and can be visited by taking Highway 199 from one end to the other. To see the scenery, take the secondary roads as well; some of these are not suitable for motor vehicles, but you can go a fair distance and then walk. Two other islands are separate, but are considered part of the archipelago: Île d'Entrée, located about 6 miles east of Havre-Aubert, and Île Brion, about 10 miles north of Gross-Île. The islands are French speaking, with the distinctive Acadian accent, which has a melodic lilt sprinkled with archaic words from ancestral France.

The topography is seemingly flat, but, when you actually near the coast, you find high sandstone cliffs. Their shapes can almost change overnight, the forces of wind and waves boring new arches and smoothing former promontories. The winds can be very strong, even in summer. The visitor is not so much conscious of travelling from one island to another as of moving between communities. The ferry from Souris arrives at the small town of Cap-aux-Meules, which is the commercial center of the islands. There are rental cars available if you need one, as well as bicycles. It is easy to see the islands in one day by car. "There is nothing out of the way here," says Paul Thériault, a young islander just back from teaching French to Thai refugees. Paul is typical of many young people here who have left the island, perhaps first to learn English in Halifax or another part of Canada, and then to pursue undergraduate and graduate degrees. Many study in Montreal, and then return there to work, relishing the cosmopolitan ambiance and having a network of friends and former classmates (in fact, there are more Madelinots in Montreal than on the islands). At the same time, most return to the islands for at least part of the summer for reunions with family and friends, and, in later life, a good many resettle on the islands.

Food in the Magdalens is excellent. "We have many good tables," says islander Claude Richard, and the fact is indisputable. A true French love of cuisine is very evident here, and, though the islands may not appear to be crowded, it is best to reserve at restaurants. The weekly newspaper *Le Radar* has a restaurant column, avidly read by locals and visitors alike. In addition to the restaurants, there are three bakeries. The Boulangerie La Fin'Croûte, Inc., at Cap-aux-Meules, has baguettes, island-style pies, croissants, and many other breads and pastries. Other bakeries are at Havre-Aubert and La Vernière.

The first historical mention of the islands was in the diary of explorer Jacques Cartier. He named them "Les Arraynes," from the Latin "arena," or "sand." He wrote that what is now Île Brion "has the best soil that we've seen, for twenty acres of this soil is worth more than Newfoundland. This island is full of beautiful trees, prairies, fields of wild wheat, and flowering pea plants as beautiful as I've ever seen in Brittany, and they seem to have been planted with much labour." The islands were named in honor of Madeleine Fontaine, wife of the islands' first lord, François Doublet de Honfleur, in 1663. In 1629, however, Samuel de Champlain wrote the name "La Magdeleine" near the vicinity of the islands on a map. The Micmac Indians named it "Menagoesenog," or "islands swept by waves."

In 1755, when the peaceful Acadian people were expelled from Nova Scotia, many were deported to an Anglo-Protestant environment in New England. A few families managed to escape the deportation and came to the Îles-de-la-Madeleine. At that time they were commercially controlled by Richard Gridley, who ran the walrus hunt and the islands' fisheries. Other familes came from the French-speaking islands of St. Pierre and Miquelon, which are French Territories near Newfoundland. The Acadians, good farmers and fishermen, really began the colonization of the Magdalens, which, in French, are called the Îles-de-la-Madeleine. The islands were annexed to Newfoundland until 1774, when they were annexed to Quebec. Isaac Coffin was granted the islands in 1787, and he exercised a feudal domination over the islands. Many islanders, exploited by merchants also, emigrated to Quebec's Lower North Shore. The Madelinots could not buy back their lands until 1895. Today there are about 15,000 inhabitants, including over 700 English-speaking islanders of Scottish descent. There are 8 municipalities: L'Île du Havre-Aubert, L'Île d'Entrée, Cap-aux-Meules, Fatima, Étang-du-Nord, Havre-aux-Maisons, Grosse-Île, and Grande-Entrée.

Island architecture is largely traditional; houses and barns are painted in a variety of bright colors. Among the conventional features, showing the Acadian and French origins of the inhabitants, are the small enclosed porch used as an entrance; roof decorations, carved in wood with a delicate design; a veranda with wooden decorations; painted or stained cedar shingles and shakes. *Baraques* — small square barns with a sliding roof, controlled by a pulley system, used to protect hay from bad weather — are particularly evident at Havre-Aubert.

The summer season is very short, from mid-June through the end of August. Avoid the last two weeks in July. The Quebec construction industry closes down July 15, and many of the workers come to the Magdalens; accommodations and restaurants are very crowded. Tourism is now the second most important industry, after fishing. The Magdalens are a source of fascination to Europeans; it is not unusual to find journalists from Milan or Paris arriving to do feature stories (one even hired a helicopter for a photography session).

Don't be surprised if you hear the stewardesses talking about the weather in "the Maggies." Weather is exceptionally important here, where the beaches and high-ridged dunes are often racked with wind, and where the summer season is shorter than in most places, from about mid-June to mid-August. It is best not to come the last two weeks of July, when the Quebec construction industry closes down and many workers vacation on the Magdalen islands. If you do come then, make reservations well ahead. The better restaurants, some of which are very good indeed, also fill up; you may not see many people on the island, but you still need to book.

POINTS OF INTEREST   The Musée de la Mer at Pointe Shea, Havre-Aubert, is well worth visiting, with a section on shipwrecks and another on the history of the island.

The Aquarium des Îles is on the dock at Havre-Aubert has an assortment of fish and aquatic life from the Gulf of St. Lawrence, including seals.

At Bassin there is a lighthouse at L'Anse-a-la-Cabane with a view of the cove, fishing port, and island landscape.

The fishing village of L'Étang-du-Nord is of interest; one landmark is the *dolosses* on the pier, cement anchors which break the waves. The cliffs here are spectacular, but here and at Old Harry they have been pounded and eroded and reshaped.

Belle-Anse at Fatima has striking red cliffs, beaten by the sea, but be very careful about going too near the edge; they are softer than they look and may collapse.

At Havre-aux-Maisons, tour the butte Chez Mounette; the Butte du Vent on the Île du Cap aux Meules has the best view of the whole archipelago.

Many craftsmen welcome visitors to their workshops; all the following are on the Chemin de la Grave in Havre-Aubert: Artisanat La Baraque (wood carvings and alabaster stone sculptures); Les Artisans du Sable (items made from sand; here you can get exquisite paperweights as well as larger sculptures); La Banquise du Golfe (sealskin items and handpainted sweaters); Creations Delphine (handwoven clothing). On the Île du Cap-aux-Meules, Chemin des Huet in Fatima, you can find pottery at Les Ateliers Art-Gil; on the Île du Havre aux Maisons, on the Chemin de la Carrière, glass-blown items are shown and glass blowing is demonstrated at Verrerie La Méduse. Also on Havre-aux-Maisons is the art gallery Point-Sud, which has exhibits of contemporary artists.

Rocky Coastline, The Magdalen Islands

The Île d'Entrée is the principal excursion for visitors (see Sightseeing Tours). It has been said that visiting this island is like visiting the Magdalens a second time. A ferry goes there from the port of Cap-aux-Meules. This is the only inhabited island not linked by land to the archipelago; it was not settled until 1870. Lobster fishing is the principal occupation. Some 195 English-speaking people live here, descended from Scottish settlers and from the stranded victims of shipwrecks. It is best to plan a full-day visit; footpaths encircle the island and entice the visitor to go hiking. The lighthouse and Anglican church are of interest. Big Hill (almost 600 feet) is the highest point in the islands.

SIGHTSEEING TOURS   There are excursions to the Île d'Entrée aboard the *Tony*, leaving at 11 a.m. from the marina at Cap-aux-Meules; call 986-2304 or 986-2245.

There are bus tours of the islands given by the Service d'Autobus Madeleinien, Cap-aux-Meules (986-2845).

There are also sightseeing tours by air; for reservations call 969-2271 or 986-6067.

From Cap-aux-Meules several companies offer boat trips. The *Gertrude-Béatrice* goes to the Île d'Entrée; call Captain Yvon Renaud, 937-2716 or 986-5690. Ferries to the Île d'Entrée leave at 8 a.m. and 3 p.m. daily except Sunday.

Fishing trips, along with excursions to Île d'Entrée and to the cliffs, leave from the port at Cap-aux-Meules; call 986-2304 or 986-2245.

From Île d'Entrée there are also deep-sea diving trips and trips to Île Brion, Rocher aux Oiseaux, and to the lagoon in Grande-Entrée; call 985-2148.

PARKS, BEACHES AND CAMPING   **Parks:** There are three wildlife reserves in the islands. One is Île Brion, about 10 miles from Gross-Île. Several families once inhabited Île Brion; later it was used seasonally for fishing, until the 1970s. Today it is uninhabited. The second, Pointe-de-l'Est in Gross-Île, is accessible from Highway 199 (between East Cape and Old Harry). The third is Rocher aux Oiseaux, which is an elevated rock 20 miles northeast of Gross-Île, which became a bird sanctuary 20 years ago. It is very windy and access is difficult, though there are the remains of an old wharf. **Beaches:** There are more than 180 miles of beaches, many of which are very scenic, nestled among red sandstone cliffs. In early August, there is a sand castle contest on the Sandy Hook beach in Havre-Aubert. The best beaches are located where there are dunes. Beware of swimming on windy days even if you are a good swimmer; waves are usually the sign of strong currents along the coast. It is best to choose a sheltered beach. Among the most visited beaches are the Dune du Nord, Plage de l'Ouest, Plage du Havre, Cap de la Pointe, and the Plage de la Pointe de l'Est on Grosse-Île. **Camping:** There are several campgrounds, at Chemin du Bassin (937-5408; the Plage du Golfe at Bassin (937-5224); Le Barachois at Fatima (986-6065); Camping Gros Cap at Gros-Cap (986-4515); and Grande-Entrée 800/361-0349). The season is usually June through August, though some are open earlier and later.

MARINAS   There are two marinas complete with services in Cap-aux-Meules and in Havre-Aubert. The Club Nautique in Cap-aux Meules (986-3774) has 60 sites, a captain's lounge, showers, electricity, and gas. In Havre-Aubert, Les Plaisanciers du Havre has 38 sites, a captain's lounge, showers and electricity. There is another marina in Havre-aux-Maisons for smaller boats. Some establishments rent sailing dinghies and give windsurfing courses to children and adults. The Centre Nautique de l'Istoriet in Havre-Aubert has a sailing school, windsurfing, and equipment rentals. For information about the weather, or other questions, at Cap-aux-Meules, call the Wharfinger's office, 986-3785.

RESTAURANTS   There are a number of excellent restaurants in the Magdalens; the following is only a selection. A full list is available from the Tourist Bureau.

The Auberge la Jetée, Cap-aux-Meules (see Lodging) is a friendly establishment with country French cuisine in a simple dining room. The pot-en-pot is very good.**$$**

The Café de la Grave, which used to be a general store and is over 100 years old, is delightful, serving croque-monsieur, special coffees, croissants, and homemade cakes. It is in the heart of Havre-Aubert, with mobiles advertising forthcoming poetry readings (held in the cafe) and such events as the Montreal Guild of Musicians. It is run by Jean-Marc Cormier and Claude Painchaud. This is a good place for lunch or dinner, as you can walk around the small town and see the aquarium also (937-5765).**$$**

La Maison de la Couline at Bassin (937-5522) has the noted island specialty "Pot-en-Pot," a casserole with seafood in a delectable cream sauce and delicate pastry on top. It also offers crab quiche, seafood crepes, and cranberry cake with butter sauce.**$$-$$$**

La Moulière (in Le Vieux Couvent), Havre-aux-Maisons (969-2233), is in an old convent, with many of the architectural features still evident, such as the ecclesiastical embossed plaster, now pale pink; the decor is stylish, with a black and pink color scheme. This is the only stone structure in the archipelago. The restaurant specializes in excellent mussels in different sauces. Be sure to reserve.**$$-$$$**

La Petite Spaghetta, L'Anse a la Cabane (937-5675), has excellent pasta dishes flavored with many types of sauces, including *spaghetti de la cheffe,* containing the famous cream of the islands. There are also Italian dishes made with seafood, such as lasagne with crab. It has a sea view and is a local favorite.**$$-$$$**

La Table des Roy, La Vernière (986-3004), is one of the top restaurants on the island; reservations are essential. They specialize in fresh fish and seafood and are closed Mondays.**$$$**

Le P'tit Cafe, Havre-aux-Maisons (969-2736), has seafood and grilled dishes, as well as patés, sandwiches, and parfaits.**$-$$**

The islands have a lively night life; during the summer season many young people routinely gather in bars, discos and clubs until 3 or 4 in the morning. The Bar-Terrasse Le Barachois in Fatima is popular, and there is a Quebeçois party every Tuesday at the Bar le Cachot, also at Fatima. Chez Gasparo, at the Hotel au Vieux Couvent, has various performers throughout the summer season. Au Vieux Treuil is the cultural center at Havre-Aubert, with shows, theater, and musicals.

LODGING   A complete list of accommodations can be obtained from the Tourist Bureau. Here is a selection:

The Auberge la Jetée, Cap-aux-Meules (986-4446) is near the ferry landing; it was once the home of a doctor. Four of the 10 rooms have shared baths.**$**

The Hotel Chateau Madelinot, Route 199, Cap-aux-Meules, C.P. 44 G0B 1B0 (986-3695), is a large establishment, with over 100 rooms, all with private baths.**$$$**

The Hotel au Vieux Couvent, Havre-aux-Maisons (969-2233), is in an old convent (see Restaurants); there are 9 rooms, 8 of which have private baths.**$**

The Motel Thériault, Dune-du-Sud, Havre-aux-Maisons C.P. 207, G0B 1K0 (969-2955) has 19 rooms, all with private baths.**$-$$**
The Motel des Îles, Route 199, Havre-aux-Maisons, C.P. 58 G0B 1K0 (969-2931) has 28 rooms, all with private baths.**$-$$**

RENTALS   There are many cottages, rooms, and houses for rent. The Madelinots, known for their hospitality, open their doors to lodge visitors. You may rent a room in a family's home, a house, a cottage, or an apartment. The Tourist Association publishes a list of available accommodations and also has a reservation service which will make bookings (see Contact).

CONTACT   Tourist Information Office, 128, Chemin du Débarcadère, Cap-aux-Meules, Îles-de-la-Madeleine, Quebec, Canada G0B 1B0 (986-2245) or Tourisme Quebec, C.P. 20 000, Quebec, Canada G1K 7X2 (418/643-2230).

PRINCE EDWARD ISLAND

Area Code 902
LOCATION   In the Gulf of St. Lawrence, off the coast of New Brunswick and Nova Scotia.

SIZE   140 miles long; width varies from 4 to 40 miles.

ACCESS   **Ferry:** From Cape Tormentine, N.B. to Borden, P.E.I. (Marine Atlantic, 121 Eden St., Bar Harbor, ME 04609; Continental US 800/341-7981; ME only 800/432-7344; Maritime Provinces 800/565-9470; Newfoundland and Labrador 800/563-7701; Quebec and Ontario 800/565-9411). From Caribou, Nova Scotia to Wood Islands, P.E.I. (Northumberland Ferries, Ltd., Box 634, Charlottetown, PEI C1A 7L3; from Nova Scotia, New Brunswick, and P.E.I. 800/565-0201). From the Magdalen Islands to Souris, P.E.I. (C.T.M.A. Traversier, C.P. 245, Cap-aux-Meules, Îles-de-la-Madeleine, Quebec, Canada G0B 1B0, 418/986-6600). **Air:** There is commercial service to Charlottetown. **Private boat.**

HISTORY AND   Anyone who has the misfortune, on P.E.I. of being
DESCRIPTION   a P.F.A. ("Person From Away") can never really compensate, but the next-best thing is to have a solid attachment to Anne of Green Gables. "I do not know whether pilgrimages to the shrines of famous men ought not to be condemned as sentimental journeys," wrote Virginia Woolf of a visit to Haworth, home of the Bronte sisters, in the first of her essays to be accepted for publication. By this standard, virtually the entire north shore of Prince Edward should be banished from the traveler's itinerary, because it is certainly pervaded by the spirit of Lucy Maud Montgomery and her fictional creation, Anne Shirley, and in many respects it is open to the charge of sentimentality. Visitors, however, in whose childhood memory Anne has assumed epic dimensions (and they are legion) would reply that there is nothing wrong with sentimentality. Sometimes it seems the island is awash with devotees seeking to identify the Lake of Shining Waters, the Haunted Wood, and the Dryad's Bubble. Their perceptions are perhaps far more alert than in their native habitat to the natural beauties of the island, which Lucy Maud Montgomery called "the only Island there is." Despite a plethora of commercial attractions

House of Green Gables, Cavendish

which have sprung up in the region near the houses with authentic Montgomery associations, the island, in many respects, seems to have changed little in the past century. Even today, it is easy to envision Anne's trip from the railway station to Avonlea in Matthew Cuthbert's cart, breathlessly admiring the blooming wild cherry-trees, slim white birches, and flowering plums.

There is no stronger testimony to the power of fiction than the bevy of small Japanese girls who throng Prince Edward Island wearing wide-brimmed "Anne" hats with red braids. American and Canadian girls have them too. "These braids only come off to get the hair washed; I'm wondering what's growing underneath," said one mother. "She's worn it five days now." Part of *Anne of Green Gables* is included in one of the junior secondary school Japanese language textbooks; each year, from 5 to 7 thousand Japanese visit the island.

The houses connected with Anne are seemingly simple to keep straight (see Points of Interest). There is the Green Gables House at Cavendish; her birthplace, in Clifton, New London; the Anne of Green Gables Museum at Silver Bush, Park Corner; and Anne's House of Dreams at French River, depicting her bridal home. There are also numerous commercial establishments invoking the names of Anne, Marilla, or Matthew. It is when you see the photographs in the museum, and begin reading manuscripts on display, that dizziness sets in. The most enduring legacies, over a century later, may well be the red roads, blossoming fruit trees and foliage, and the sense of Anne's whimsical imagination. Mark Twain, then 73, wrote Lucy Maud Montgomery that Anne was "the dearest, and most lovable child in fiction since the immortal Alice."

The island tends to be overshadowed by the legend of Lucy Maud Montgomery, but there are many other aspects well worth exploring. The countryside, with its lush green pastures and small farms, has been compared with that of Ireland. Sometimes the entire landscape seems to take on a red hue, with red cliffs, sand dunes, and soil; the base of the island is a red sandstone.

The first inhabitants were the Micmac Indians, some 2,000 years ago. They were followed by French settlers in the early 1700s; there is still a strong French presence on the island. This is especially evident in the Evangeline section. Located in the western portion of the island, it is surrounded by the Lady Slipper Scenic Drive between Miscouche and Mount Pleasant, a town which dates back to the mid-1700s. Descendants of the original French (Acadian) settlers survived a sweeping expulsion from the region by the British in 1758 and, since then, have toiled to keep their language, culture, and traditions alive.

There are more than 60 ports and harbors around the island; with their lobster traps, wharves, breakwaters, boat pens, and capstans they are well worth exploring. The fishermen are usually affable, ready to talk about what's biting. There are bays, coves, and creeks, especially on the south shore; the north shore is more rugged, with cliffs.

POINTS OF INTEREST   The leading places of interest on the island are aligned along three scenic drives, which are clearly marked on road maps and signs.

Blue Heron Scenic Drive, south-central:

This ends at Charlottetown, which has many sites of interest, including the Confederation Centre of the Arts, which is a memorial to the Fathers of Confederation. The Centre has a museum, a provincial library, and a handsome theater where, each summer since 1964, the musical *Anne of Green Gables* has delighted visitors. One or two of the "children" are over 40, but you would be hard put to tell them from the actual children in the cast. A number of actresses have portrayed Anne over the years.

St. Dunstan's Basilica is one of Canada's largest churches; it is known for its twin Gothic spires and Italian carvings.

The Anglican Cathedral has murals by Robert Harris, the noted Canadian portrait painter.

Government House overlooks Charottetown Harbour.

Victoria is a small seaside village which is home to the Victoria Playhouse, a repertory theater company.

Blue Heron Drive, north-central:

This drive goes past or near most of the Lucy Maud Montgomery historic sites.

The House of Green Gables at Cavendish, in the National Provincial Park, is free; it belonged to cousins of Lucy Maud Montgomery with whom she played as a child. This is the original building which opened in 1938 and which was approved by the author. Her grave is nearby in Cavendish Cemetery.

The Lucy Maud Montgomery birthplace, in Clifton, New London, is where she lived until she was 21 months old and her mother died.

The Anne of Green Gables Museum at Silver Bush, Park Corner, is still owned by Montgomery relations. She lived here at various times with her aunt and uncle, and the "Lake of Shining Waters" is nearby.

Anne's House of Dreams at French River was the model for the home of the fictional characters "Anne" and "Gilbert" as newlyweds; furnishings are from the turn of the century and there are scale models of the old Presbyterian Church in Cavendish and Diana Barry's house on the grounds.

Also of interest on the Blue Heron Drive are Woodleigh, at Burlington, a miniature English village with lawns, gardens, and reproductions of castles, cathedrals, and fortifications, some of which are large enough to enter.

Lady Slipper Drive, western Prince Edward Island:

The Bottle Houses at Cap-Egmont are made of varicolored bottles of all shapes and sizes; they were made by the late Edouard T. Arsenault.

The Acadian Museum in Miscouche depicts the history of the Acadian people through a collection of artifacts, illustrations, and texts.

Malpeque Bay is famous for Malpeque Oysters, whose sharp, clean taste was world renowned before a 1917 epidemic decimated the oyster beds. Today the beds are farmed, and over 10 million oysters are harvested annually.

Le Village des Pionniers Acadiens in Mont-Carmel is a re-created Acadian pioneer village, circa 1820, which even has a French dinner theater.

Lennox Island is the province's largest Indian reservation, with a variety of distinctive crafts.

The Green Park shipbuilding museum near Bideford has restored houses and artifacts of interest.

Summerside is the island's second-largest community; it is a port, which also has beautiful old homes, a marina, a dinner theater, and, in summer, harness racing, fiddling and step-dancing contests, and lobster suppers. It is well known for many sports events; the P.E.I. Sports Hall of Fame is a permanent display in the Eptek National Exhibition Centre.

West Point Lighthouse

The West Point Lighthouse (see Lodging) is an example of preservation at its best. Carol Livingstone, granddaughter of William Anderson MacDonald, first lighthouse keeper (called "Lighthouse Willie"), was the moving spirit behind a community effort to save the lighthouse, abandoned once the Coast Guard put in electricity. Through a Community Development Program, the lighthouse was once again put into use. It houses a museum of lighthouse history, and is filled with some of the original keeper's furniture, rooms for guests, a craft shop in which local women display beautiful needlework, and a restaurant. Hiking walks through the nearby hollows, planned by history researchers and environmentalists, leave from here. There is a Provincial Park nearby also, as well as a beach, and there is a summer festival the third weekend in July.

Kings Byway Drive (southeast):

Orwell Corner is a small village restored to the late 1800s; Island author and physician, Sir Andrew Macphail, was born here.

Montague, an old town, features the Garden of the Gulf Museum, which displays pioneer farm and cooking implements.

Just off the drive is Point Prim, where the oldest lighthouse on the island, built on Point Prim in 1846, is still in use.

Kings Byway Drive, northeast:

Georgetown has the King's Playhouse, a summer theater presenting professional repertory productions.

Murray Harbour is a pretty fishing village; there is also a log-cabin museum near here with antiques over two centuries old.

Souris is a pleasant town, the terminus of the ferry to the Magdalen Islands. The name, meaning "mice," derives from the proliferating mice brought over on ships during the settlement of the island; the town was so named by French settlers.

SIGHTSEEING TOURS   At Wood Islands, next to the ferry wharf, cruises aboard a 40-foot Newfoundland schooner may be booked.

In front of the Confederation Centre in Charlottetown there is a tour booth where city tours aboard a double-decker London bus may be booked; the same company runs longer tours to other parts of the island, including the Green Gables house.

Heritage P.E.I. Tours, Ltd. (Clara J. Howard, 892-7243) offers walking tours of Charlottetown.

Innova Tours, Inc. (H. Shirley Horne, 894-3074) organizes custom tours to the countryside and fishing villages of the island.

Headland Nature Tours, Ltd. (Katherine Clough, 566-4961) offers off-the-beaten-track tours of the island.

Prince Edward Sightseeing Tours, located in the Prince Edward Hotel (Box 2644, Charlottetown, C1A 8C3, 566-5466), offers personalized island tours in town cars and vans with English, French, and Japanese-speaking guides.

North Shore Sea Tours and Water Taxi leave from North Rustico (Mike Doyle, 675-2501 or reserve at the Seagull's Nest gift shop on Court's Wharf).

Charlottetown Harbour Cruises (892-5889 or 894-9207) offers tours of the harbor.

Victoria Sailing Excursions leave from the wharf at Victoria (Captain Ray Belanger, 658-2227).

Seal-watching cruises leave from Montague (Captain Dan Bears, 838-3444) and Murray River (Garry's Boat Tours and Deep-Sea Fishing, 962-2494).

PARKS, BEACHES
AND CAMPING

Parks: Prince Edward Island has 30 provincial parks and 1 national park. One of the most scenic of the national park areas is at Cavendish, site of the Green Gables House; the beach here has huge striated red rocks. Red Point Provincial Park, near Souris, is also attractive and features an ocean beach. The national park (at Rustico Island) has an outdoor theater with evening slide and film presentations. *Beaches:* Prince Edward Island has dozens of beaches. The one at Red Point Provincial Park is very popular, as is the one at Stanhope. Another appealing beach is in the western part of the island, at the West Point Lighthouse, near the Cedar Dunes Provincial Park; this is more isolated. Panmure Island Provincial Park has a supervised ocean beach with fine white sand and dunes nearly 20 feet high. The Jacques Cartier Provincial Park also has a supervised beach. *Camping:* There is camping at many of the provincial parks and at more than 30 private campgrounds; their facilities are fully listed in the *P.E.I. Visitors Guide.* Campsites vary; some are wooded, others are in grassy fields, and still others are on the ocean or at resorts. None of the campgrounds is far from the three scenic drives. The provincial and national park campgrounds do not permit fires on the beaches.

MARINAS

The Silver Fox Curling and Yacht Club, Summerside (436-2153), managed by Colleen Marsh, is glad to have visiting boaters. There are ample transient slips handling boats of almost any length and depth is not a problem; they have had yachts up to 180 feet long as well as tugboats. The marina is in the middle of town, ideal for exploring; a shopping mall and museum are very near. Facilities include dockside electricity, lounge, showers, and eating place. There are other restaurants also within walking distance.

The Charlottetown Yacht Club (892-9065) welcomes visiting boaters, but has limited docking facilities; yachts must be moored in the Charlottetown Harbour.

RESTAURANTS

The Claddagh Room, 129 Sydney St., Charlottetown (892-9661), is a small restaurant in a restored building not far from the Confederation Centre. One specialty is Galway Bay Delight (scallops and shrimp sauteed and flambeed in Irish Mist finished with fresh cream). Reserve well ahead.**$$**

The Off Broadway Cafe, 125 Sydney St., Charlottetown (892-0632), is in a restored building of the 1870s, with attractive padded booths, woodbeams, and brick. Crepes are a specialty. Reserve well ahead; in summer there are more prospective diners than can be accommodated.**$$**

The Lord Selkirk Dining Room, in the C.P. Prince Edward Hotel (see Lodging) has a very pleasant atmosphere and excellent food.**$$$**

If you have a chance, stop in at one of the lobster suppers. These dot the island; one is the Saint Ann's Church Lobster Supper in Hunter River; it has been operating since 1964. These suppers are usually held from the last week in June through the second week in September. They are very reasonable, and usually include lobster, potato, seafood chowder, vegetables, and dessert such as strawberry shortcake. A special plus is having a chance to talk with islanders and exchange notes with other tourists.**$**

An excellent lunch or tea is available at the Green Gables House restaurant. "Marilla's Tea" and "Matthew's Tea" are served all day. "Marilla's" consists of delectable tiny sandwiches and pastries, along with beverage; "Matthew's" is heartier.**$**

LODGING There are over 650 establishments offering accommodation on Prince Edward Island, including hotels, inns, motels, bed-and breakfast homes, and housekeeping cottages. The list which follows is necessarily brief, but should suggest the type of accommodation available. The island is small enough that the major attractions are easily accessible from most places. However, if you should stay in Charlottetown and want to visit the far west section, the drive can take several hours.

C. P. Prince Edward Hotel and Convention Centre, 18 Queen St., Box 2170, Charlottetown C1A 8B9 (566-2222). This hotel is on the waterfront, and has very large, comfortable, modern rooms. Those in business class are almost suite-sized, with a low divider separating the bed from the seating area, which has sofas, easy chairs and a large desk. It is near several interesting restaurants and the Confederation Centre (see Points of Interest).**$$$**

The Charlottetown, Box 159, Charlottetown C1A 7K4 (Eastern U.S. 800/565-9077; Maritimes 800/565-0207) is situated in downtown Charlottetown (corners of Kent and Pownal Sts.) This 108-room hotel has a a popular summer dinner theater, a marble-floored lobby, a Georgian ballroom, and many other amenities.**$$$**

Elmwood, Box 3128, Charlottetown, P.E.I. C1A 7N8 (368-3310) is a 24-room Victorian manor house, once in Jay Macdonald's family, which Jay his wife Carol are converting into an elegant inn. The Macdonalds are from Connecticut, but have returned to the island which was the home of Jay's ancestors. The rooms are appealing enough to be on a house tour; one, in an octagonal shape, has been richly decorated with a custom-made rose and green bordered rug, colors echoed in the lamps and other furnishings. There are antiques, hand-made quilts, and luxuriously thick towels. Jay often makes his special immense popovers for breakfast, which is served in a large and elegant dining room. The inn is within walking distance of the downtown attractions, which is handy if you arrive in a leased plane, as some of their guests do.**$$**

Lobster Traps, North Lake

Inn at Bay Fortune, Souris RR #4, C0A 2B0 (687-3745), is undergoing masterful renovation by innkeeper David Wilmer. The inn was built in 1910 by playwright Elmer Harris, author of *Johnny Belinda* (a 1940 Broadway hit); in 1972, it was bought by the actress Colleen Dewhurst (among her roles was Marilla in the television production of *Anne of Green Gables*); she brought up her children here. It has a tower, the fourth level of which is an observation room and sanctuary for reading. The inn has ten spacious suites, each with a private bath, a view of the sea, and a fireplaced sitting area.**$$$**

Kindred Spirits Country Inn and Cottages, Cavendish C0A 1N0 (963-2434) is a large home, which Al and Sharon James have restored, in the resort area adjacent to the Green Gables House. It has large rooms and suite, all with private bath and color television. They also have a number of housekeeping cottages (see Rentals).**$$**

Silver Fox Inn, 61 Granville St., Summerside C1N 2Z3 (436-4033), owned by Julie Simmons, is in an historic house with period furnishings and a pleasant atmosphere with personalized service. Each of the six rooms has a private bath; rates include a continental breakfast, and there is a sitting room with television for guests.**$$**

Shining Waters Lodge and Cottages, Cavendish C0A 1NO (963-2251), owned by Barry and Judy Clark, is also located in the Cavendish area, 500 meters from the main ocean beach. It was once the home of the prototype of Rachel Lynde, who is a principal character in *Anne of Green Gables*. There are ten rooms with private baths and color television. There is a whirlpool-spa, a library, and a sundeck overlooking the ocean. There are also housekeeping cottages (see Rentals).**$$**

Stanhope by the Sea, Box 2109, Charlottetown C1A 7N7 (672-2047) overlooks Covehead Bay and the National Park. This has been a country inn since 1917. The original inn has 35 rooms; they are slowly being refurbished, but some of the furniture is rickety and the rooms do not have private telephones. There is a new annex with 24 rooms. Swimming, boats, and tennis are offered.**$$-$$$**

The West Point Lighthouse, O'Leary RR2, C0B 1V0 (June–September 859-3605; September–May 859-3117; see Points of Interest), with its rooms, museum, craft shop, and restaurant, is a much cherished community enterprise. "Everybody is willing to do their bit for the lighthouse," says Carol Livingstone, who was responsible for its conversion into an inn. One room is especially for honeymooners, with a high lace canopy over the bed; honeymoon rates include champagne, a fruit basket, and a continental breakfast. The curtains are designed to accommodate the tapered walls of the lighthouse. The nearby beach and the isolated position of the lighthouse make this an unusual and appealing place to stay.**$**

RENTALS   There are hundreds of housekeeping cottages on the island, but not all are on the coast; for a complete listing, consult the *Visitors Guide*. Here are a few which are particularly appealing:

Kindred Spirits Country Inn and Cottages (see Lodging) offers 13 housekeeping cottages. They are heated, and amenities include decks, color television, barbecues, toys, children's movies, campfires, and babysitting.

Rodd Brundenell River Resort is at the Brundenell River Provincial Park, Roseneath, Box 67, Cardigan, C0A 1G0 (652-2332; 800/565-9077 from Eastern

Festival, St. Pierre and Miquelon

US). This complex is on spacious landscaped grounds overlooking the Brundenell River. There are modular designed resort chalets in cluster formation (some with kitchen; some without), as well as tennis courts, an 18-hole golf course, two pools, rental boats and canoes, nature trails, and a playground.

Shining Waters Lodge and Cottages (see Lodging) has 20 housekeeping cottages (1–3 bedrooms) with many amenities — sundecks, picnic tables, barbecues, cribs, toys, shuffleboatd, campfires, and babysitting.

CONTACT   Department of Tourism and Parks, Box 940E, Charlottetown, Prince Edward Island, Canada C1A 7M5 (North America 800/565-0267; also 902/368-4444).

ST. PIERRE AND MIQUELON
Territory of France

LOCATION   The islands are located about 9 miles from the southernmost tip of the Burin peninsula in Newfoundland and about 186 miles from Cape Breton.

SIZE   St. Pierre is 5 by 6 miles; Miquelon is about 80 square miles. The area of the islands is about 242 square kilometers.

ACCESS   *Ferry:* Two boats run from Fortune. The first is the *MV St. Eugene V,* a large, sleek hydrofoil; for information, call in St. John's 709/722-2606 or in

Fortune 709/832-2006. It begins running in mid June and runs to the end of September. It takes 55 mins. and leaves Fortune at 2:30 p.m. and St. Pierre at 1 p.m. The second is the *MV Arethusa* (38 Gear St., St. Johns, Newfoundland, A1C 2J5; 709/738-1357 or Box 39, Fortune, Newfoundland; 709/832-0429). It runs from mid-June through mid-September, leaving Fortune at 1:30 p.m. and St. Pierre at 11:15 a.m. Both companies work with tour groups offering boat/hotel packages (see Lodging); if you do not have a car and wish to fly to St. John's and make a side trip to St. Pierre and Miquelon, these are highly recommended. Vans transport passengers to Fortune from St. John's. *Air:* From Montreal, Halifax, and Sydney, N.S.: Air Saint-Pierre, B.P. 4225, Saint-Pierre 97500, tel. 41.47.18; Miquelon tel. 41.65.85; Halifax 902/873-3566, or Sydney, 902/562-3140. Flights vary in frequency but do not run every day. From St. John's: Air Atlantic; in Newfoundland 709/722-3892; in St. Pierre tel. 41.24.26. A regular airline from Sydney, N.S. to St. Pierre is expected to begin running in the spring of 1990. *Private boat*.

HISTORY AND DESCRIPTION	It is hard to realize that a territorial part of France lies just off Newfoundland, in the form of a group of islands. St. Pierre is the administrative capital

and commercial center of the islands. Miquelon is linked by a narrow sandy isthmus to a third island, Langlade. There are another dozen rocky islets just barely showing above sea level.

The islands were discovered about 1520 by the Portugese navigator Jose Alvarez Faguendes, who called them "The Islands of the 11,000 Virgins" (because he arrived on the feast day of St. Ursula, martyred in Cologne with 11,000 virginal devotees). In 1535, Jacques Cartier took possession of the archipelago for the King of France. At this time, St. Pierre was being settled by people coming from Brittany, Normandy, and the Basque country, fishermen who were working on the Banks from early in the sixteenth century onward. In the seventeenth century it became an official French territory, and during the struggles of the eighteenth century, France managed to retain these islands as a pied à terre for her fishing fleets.

The inhabitants were originally fishermen from Normandy, Brittany, and the Basque country, though a few families may be traced back to Acadia and Ireland. The population was deported to Canada, the U.S.A., and to France, only to come back each time with a dogged determination. The islands were finally ceded to France in 1816. In 1976, the islands became a Department of France. In 1985, they were granted the status of "Territorial Collectivity of the French Republic," so they now enjoy representation in the French National Assembly and the Senate. There is a high quality of French spoken on the islands. Cod fishing is still the principal occupation of the people, though the new fishing technologies and factory ships are tending to deplete the supply of fish. There are two fishing companies, Interpêche and La Miquelonnaise, which have fleets and fish processing plants. Tourism is the only supplemental source of income.

The landscape is rugged and rocky, with extensive moors broken by low hills. The shoreland consists of cliffs and unpolluted beaches of sand or pebbles. The climate is harsh, humid and windy, with a good deal of fog. It is best to visit between the end of June and the end of September, though the season really begins coming to an end in late August. The population of St. Pierre, the administrative and commercial center, is about 5,800; Miquelon has about 700 people. A container ship calls there every week to stock the Miquelon shops. Langlade is a summer vacation spot, which has a small inlet, numerous summer cottages, nature walks, a pretty river, and a very good beach with fine sand.

The theory held by cultural anthropologists such as Pierre Bourdieu that cultures can be transmitted is virtually proved in St. Pierre and Miquelon. There is a startling French quality to the island, as opposed to the English quality of the Newfoundland mainland; one feels the differences stretch back over time, back to the colonial settlements, back to the time of Agincourt and Henry V, back to the Norman Conquest. There is a grace and charm to St. Pierre; the very telephone book, which is sold in hotels for a modest fee, has a splendid coat of arms, that of St. Pierre, with a sailing ship, lions couchant, fleur de lys, and ropes entwined about anchors and sails. Inside, there is a portfolio of color pictures of the islands at various seasons. For an analogy to France in the appearance of St. Pierre, one must look not so much to the lavender-hued soft landscape of Provence or the hillside villages near the Mediterranean as to the harder contours of the northern towns of Dieppe or Rouen. The tall stone houses have lace curtains, picket fences, flower gardens, and French house numbers; the streets are narrow, with a decidedly European flavor. There are pealing cathedral bells and crusty baguettes. In the summer evenings, carousel music jingles as a small train, "Le P'tit Saint-Pierre," winds around the misty docks, with the lights of large container ships reflected in the water, and the hilly streets of the small town. The Mediterranean game of "La Petanque" is played on a city court; Basque games are also popular, as the Basque folklore is the last to survive here. Gendarmes are sent from France for 3-year tours of duty; at certain times they are visible in full regalia. Some of the houses are painted in pastel colors, like those on Faro in Iceland. There are frustrations for the American (and Canadian) visitor: shop doors slam shut between 12 and 2, restaurants do not open until 7 p.m., and the plugs and current are European (no laptop computers unless they use batteries; no hair-dryers; no electric shavers). The island is not, in a way, tourist-oriented; there is no surfeit of cheap souvenir and T-shirt shops and fast-food places. Visitors are, however, welcome, and the food is excellent.

Watch out for cars; there are 3,000 cars on St. Pierre for 6,000 people. The car to the right has the right-of-way. The roads are not always in good repair, as the island looks to France for road repair money, and it is not always forthcoming. The island has its own television station, and also receives programs from France beamed by satellite. In addition, the island also receives the Canadian Broadcasting Company (CBC) from Marystown in Newfoundland. You really need to plan a visit of 2 or 3 days in order to make side trips, do a little shopping and touring, and allow for bad weather to cause cancellation of side trips, which often happens, even in summer. Part of the reason the island does not seem geared wholly to visitors is that the season is very short, mainly from late June through late August. To land on the islands, citizens of the U.S. and Canada need some form of identification; citizens of other countries need a valid passport.

Many of the inhabitants of St. Pierre have summer homes on the winding road which goes around the back of the island. Most have names, such as the "Chateau Savoyard," after the nearby fresh-water lake. They have no electricity, though some homes have wind generators. They do have telephones. Most people have lavished more care and attention on their summer homes than on the winter ones. "Cutty Sark Villa" was built of Scotch whiskey crates from the era of Al Capone. From 1920–1933, the island was a notorious smuggling center, which brought prosperity. Sometimes as many as 300,000 cases of whiskey a month passed through St. Pierre. There is a small Al Capone museum in the lobby and dining room of the Hotel Robert, with photographs of that era. French goods are of great interest to tourists, as they are duty-free; wines, cheeses, and perfumes, especially, are in demand. There is a Cultural and Sports Centre on the island, where two or three productions per year are put on by a local amateur theater group, "Les Tréteaux du Centre." Music, photography, and pottery classes are taught; there is a library, a gym, a swimming pool, and an auditorium with a good sound system, attracting concert artists.

Miquelon has a small settlement. At the northern tip, Le Cap is known for its scenic cliffs and the many seagulls which swoop past. The island has a sandspit known as the dune of Langlade in the middle. The remains of over 600 shipwrecks are visible from the island.

There has been speculation that, one day, the islands might revert to Canada, but this is not within the realm of possibility for most islanders. "We are too French deep inside to accept a Canadian suzerainty," says Stephané Claireaux of St. Pierre. One feels that St. Pierre and Miquelon will always be profoundly Gallic; there will be the vowels of pure French, the aroma of crusty baguettes, and, more tangibly, the pure Norman cheeses and Quimper pottery gracing the shop windows and the incomparable flavor of French cuisine.

POINTS OF INTEREST   The museum has historical artifacts, boat models, wildlife exhibits, and memorabilia from the two world wars. The cemetery is of special interest, with its situation overlooking the sea, individually tended graves, elaborate sculpture, and unusual architecture. Some graves incorporate the portholes from shipwrecks.

The Roman Catholic Cathedral of St. Pierre has 5 priests and 1 bishop.

There is a grotto modeled after that of Bernadette in Lourdes.

SIGHTSEEING TOURS   In the evening, there is "Le P'tit Saint-Pierre," leaving from the street in front of the main pier (tel. 41.38.39); it tours the little city of Saint-Pierre and there is a bilingual commentary.

Sightseeing buses (run by H. Roulet, BP 45, 43, rue Raymond Poincare; tel. 41.22.41) make a more extensive tour of the island of St. Pierre, both morning and evening. Mr. Roulet speaks excellent English and also offers taxi tours of the island.

There are trips to Miquelon aboard the *St. Eugene V;* the crossing takes 55 minutes. A bus takes visitors around the principal points of interest on Miquelon, then crosses to Langlade over the Dune (the sand isthmus joining the two islands). Seals and wild horses can often be seen. The noon meal is included in the price.

There is also a crossing to Langlade aboard the *St. George,* which takes 60 minutes; here you can take nature walks. The island is unhabited except in summer, when summer vacationers from St. Pierre retreat to their small cottages.

There is a launch near the Tourist Bureau which goes to L'Ile aux Marins (Sailors' Island), 7 minutes away, for a 2-hour tour. Here there are a church and some other buildings, and it is hoped to restore them and make the island more of a tourist attraction.

PARKS, BEACHES   **Parks:** At present there are no parks, but there
AND CAMPING   may eventually be a nature reserve. On Langlade there are many wild deer and birds; people often go there by speedboat to enjoy the wildlife and beaches. **Beaches:** There are rocky beaches on the north side of St. Pierre, but they are cold. One side of the island is fresh and one is salty. The best beaches are on Langlade. **Camping:** "In St. Pierre, it's allowed everywhere but the airfield and the town streets," says Marc Comier of the Tourist Bureau. On Miquelon, the Amenage campground is free; it has a barbecue, picnic tables, a toilet and sink with cold water; for

information, contact the Tourist Bureau, Miquelon (tel. 41.61.87). There is also camping in Fortune at the Horse Brook Trailer Park; contact the Fortune Town Office, 709/832-2810.

MARINAS	The harbor at St. Pierre has a deep-water quay which can accommodate vessels with up to a 32-foot draft.

RESTAURANTS   **St. Pierre:**

Le Chantecler, at the Hotel Ile de France (see Lodging) is a delightful dining room with beams and a stone fireplace. There are many seafood specialties, and the service is gracious.**$$$**

Chez Dutin, 20 rue Amiral Muselier; tel. 41.24.92, is in the home of Madame Josephine Dutin; it is open daily, offering one menu. The food is excellent. Reservations are preferred.**$$-$$$**

Chez Eric, at the Hotel Central (see Lodging), offers local specialties; it is closed Mondays.**$$$**

Le Caveau, 2 bis rue Maître Georges Lefèvre, tel. 41.30.30, specializes in boudin de St. Jacques; closed Mondays.**$$-$$$**

Miquelon: Chez Mimi, 5 rue Victor Briand; tel. 41.62.55, offers local specialties.**$$**

Entre-Nous, 34 rue Baron de l'Espérance, tel. 41.61.24, offers traditional French cooking; it is open daily.**$$-$$$**

LODGING   **St. Pierre:**

The Auberge des Vacances, 18 rue Ducouédic; tel. 41.39.19, has six rooms and is very reasonable.**$**

The Hotel Central, 32 rue Maréchal Foch; tel. 41.32.90,, has 10 rooms and a restaurant, Chez Eric.**$**

The Hotel Ile de France, M. Georges Lefèvre; tel. 41.31.62 or tel. 41.28.36, is a 3-star and extremely pleasant hotel, with very nice rooms. It is centrally located and rates include a continental breakfast. You may book directly or take a van/boat/hotel package tour offered by Lloyd G. Lake, Ltd., Fortune, Newfoundland, 709/832-2006 or 832-1955; Loveless Bus Service brings passengers to and from St. John's, a 4-hour trip with one rest stop where you can get a snack or meal. They also handle smaller guest houses. The boat crossing is on the *MV Eugene V.***$$$**

The Hotel Robert, Quai de la République, tel. 41.24.19 or, in Newfoundland, 709/722-3892, is the other 3-star hotel in St. Pierre, with a small gift boutique. Around the walls of the dining room and lobby are photographs from the Al Capone era. The hotel only accepts its own lodgers for meals. The dining room is not so elegant as that in the Ile de France, but the personnel are extremely pleasant. You may book directly or through SPM Tours Ltd., 38 Gear St., St. John's, Newfoundland, A1C 2J5, 709/722-3892; Fortune office Box 39, Fortune, Newfoundland A0E 1P0; 709/832-0429 or, after hours, Mrs. Brenda Patten, Fortune, 709/832-1199. Transportation from St. John's is by van and the boat crossing is on the *MV Arethusa*. You can also drive to Fortune and take a package tour, including the boat and hotel, from either tour company but it is wise to reserve first.**$$$**

The Motel Rode has housekeeping units (see rentals).

There are also several boarding houses on St. Pierre; write Tourist Bureau for a full list.

Miquelon:
The Hotel L'Escale, 24 rue Victor Briand; tel. 41.62.04,, has six rooms with bath.**$$**

RENTALS   The Motel Rode, 27 rue Beaussant, BP 1033, St. Pierre and Miquelon; tel. 41.37.47, has efficiency units featuring kitchennete/living room, bedroom, and bathroom, accommodating up to 6 persons.

CONTACT   St. Pierre and Miquelon Tourist Office, B.P. 4274, Saint-Pierre and Miquelon, 97500; tel. 41.22.22/41.23.84. Also the French Government Tourist Office, 1981 McGill College Ave., Suite 490, Montreal, Quebec, Canada H3A 2W9; 514/288-4264, and the French Government Tourist Office, Dundas St. West, Suite 2405, Box 8, Toronto, Ont. M5B 1Z3; 416/593-4717. You can also contact the Goora Travel Service, Box 308, North Sydney, N.S., Canada B2A 3M4.

Sculpture at the Airport, St. Pierre and Miquelon

ACKNOWLEDGMENTS

I have been greatly indebted, in the preparation of this volume, to a number of individuals who have taken time from their busy schedules to read and offer suggestions on the drafts of various entries: Ned Cameron on Thacher Island, Massachusetts; Christine Bogdanowicz of the Shoals Marine Lab and Dr. Faith Harrington on the Isles of Shoals, New Hampshire; West Elliot of Boothbay Harbor on Squirrel Island, Maine; Jeffrey Burke on the Isle au Haut, Maine; Rebecca J. Lunt of Frenchboro, Maine; Stephané Claireaux of St. Pierre/ Miquelon, Canada; Donald Grant, Gillette Castle, Connecticut, on Seldon Neck State Park; Beverly Anne Deans on the Thousand Islands, New York; Afton Green on Campobello, Canada; Bill Daggett on Grand Manan, Canada; and Audrey Cline on Deer Island, Canada. Beverly, Afton, Bill, and Audrey also offered tours and substantive help on visits to their respective islands. Barbie Bornemann Stainton not only read my entry on Great Cranberry Island, Maine, but also photographed the island for me. Barbie and Agatha Cabaniss of Islesboro, Maine, are both Bryn Mawr classmates who are fortunate enough to live on islands and who were very generous in sharing their impressions; Agatha also offered kind hospitality while I was on Islesboro.

Friends who have given extensive assistance include Shirley Uber of North Kingstown, Rhode Island, with whom I made a delightful trip to the Maine islands; Betty and Fred Scott of Richmond, Virginia, who shared their intimate knowledge of Squam Lake and Chocorua Island, New Hampshire; Peter Arne Hutchinson of Rockville, Maryland, a native of Maine and enthusiastic supporter of this volume from its inception; Ruth Fritz of Cambridge, Massachusetts, who first disclosed the existence of that remarkable island off Rockport, Thacher; and Ruth and George Ursul of Brookline, Massachusetts, who have long been conversant with Mount Desert and other New England islands. Prudence Heller of Manhattan supplied extensive help in sorting out some of the New York islands, especially City, Shelter, and Fishers. My aunt, Dorothy Williams, has as always been a wonderful listener and perceptive critic. My brothers Martin and Oscar Grant and Oscar's wife, Jane, have assisted me in every way; Oscar and Jane first suggested including the Thousand Islands in New York. My cousins Jean and Myron Kauffman of Richmond made a fortuitous trip to Vermont just as the manuscript was in its final stages, and gave me welcome impressions of fall on the islands in Lake Champlain. The scholar and critic Mary Ann Caws, with whom I grew up on an island, has explored a great many herself and, as always, inspired me with her high standards of writing and of travel. Jean Davis has sustained me through many crises, and Estelle Crump has patiently assisted me in ways too numerous to count. Cynthia Rider of Newark, Delaware, also a Bryn Mawr classmate, and her mother, Hazel Josselyn of Providence, first introduced me to the wonders of New England and interpreted Nantucket long before I was privileged to explore it. Ken Stein, of Sayville, New York, made very perceptive suggestions regarding Fire Island and enabled me to go there aboard one of the ships of his Sayville Ferry Service fleet. Joseph and Viola Connolly gave me a memorable morning on Block Island and shared their very valuable knowledge of that community.

A number of people have answered minute queries with great patience and sent special literature on various islands: Robert J. Cole of the Winnipesaukee Flagship in New Hampshire; Alberta Buswell of Swans Island, Maine; Jim Brown of North Haven Island, Maine; Harriet Williams of Matinicus Island, Maine; Bob and Mary Burton of Monhegan, Maine; Diana Pardue of the Statue of Liberty National Monument; and Johanna Sherwood of Deer Isle, Maine.

I was made especially welcome in Canada and given every assistance by Frank LaFleche of the Canadian Embassy; Ralph Burtt of New Brunswick, who offered invaluable insights into the province and gave me the pleasure of his company visiting Grand Manan, Deer, and Campobello, as well as St. Andrews; Nancy Harris of Nova Scotia, who arranged a memorable visit to Cape Breton and even descended with me into the Glace Bay Miners Museum; Lynda Hanscome and Laurie MacCormack of Prince Edward Island; Claude Richard and Paul Thériault of the Magdalens (Paul gave me an excellent all-day tour).

In addition I was greatly assisted by Nancy Martin of the Boston Harbor Association; George Fowler of the Lake Champlain Islands Chamber of Commerce, Barbara J. Beeching of the Connecticut Department of Economic Development; Bettie Perreault of the Connecticut Valley Tourism Commission; Cindy M. Chaltain of the 1000 Islands International Council; Teresa Mitchell of the Seaways Trail, in the Thousand Islands; Michael Quencer of the New York Office of Parks, Recreation, and Preservation; E. T. Jones of Wellesley Island, Thousand Islands, New York; Laura Chase of Fredericton, New Brunswick; and Marianne Murray of the New York Convention and Visitors Bureau, Inc. This volume and my previous books have been greatly enriched by the maps drawn by cartographer Tom Roberts.

My Peachtree editor, Susan Thurman, has presided over the publication process with aplomb and care; my copy-editor, Helen Weil, has saved me from grievous errors and gently restrained stylistic extravagances. My agent, Susan Urstadt, has encouraged me in the conception and execution of the island series and always been accessible and helpful. My husband, Lewis, has, as Henry James might say, "seen me through," assisting and encouraging me in countless ways. My son, Alex, has given valuable material assistance with the Boston Harbor Islands and has been immensely supportive. My other indebtedness is expressed all too impersonally in the list of *Sources for Further Reading*.

SOURCES
FOR FURTHER READING

Non-fiction

Barrette, Roy. *A Countryman's Journal; Views of Life and Nature from a Maine Coastal Farm*. Boston: Godine, 1986.

Beaubelle, March. *Coastal Connecticut*. New York: Peregrine Press, 1979.

Burroughs, Polly. *Guide to Martha's Vineyard; Guide to Nantucket*. New York: Globe Pequot, 1985.

Caldwell, Bill. *Islands of Maine*. Portland, ME: Gannett, 1981.

Coffin, Robert P. Tristram. *Yankee Coast*. New York: Macmillan, 1947.

Conkling, Philip W. *Islands in Time*. Camden, ME: Down East, 1981.

Dow, Richard A. and E. Andrew Mowbray. *Newport*. Lincoln, R.I.: A. Mowbray, Inc., 1976. (Write Box 460, Lincoln, R.I. 02865).

Duncan, Roger F. and John P. Ware. *A Cruising Guide to the New England Coast*. New York: Dodd, Mead & Co., 1983.

Eliot, Charles W. *John Gilley of Baker's Island*. Originally published in 1899 by *The Century Magazine*; reprinted 1985 by Acadia Publishing Co., in cooperation with Acadia National Park, Maine.

Fardelmann, Charlotte. *Islands Down East: A Visitor's Guide*. Camden, ME: Down East, 1984.

Gambee, Robert. *Nantucket Island*. New York: Norton, 1986.

Hill, Ralph Nading. *Yankee Kingdom: Vermont and New Hampshire*. New York: Harper & Row, Publishers, 1960.

Kales, Emily and David. *All About the Boston Harbor Islands*. Hingham, MA: Hewitts Cove Publishing Co., Inc., Hingham Shipyard, 349 Lincoln St., Hingham, MA 02043.

Lombard, Asa Cobb Paine, Jr. *Cuttyhunk: Bartholomew Gosnold's Contribution to Our Country and the Plymouth Colony*. Cuttyhunk Island, MA: 1976 (Reynolds-DeWalt Printing, Inc., New Bedford, MA).

Long, Charles A. E. *Matinicus Isle: Its Story and Its People*. Lewiston, ME: Lewiston Journal Print Shop, 1926.

Lunt, Vivian. *A History of Frenchboro, Long Island Plantation, Hancock County, Maine*. Frenchboro, Maine: 1976. (For copies, write the Frenchboro Historical Society, Frenchboro, Maine, 04635.)

MacBeath & Taylor. *Steamboat Days on the St. John 1816-1946*. St. Stephen, N.B., Canada: Print n' Press, Ltd., 1982.

McLane, Charles B. *Islands of the Mid-Maine Coast: Blue Hill Bay*. Woolwich, ME: The Kennebec River Press, 1982.

Manley, Seon and Robert. *Islands: Their Lives, Legends, and Lore*. New York: Chilton, 1970.

Maynard, Mary. *Island Hopping in New England*. Dublin, NH: Yankee Books, 1986.

Muskie, Stephen O. *Campobello*. Camden, ME: Down East, 1982.

Parsons, Eleanor C. *Thachers: Island of the Twin Lights*. Canaan, NH: Phoenix Publishing, 1985.

Perrin, Noel. *Second Person Rural*. Boston: David R. Godine, 1980. (Vermont).

Pratson, Frederick. *Guide to Eastern Canada*. New York: Globe Pequot, 1983.

Rich, Louise Dickinson. *My Neck of the Woods*. Camden, ME: Down East, 1976 (first published 1950).

Rich, Louise Dickinson. *The Coast of Maine*. New York: Thomas Y. Crowell Co., 1962.

Russell, Robert. *The Island*. New York: Vanguard Press, 1973. (Thousand Islands, NY).

Rutledge, Lyman V. *The Isles of Shoals in Lore and Legend*. Boston: The Star Island Corporation, 1971.

Snow, Edward Rowe. *The Islands of Boston Harbor* 1630-1971. New York: Dodd, Mead & Company, 1936, 1971.

Spurling, Ted. *The Town of Cranberry Isles: A Thumbnail Sketch of Five Main Islands*. Brownsville, Vermont: Van Houten Graphics, 1979, 1986. Copyright 1979 by Theodore and Cara Spurling under the title: *The Town of Five Islands*.

Thaxter, Celia. *Among the Isles of Shoals*. Boston: Houghton Mifflin, 1873; reprinted Bowie, Maryland and Hampton, New Hampshire: Heritage Books, Inc., 1978.

Tree, Christina. *Maine: An Explorer's Guide*. Woodstock, VT: Countryman Press, 1984.

Tree, Christina and Peter S. Jennison. *Vermont: An Explorer's Guide*. Woodstock, VT: Countryman Press, 1983.

Whitman, Herbert. *Exploring Old Block Island*. New York: Chatham, 1980.

Verrill, A. Hyatt. *Along New England Shores*. New York: G. P. Putnam's Sons, 1936.

The WPA Guides to Connecticut, Maine, Massachusetts, New Hampshire, New York, Rhode Island, and Vermont are very useful.

Yeadon, David. *Secluded Islands of the Atlantic Coast*. New York: Crown, 1984.

Fiction

Auchincloss, Louis. *The House of Five Talents*. Boston: Houghton Mifflin, 1960. (Newport, RI).

Benchley, Peter. *Jaws*. New York: Doubleday, 1974. (About Long Island, NY; filmed on Martha's Vineyard, MA).

Benchley, Nathaniel. *The Off-Islanders*. New York: McGraw-Hill, 1961. (Nantucket, MA).

Hirschfield, Burt. *Return to Fire Island*. New York: Avon, 1984.

Jewett, Sarah Orne. *The Country of the Pointed Firs*. Arden Lib.; first pub. 1896. (Deer Isle, ME).

Montgomery, Lucy Maud. *Anne of Green Gables* (and sequels). First published by L. C. Page 1908; 68 printings through 1942. New York: Bantam Books, 1982. (Prince Edward Island, Canada).

Ogilvie, Elisabeth. The Bennett Island series of novels: *High Tide at Noon*, 1944, *Storm Tide*, 1945, and *Ebbing Tide*, 1947 (all published by Thomas Y. Crowell, N.Y.) and *How Wide the Heart*, 1959, and *An Answer in the Tide*, 1978 (both published by McGraw-Hill, N.Y.) are set on Matinicus and Criehaven, ME.

Rich, Virginia. *The Nantucket Diet Murders*. New York: Delacorte Press, 1985. (Nantucket, MA).

Whitney, Phyllis A. *Spindrift*. New York: Doubleday, 1975. (Newport, RI).

Wilder, Thornton. *Theophilus North*. New York: Har-Row, 1973. (Newport, RI).

PHOTO CREDITS

Canoeists with Selden Island in Background, courtesy David Harraden, North American Canoe Tours, Inc., Page 6.

Sheffield Island Lighthouse, courtesy Norwalk Seaport Association, Page 7.

Volsunga III, courtesy Connecticut Dept. of Economic Development, Page 9.

Peaks Island, photo by Christopher Ayres, Page 19.

Great Cranberry Island, photo by Barbara Bornemann Stainton, Page 22.

The *Mink* and *Miss Lizzie*, photo by Sarah Bird Wright, Page 26.

Frenchboro Congregational Christian Church Parsonage, courtesy Rebecca Lunt, Page 31.

Shoreline, Isle au Haut, photo by Jeffrey Burke, Page 34.

Isle au Haut Light, photo by Jeffrey Burke, Page 36.

Grindle Point Lighthouse and Museum, photo by Sarah Bird Wright, Page 38.

Centennial Building and Wharf, Matinicus, photo by Warren Williams, Page 42.

White Head, Monhegan Island, photo by Sarah Bird Wright, Page 47.

Bass Harbor Head Light, Mt. Desert, photo by Sarah Bird Wright, Page 50.

North Haven ferry, photo by Christopher Ayres, Page 55.

Squirrel Island, photo by Ross Edwards, Page 58.

Swans Island, photo by Christopher Ayres, Page 61.

Vinalhaven, photo by Christopher Ayres, Page 63.

Gallop's Island, courtesy Mass Dept. of Environmental Management, Page 70.

Edgartown Harbor, Martha's Vineyard, photo by Sarah Bird Wright, Page 77.

Gay Head Cliffs, Martha's Vineyard, photo by Sarah Bird Wright, Page 80.

Brant Point Light, Nantucket, photo by Sarah Bird Wright, Page 82.

Beach, Nantucket, photo by Sarah Bird Wright, Page 84.

White-Tail Deer in Winter, Plum Island, photo by Bonnie Manning, Page 88.

Gosport Church and Star Island Conference Center, photo by Peter E. Randall, Page 97.

Island in Lake Winnipesaukee, courtesy Captain Robert J. Cole, Page 101.

Ellis Island, courtesy National Park Service, Page 108.

Cherry Grove, Fire Island, photo by Sarah Bird Wright, Page 112.

Statue of Liberty, Liberty Island, courtesy National Park Service, Page 118.

House on Shelter Island, photo by Prudence Heller, Page 122.

Chimera Guarding Casa Blanca, photo by Sarah Bird Wright, Page 124.

Boldt Castle, Heart Island, courtesy Thousand Islands International Council, Page 128.

Griffins Guarding Casa Blanca, photo by Sarah Bird Wright, Page 135.

Newport and Harbor, photo by John Corbett, courtesy Newport County Convention & Visitors Bureau, Page 141.

The Chinese Teahouse, Marble House, Newport, photo by Sarah Bird Wright, Page 143.

Southeast Light, Block Island, photo by Malcolm Greenaway, Page 145.

Southeast Light and Mohegan Bluffs, courtesy of the R.I. Dept. of Economic Development, Page 148.

Prudence Island, courtesy of the R.I. Dept. of Economic Development, Page 150.

The Hyde Log Cabin, Grand Isle, courtesy Vermont Travel Division, Page 158.

Apple Blossom Time, Grand Isle, courtesy Vermont Travel Division, Page 159.

St. Anne Shrine, Isle La Motte, courtesy Vermont Travel Division, Page 161.

The Adirondack ferry, Lake Champlain, courtesy Vermont Travel Division, Page 163.

Head Harbour Lighthouse, Campobello, photo by Sarah Bird Wright, Page 168.

The Roosevelt Summer Home, photo by Sarah Bird Wright, Page 169.

Scenery on the Cabot Trail, Cape Breton, photo by Sarah Bird Wright, Page 172.

Fortress of Louisbourg, Cape Breton, courtesy Canadian Office of Tourism, Page 174.

Deer Island Ferry, New Brunswick, photo by Sarah Bird Wright, Page 178.

Herring Smokehouses, Grand Manan, photo by Sarah Bird Wright, Page 182.

Shoreline, Grand Manan, photo by Sarah Bird Wright, Page 186.

Grosse-Île, The Magdalen Islands, photo by Sarah Bird Wright, Page 188.

Rocky Coastline, The Magdalen Islands, photo by Sarah Bird Wright, Page 191.

House of Green Gables, Cavendish, courtesy Canadian Government Office of Tourism, Page 195.

West Point Lighthouse, P.E.I., photo by Sarah Bird Wright, Page 197.

Lobster Traps, North Lake, P.E.I., courtesy Canadian Government Office of Tourism, Page 200.

Festival, St. Pierre and Miquelon, courtesy Agence Regionale du Tourism, Saint-Pierre and Miquelon, Page 202.

Sculpture at the Airport, St. Pierre and Miquelon, photo by Sarah Bird Wright, Page 207.

INDEX

Photo by Laurie MacCormack

Sarah Bird Wright continues her highly praised **ISLANDS** travel series with this second volume. Her first book, **FERRIES OF AMERICA** (Peachtree) was named by *Library Journal* as "one of the best reference books of 1987." Her travel writing has appeared in *Travel-Holiday, The New York Times, The Christian Science Monitor, The Toronto Globe and Mail, Woman's World,* and many other publications. She teaches part-time at the University of Richmond and lives in Midlothian, Virginia.